W9-BUB-872

The best projects from a year of *Bead&Button* magazine

Creative Beading

Vol. 6

KALMBACH BOOKS

Kalmbach Books
21027 Crossroads Circle
Waukesha, Wisconsin 53186
www.Kalmbach.com/Books

© 2011 Kalmbach Books
All rights reserved. Except for brief excerpts for review, this book may not be reproduced in part or in whole by
electronic means or otherwise without written permission of the publisher.

The designs in *Creative Beading Vol. 6* are copyrighted. Please use them for your education and personal enjoyment
only. They may not be taught or sold without permission.

Published in 2011
15 14 13 12 11   1 2 3 4 5

Manufactured in China

ISBN: 978-0-87116-419-3

The material in this book has appeared previously in *Bead&Button* magazine. *Bead&Button* is registered as
a trademark.

Publisher's Cataloging-in-Publication Data

Creative beading. Vol. 6 : the best projects from a year of Bead&Button
   magazine.

   p. : col. ill. ; cm.

"The material in this book has previously appeared in Bead&Button magazine."
Includes index.

ISBN: 978-0-87116-419-3

   1. Beadwork--Handbooks, manuals, etc. 2. Beads--Handbooks, manuals, etc. 3. Jewelry making--Handbooks,
manuals, etc. I. Title: Bead&Button magazine.

TT860 .C743 2011
745.594/2

Contents

26

30

59

62

132

138

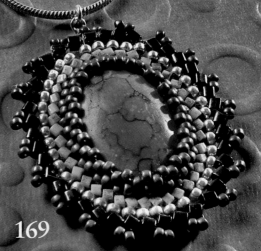

157

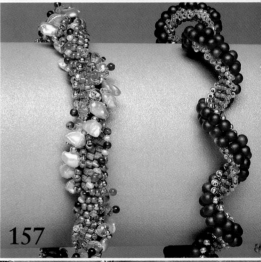

169

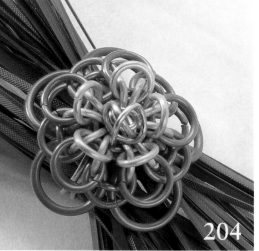

184

204

208

216

228

238

240

245

Introduction

At *Bead&Button* magazine, we've just completed our biannual survey, and here's what we've confirmed about our readers:

- You love to collect instructions for jewelry projects in many different techniques.
- Books run a close second to magazines in your jewelry-project collections.
- BeadAndButton.com is your leading online resource for information about jewelry making.
- You enjoy learning about jewelry techniques and like to challenge yourselves to try new skills.
- Beading makes you happy.

The editors of *Bead&Button* all can relate to these essential characteristics — especially the "happy" part — and this new, sixth volume of *Creative Beading* makes us very happy. In all, it has 77 projects from *Bead&Button*: 56 stitched projects, 13 wirework pieces, and eight projects in miscellaneous techniques. We selected each of these projects with care and attention to detail, tested every step, and "packaged" them in easy-to-follow articles with how-to photos and illustrations. To our delight, they make a winning collection when bound together in this hardcover book.

We're glad that you added *Creative Beading Vol. 6* to your jewelry-project collection. It will bring you years of pleasure and scores of new pieces of jewelry to make, wear, and give to others.

Happy beading,

Julia Gerlach

Julia Gerlach
Editor, *Bead&Button*

Tools & Materials

Excellent tools and materials for making jewelry are available in bead and craft stores, through catalogs, and on the Internet. Here are the essential supplies you'll need for the projects in this book.

TOOLS

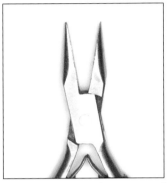

Chainnose pliers have smooth, flat inner jaws, and the tips taper to a point. Use them for gripping and for opening and closing loops and jump rings.

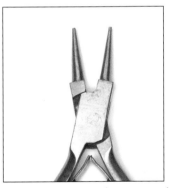

Roundnose pliers have smooth, tapered, conical jaws used to make loops. The closer to the tip you work, the smaller the loop will be.

Use the front of a **wire cutters'** blades to make a pointed cut and the back of the blades to make a flat cut. Do not use your jewelry-grade wire cutters on memory wire, which is extremely hard; use heavy-duty wire cutters or bend the memory wire back and forth until it breaks.

Crimping pliers have two grooves in their jaws that are used to fold or roll a crimp bead into a compact shape.

Make it easier to open split rings by inserting the curved jaw of **split-ring pliers** between the wires.

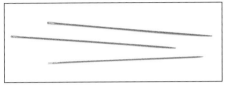

Beading needles are coded by size. The higher the number, the finer the beading needle. Unlike sewing needles, the eye of a beading needle is almost as narrow as its shaft. In addition to the size of the bead, the number of times you will pass through the bead also affects the needle size that you will use; if you will pass through a bead multiple times, you need to use a smaller needle.

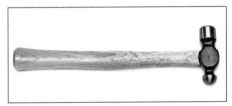

A **hammer** is used to harden wire or texture metal. Any hammer with a flat head will work, as long as the head is free of nicks that could mar your metal. The light ball-peen hammer shown here is one of the most commonly used hammers for jewelry making.

A **bench block** provides a hard, smooth surface on which to hammer your pieces. An anvil is similarly hard but has different surfaces, such as a tapered horn, to help form wire into different shapes.

Tools & Materials

A **head pin** looks like a long, blunt, thick sewing pin. It has a flat or decorative head on one end to keep beads on. Head pins come in different diameters (gauges) and lengths.

Eye pins are just like head pins except they have a round loop on one end instead of a head. You can make your own eye pins from wire.

A **jump ring** is used to connect two loops. It is a small wire circle or oval that is either soldered closed or comes with a split so it can be opened and closed.

Split rings are used like jump rings but are much more secure. They look like tiny key rings and are made of springy wire.

Crimp beads are small, large-holed, thin-walled metal beads designed to be flattened or crimped into a tight roll. Use them when stringing jewelry on flexible beading wire.

Clasps come in many sizes and shapes. Some of the most common (clockwise from the top left) are the toggle, consisting of a ring and a bar; lobster claw, which opens when you pull on a tiny lever; S-hook, which links two soldered jump rings or split rings; slide, consisting of one tube that slides inside another; and box, with a tab and a slot.

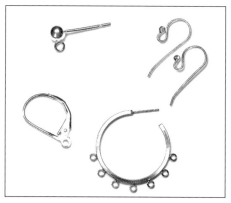

Earring findings come in a huge variety of metals and styles, including (clockwise from the top left) post, French hook, hoop, and lever-back. You will almost always want a loop (or loops) on earring findings so you can attach beads.

WIRE

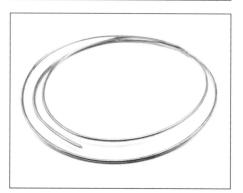

Wire is available in a number of materials and finishes, including brass, gold, gold-filled, gold-plated, fine silver, sterling silver, anodized niobium (chemically colored wire), and copper. Brass, copper, and craft wire are packaged in 10- to 40-yd. (9.1–37 m) spools, while gold, silver, and niobium are sold by the foot or ounce. Wire thickness is measured by gauge — the higher the gauge number, the thinner the wire. It is available in varying hardnesses (dead-soft, half-hard, and hard) and shapes (round, half-round, square, and others).

STITCHING & STRINGING MATERIALS

Selecting beading thread and cord is one of the most important decisions you'll make when planning a project. Review the descriptions below to evaluate which material is best for your design.

Threads come in many sizes and strengths. Size (diameter or thickness) is designated by a letter or number. OO and A/O are the thinnest; B, D, E, F, and FF are subsequently thicker. **Cord** is measured on a number scale; 0 corresponds in thickness to D-size thread, 1 equals E, 2 equals F, and 3 equals FF.

Parallel filament nylon, such as Nymo or C-Lon, is made from many thin nylon fibers that are extruded and heat set to form a single-ply thread. Parallel filament nylon is durable and easy to thread, but it can be prone to fraying and stretching. It is best used in bead weaving and bead embroidery.

Plied nylon thread, such as Silamide, is made from two or more nylon threads that are extruded, twisted together, and coated or bonded for further strength, making them strong and durable. It is more resistant to fraying than parallel filament nylon, and some brands do not stretch. It's a good material to use for twisted fringe, bead crochet, and beadwork that needs a lot of body.

Plied gel-spun polyethylene (GSP), such as Power Pro or DandyLine, is made from polyethylene fibers that have been spun into two or more threads that are braided together. It is almost unbreakable, it doesn't stretch, and it resists fraying. The thickness can make it difficult to make multiple passes through a bead. It is ideal for stitching with larger beads, such as pressed glass and crystals.

Parallel filament GSP, such as Fireline, is a single-ply thread made from spun and bonded polyethylene fibers. It's extremely strong, it doesn't stretch, and it resists fraying. However, crystals will cut through parallel filament GSP, and some varieties can leave a black residue on hands and beads. It's most appropriate for bead stitching.

Polyester thread, such as Gutermann, is made from polyester fibers that are spun into single yarns and then twisted into plied thread. It doesn't stretch and comes in many colors, but it can become fuzzy with use. It is best for bead crochet or bead embroidery when the thread must match the fabric.

Flexible beading wire is composed of wires twisted together and covered with nylon. This wire is stronger than thread and does not stretch. The higher the number of inner strands (between 3 and 49), the more flexible and kink-resistant the wire. It is available in a variety of sizes. Use .014 and .015 for stringing most gemstones, crystals, and glass beads. Use thicker varieties, .018, .019, and .024, for heavy beads or nuggets. Use thinner wire, .010 and .012, for lightweight pieces and beads with very small holes, such as pearls. The thinnest wires can also be used for some bead-stitching projects.

Tools & Materials

SEED BEADS

A huge variety of beads is available, but the beads most commonly used in the projects in this book are **seed beads**. Seed beads come in packages, tubes, and hanks. A standard hank (a looped bundle of beads strung on thread) contains 12 20-in. (51 cm) strands, but vintage hanks are usually much smaller. Tubes and packages are usually measured in grams and vary in size.

Seed beads have been manufactured in many sizes ranging from the largest, 5º (also called "E beads"), which are about 5 mm wide, to tiny size 20º or 22º, which aren't much larger than grains of sand. (The symbol º stands for "aught" or "zero." The greater the number of aughts, e.g., 22º, the smaller the bead.) Beads smaller than Japanese 15ºs have not been produced for the past 100 years, but vintage beads can be found in limited sizes and colors. The most commonly available size in the widest range of colors is 11º.

Most round seed beads are made in Japan and the Czech Republic. **Czech seed beads** are slightly irregular and rounder than **Japanese seed beads**, which are uniform in size and a bit squared off. Czech beads give a bumpier surface when woven, but they reflect light at a wider range of angles. Japanese seed beads produce a uniform surface and texture. Japanese and Czech seed beads can be used together, but a Japanese seed bead is slightly larger than the same size Czech seed bead.

Seed beads also come in a sparkly cut version. Japanese **hex-cut** or hex beads are formed with six sides. **2-** or **3-cut** Czech beads are less regular. **Charlottes** have an irregular facet cut on one side of the bead.

The Japanese **cylinder bead,** otherwise known as Delica (the Miyuki brand name), Toho Treasures (the brand name of Toho), and Toho Aikos are extremely popular for peyote stitch projects. These beads are very regular and have large holes, which are useful for stitches requiring multiple thread passes. The beads fit together almost seamlessly, producing a smooth, fabric-like surface.

Bugle beads are thin glass tubes. They can be sized by number or length, depending on where they are made. Japanese size 1 bugles are about 2 mm

long, but bugles can be made even longer than 30 mm. They can be hex-cut, straight, or twisted, but the selection of colors, sizes, shapes, and finishes is limited. Seed beads also come in a variety of other shapes, including **triangles, cubes,** and **teardrops.**

In stitches where the beads meet each other end to end or side by side — peyote stitch, brick stitch, and square stitch — try using Japanese cylinder beads to achieve a smooth, flat surface. For a more textured surface, use Czech or round Japanese seed beads. For right-angle weave, in which groups of four or more beads form circular stitches, the rounder the seed bead, the better; otherwise you risk having gaps. Round seed beads also are better for netting and strung jewelry.

Basics

THREAD AND KNOTS

Adding thread

To add a thread, sew into the beadwork several rows prior to the point where the last bead was added. Sew through the beadwork, following the thread path of the stitch. Tie a few half-hitch knots (see **Half-hitch knot**) between beads, and exit where the last stitch ended.

Conditioning thread

Use either beeswax or microcrystalline wax (not candle wax or paraffin) or Thread Heaven to condition nylon thread. Wax smooths the nylon fibers and adds tackiness that will slightly stiffen beadwork. Thread Heaven adds a static charge that causes the thread to repel itself, so don't use it with doubled thread. Stretch the thread, then pull it through the conditioner.

Ending thread

To end a thread, sew back into the beadwork, following the existing thread path and tying two or three half-hitch knots (see **Half-hitch knot**) between beads as you go. Change directions as you sew so the thread crosses itself. Sew through a few beads after the last knot, and trim the thread.

Half-hitch knot

Pass the needle under the thread between two beads. A loop will form as you pull the thread through. Cross back over the thread between the beads, sew through the loop, and pull gently to draw the knot into the beadwork.

Overhand knot

Make a loop with the thread. Pull the tail through the loop, and tighten.

Slip knot

Make a loop in the thread, crossing the ball end over the tail. Insert your hook into the loop, yarn over the hook, and pull through the loop. Pull to tighten.

Square knot

[1] Cross the left-hand end of the thread over the right, and bring it under and back up.

[2] Cross the end that is now on the right over the left, go through the loop, and pull both ends to tighten.

Surgeon's knot

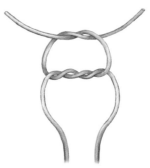

[1] Cross the left-hand end of the thread over the right twice. Pull to tighten.
[2] Cross the end that is now on the right over the left, go through the loop, and tighten.

Stop bead

Use a stop bead to secure beads temporarily when you begin stitching. Choose a bead that is distinctly different from the beads in your project. String the stop bead, and sew through it again in the same direction. If desired, sew through it one more time for added security.

Basics

STITCHES

Beaded backstitch

To stitch a line of beads, come up through the fabric from the wrong side. Pick up three beads. Place the thread where the beads will go, and sew through the fabric right after the third bead. Come up between the second and third beads, and go through the third bead again. Pick up three more beads, and repeat. For a tighter stitch, pick up only one or two beads at a time.

Brick stitch
Traditional

[1] Begin with a ladder of beads (see **Ladder stitch**), and position the thread to exit the top of the last bead. The ends of each new row will be offset slightly from the previous row. To work the typical method, which results in progressively decreasing rows, pick up two beads. Sew under the thread bridge between the second and third beads in the previous row from back to front. Sew up through the second bead added, down through the first bead, and back up through the second bead.

[2] For the row's remaining stitches, pick up one bead per stitch. Sew under the next thread bridge in the previous row from back to front, and sew back up through the new bead. The last stitch in the row will be positioned above the last two beads in the row below, and the row will be one bead shorter than the previous row.

Increase

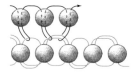

[1] To increase within a row, add a second stitch to the same thread bridge as the previous stitch.

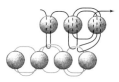

[2] To increase at the end of the row, add a second stitch to the final thread bridge in the row.

Tubular

[1] Begin with a ladder of beads, and join the ends to form a ring (see **Ladder stitch**). Position the thread to exit the top of a bead.

[2] Following the instructions for flat brick stitch, pick up two beads to begin the row. Stitch around the ring in brick stitch.

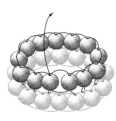

[3] Join the first and last beads of the round by sewing down through the first bead and up through the last bead.

Circular

Circular brick stitch is often worked off of a thread bridge surrounding a large central bead. To begin, pick up two smaller beads, (such as seed beads), sew under the thread bridge, and sew back through the second bead. Continue around the central bead, picking up one bead per stitch. When you've gone all the way around, sew down through the first bead in the round and up through the last bead in the round.

For subsequent rounds, work as in traditional brick stitch, increasing or using larger beads as needed to fill any gaps. Connect the first and last beads in each round as in the initial round.

Crossweave technique

Crossweave is a beading technique in which you string beads on both ends of a length of thread or cord and then cross the ends through another bead.

Herringbone stitch
Flat

[1] Start with an even number of beads stitched into a ladder (see **Ladder stitch**). Turn the ladder, if necessary, so your thread exits the end bead pointing up.

[2] Pick up two beads, and sew down through the next bead in the ladder (a–b). Sew up through the third bead in the ladder, pick up two beads, and sew down through the fourth bead (b–c). Repeat across the ladder.

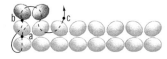

[3] To make a turn, sew down through the end bead in the previous row and back through the last bead of the pair you just added (a–b). Pick up two beads, sew down through the next bead in the previous row, and sew up through the following bead (b–c). Continue adding pairs of beads across the row. You may choose to hide the edge thread by picking up an accent or smaller bead before you sew back through the last bead of the pair you just added.

Tubular

[1] Stitch a ladder (see **Ladder stitch**) with an even number of beads, and form it into a ring. Your thread should exit the top of a bead.

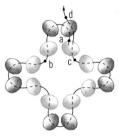

[2] Pick up two beads, and sew through the next bead in the previous round (a–b). Sew up through the next bead, and repeat around the ring to complete the round (b–c). To step up, sew up through the first bead in the previous round and the first bead added in the new round (c–d).
[3] Continue adding two beads per stitch. As you work, snug up the beads to form a tube, and step up at the end of each round until your rope is the desired length.

Twisted tubular

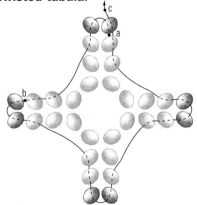

[1] Work a ladder and two rounds of tubular herringbone as explained above.
[2] To create a twist in the tube, pick up two beads, sew down through one bead in the next stack, then up through two beads in the following stack (a–b). Repeat around, adding two beads per

stitch. Step up to the next round through three beads (b–c). Snug up the beads. The twist will begin to appear after the sixth round. Continue until your rope is the desired length.

Ladder stitch
Traditional method

[1] Pick up two beads, sew through the first bead again, and then sew through the second bead (a–b).
[2] Add subsequent beads by picking up one bead, sewing through the previous bead, and then sewing through the new bead (b–c). Continue for the desired length.

This technique produces uneven tension, which you can easily correct by zig-zagging back through the beads in the opposite direction.

Crossweave method
[1] Center a bead on a length of thread with a needle attached to each end.

[2] Working in crossweave technique, pick up a bead with one needle, and cross the other needle through it (a–b and c–d). Add all subsequent beads in the same manner.

Alternative method

[1] Pick up all the beads you need to reach the length your pattern requires. Fold the last two beads so they are parallel, and sew through the second-to-last bead again in the same direction (a–b).

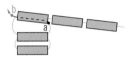

[2] Fold the next loose bead so it sits parallel to the previous bead in the ladder, and sew through the loose bead in the same direction (a–b). Continue sewing back through each bead until you exit the last bead of the ladder.

Forming a ring
If you are going to work in tubular brick or herringbone stitch, form your ladder into a ring to provide a base for the new technique: With your thread exiting the last bead in the ladder, sew through the first bead and then through the last bead again.

Basics

Peyote stitch
Flat even-count

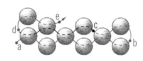

[1] Pick up an even number of beads (a–b). These beads will shift to form the first two rows.

[2] To begin row 3, pick up a bead, skip the last bead strung in the previous step, and sew through the next bead in the opposite direction (b–c). For each stitch, pick up a bead, skip a bead in the previous row, and sew through the next bead, exiting the first bead strung (c–d). The beads added in this row are higher than the previous rows and are referred to as "up-beads."

[3] For each stitch in subsequent rows, pick up a bead, and sew through the next up-bead in the previous row (d–e). To count peyote stitch rows, count the total number of beads along both straight edges.

Flat odd-count

Odd-count peyote is the same as even-count peyote, except for the turn on odd-numbered rows, where the last bead of the row can't be attached in the usual way because there is no up-bead to sew through.

Work the traditional odd-row turn as follows:

[1] Begin as for flat even-count peyote, but pick up an odd number of beads. Work row 3 as in even-count, stopping before adding the last two beads.

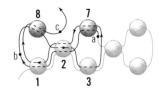

[2] Work a figure-8 turn at the end of row 3: Pick up the next-to-last bead (#7), and sew through #2, then #1 (a–b). Pick up the last bead of the row (#8), and sew through #2, #3, #7, #2, #1, and #8 (b–c).

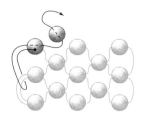

[3] You can work this turn at the end of each odd-numbered row, but this edge will be stiffer than the other. Instead, in subsequent odd-numbered rows, pick up the last bead of the row, then sew under the thread bridge immediately below. Sew back through the last bead added to begin the next row.

Tubular

Tubular peyote stitch follows the same stitching pattern as flat peyote, but instead of sewing back and forth, you work in rounds.

[1] Start with an even number of beads in a ring.

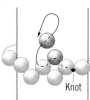

[2] Sew through the first bead in the ring. Pick up a bead, skip a bead in the ring, and sew through the next bead. Repeat to complete the round.

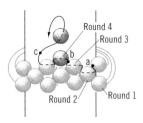

[3] You need to step up to be in position for the next round. Sew through the first bead added in round 3 (a–b). Pick up a bead, and sew through the second bead in round 3 (b–c). Repeat to achieve the desired length.

Circular

Circular peyote is also worked in continuous rounds like tubular peyote, but the rounds stay flat and radiate outward from the center as a result of increases or using larger beads. If the rounds do not increase, the edges will curve upward and become a tube.

Bezels

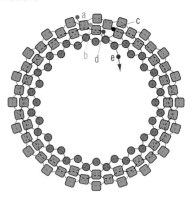

[1] Pick up enough 11º cylinder beads to fit around the circumference of a rivoli or stone, and sew through the first cylinder again to form a ring (a–b).

[2] Pick up a cylinder, skip the next cylinder in the ring, and sew through the following cylinder (b–c). Continue working in tubular peyote stitch to complete the round, and step up through the first cylinder added (c–d).

[3] Work the next two rounds in tubular peyote using 15º seed beads (d–e). Keep the tension tight to decrease the size of the ring.

[4] Position the rivoli or stone in the bezel cup. Using the tail thread, work one round of tubular peyote along the other edge using cylinder beads, and work two rounds using 15ºs.

Decrease

[1] At the point of decrease, go through two beads in the previous row.

[2] In the next row, when you reach the two-bead space, pick up one bead.

Increase

[1] At the point of increase, pick up two beads instead of one. Sew through the next bead.

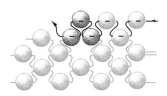

[2] When you reach the two beads in the next row, sew through the first bead, pick up a bead, and sew through the second bead.

Two-drop

Two-drop peyote follows the same stitching pattern as basic flat or tubular peyote, but you work with pairs of beads instead of single beads.

Start with an even number of beads divisible by four. Pick up two beads (stitch 1 of row 3), skip two beads, and sew through the next two beads. Repeat across the row or round.

Zipping up or joining

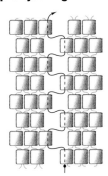

To join two sections of a flat peyote piece invisibly, match up the two pieces so the end rows fit together. "Zip up" the pieces by zigzagging through the up-beads on both ends.

Right-angle weave
Flat

[1] To start the first row of right-angle weave, pick up four beads, and tie them into a ring. Sew through the first three beads again.

[2] Pick up three beads. Sew through the last bead of the previous ring (a–b), and continue through the first two beads picked up in this stitch (b–c).

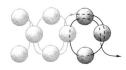

[3] Continue adding three beads per stitch until the first row is the desired length. You are sewing rings in a figure-8 pattern, alternating direction with each stitch.

Tubular

[1] Work a flat strip of right-angle weave that is one stitch fewer than needed for the desired circumference of the tube.

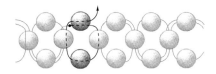

[2] Connect the last stitch to the first stitch as follows: Exit the end bead of the last stitch, pick up one bead, sew through the first bead of the first stitch, and pick up one bead. Complete the connecting stitch by retracing the thread path. Exit as shown above.

[3] In subsequent rounds, add three beads in the first stitch, two beads in the next stitches, and only one bead in the final stitch.

Square stitch

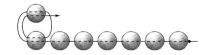

[1] String all the beads needed for the first row, then pick up the first bead of the second row. Sew through the last bead of the first row and the first bead of the second row again. The new bead sits on top of the bead in the previous row, and the holes are parallel.

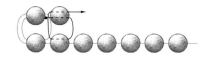

[2] Pick up the second bead of row 2, and sew through the next bead in row 1 and the new bead in row 2. Repeat this step for the entire row.

Whip stitch

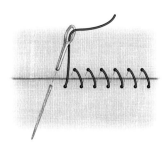

To join two layers of fabric with a finished edge, exit one layer. Cross over the edge diagonally, and stitch through both layers in the same direction about 1/16 in. (2 mm) away from where your thread exited. Repeat.

WIRE TECHNIQUES

Crimping

Use crimp beads to secure flexible beading wire. Slide the crimp bead into place, and squeeze it firmly with chainnose pliers to flatten it. For a more finished look, use crimping pliers:

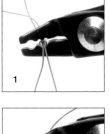

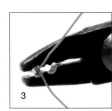

[1] Position the crimp bead in the hole that is closest to the handle of the crimping pliers.

[2] Holding the wires apart, squeeze the pliers to compress the crimp bead, making sure one wire is on each side of the dent.

[3] Place the crimp bead in the front hole of the pliers, and position it so the dent is facing the tips of the pliers. Squeeze the pliers to fold the crimp in half. Tug on the wires to ensure that the crimp is secure.

Loops and jump rings: opening and closing

[1] Hold a loop or a jump ring with two pairs of pliers.

[2] To open the loop or jump ring, bring the tips of one pair of pliers toward you, and push the tips of the other pair away from you.

[3] The open jump ring. Reverse the steps to close the open loop or jump ring.

Loops, plain

[1] Using chain-nose pliers, make a right-angle bend approximately ⅜ in. (1 cm) from the end of the wire.

[2] Grip the tip of the wire with roundnose pliers. Press downward slightly, and rotate the wire into a loop. The closer to the tip of the roundnose pliers that you work, the smaller the loop will be.

[3] Let go, then grip the loop at the same place on the pliers, and keep turning to close the loop.

[4] The plain loop.

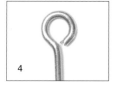

Loops, wrapped

[1] Using chain-nose pliers, make a right-angle bend approximately 1¼ in. (3.2 cm) from the end of the wire.

[2] Position the jaws of the roundnose pliers in the bend.

[3] Curve the short end of the wire over the top jaw of the roundnose pliers.

[4] Reposition the pliers so the lower jaw fits snugly in the loop. Curve the wire downward around the bottom jaw of the pliers. This is the first half of a wrapped loop.

[5] To complete the wraps, grasp the top of the loop with chainnose pliers.

[6] Wrap the wire around the stem two or three times. Trim the excess wire, and gently press the cut end close to the wraps with chainnose pliers.

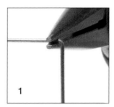

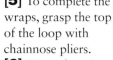

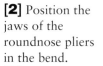

Stitching

Ropes
and rings

A network of connected rings showcases the sparkle of crystals and the luster of pearls

designed by **Laura McCabe**

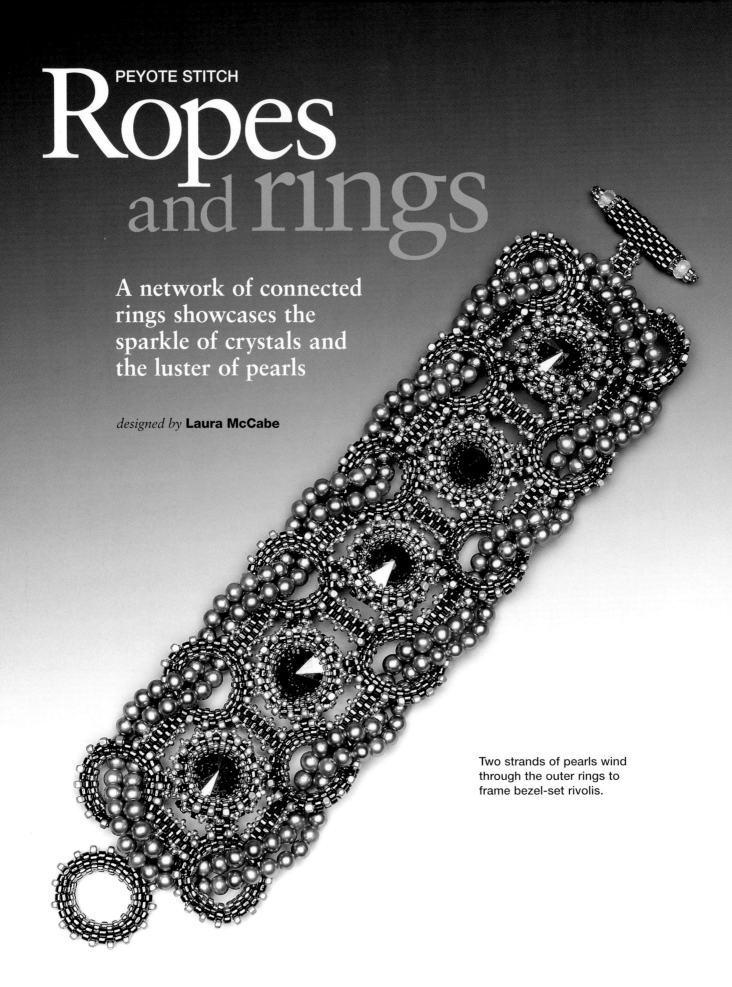

Two strands of pearls wind through the outer rings to frame bezel-set rivolis.

a

b

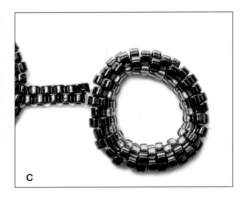

c

Inspired by the lavish opulence of late 18th century French jewelry and apparel, this bracelet pairs richly colored crystal stones and metallic Charlottes with small freshwater pearls to create a stunning look.

step by step

End and add Fireline (Basics, p. 13) as needed.

Rings

[1] On 1 yd. (.9 m) of Fireline, pick up 32 15º seed beads, and, leaving a 12-in. (30 cm) tail, sew through the first few 15ºs again to form a ring. Using 15ºs, work a round in tubular peyote stitch (Basics), and step up.

[2] Work three rounds in tubular peyote using 11º cylinder beads.

[3] Thread a needle on the tail, and work two rounds using cylinders.

[4] Zip up (Basics) the last round of cylinders in step 3 and the last round of cylinders in step 2. Tie a few half-hitch knots (Basics) to secure the thread, but do not trim.

[5] Repeat steps 1–4 to make a total of 18 rings.

Stone bezels

[1] Sew through the beadwork of a ring to exit a cylinder in the first round of cylinders. Work two rounds of tubular peyote using cylinders (photo a), and step up.

[2] Place a 12 mm rivoli or cubic zirconia stone in the bezel face up, and work a round of tubular peyote with 15º seed beads. Work another round using 15º Czech Charlottes. Tie a few half-hitch knots to secure the thread, but do not trim.

[3] Sew through the beadwork to exit a cylinder in the first round on the back side of the bezel. Work two rounds with 15º seed beads. Work a round with 15º Czech Charlottes. Tie a few half-hitch knots to secure the thread, but do not trim.

[4] Repeat steps 1–3 to make a total of five stone bezels.

Linking components

[1] Sew through the beadwork of a ring to exit an outer cylinder in the center round. Work a peyote stitch using a cylinder. Pick up a cylinder, turn, and sew through the cylinder just added (photo b). Working in flat even-count peyote (Basics), make a strip that is two cylinders wide by 10 rows long with five cylinders on each edge. Zip up the last two rows of the strip to the center round of cylinders in a new ring (photo c).

materials

bracelet 6¼ in. (15.9 cm)

- 5 12 mm rivolis or cubic zirconia stones with pointed backs
- 2 4 mm rondelles
- 2 16-in. (41 cm) strands 3 mm freshwater pearls
- 15 g 11º cylinder beads
- 6 g 15º seed beads
- 6 g 15º Japanese Charlottes (justletmebead.com)
- 5 g 15º Czech Charlottes
- Fireline, 6 lb. test
- beading needles, #12 and #13
- beading wax (optional)

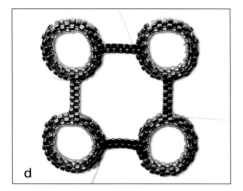

d

e

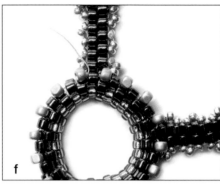

f

g

h

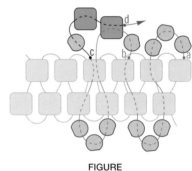

FIGURE

[2] Connect two more rings to the first two rings in the same manner, stitching the strips at right angles to form the four rings into a square. There should be six cylinders between each pair of strips on a ring to form the right angle (photo d).

[3] Continuing in the pattern of groups of four, connect 12 rings in this manner for the length of the bracelet.

[4] To add picots along the edges of the strips, sew through the beadwork to exit the first cylinder on a strip. Pick up three 15° Czech Charlottes, and sew through the next two cylinders. Repeat (photo e) to add picots along both edges of the strip. Add picot trim to all the strips except the end strips, which is where the clasp will be attached.

[5] To embellish each ring, work a round of peyote stitch off the second round of cylinders using 15° Japanese Charlottes (photo f).

[6] To add a bezel-set stone, use the tail from the bezel to work a strip as in step 1

that is two beads wide by two rows long with one cylinder on each edge. Align the strip with the "corner" of a ring in a square of rings, and zip up the strip to the ring (photo g). Add picot trim to the strip as in step 4. Work three more strips around the bezel-set stone at right angles to each other with six cylinders between each pair of strips.

[7] Sew through the beadwork to exit the top round of cylinders in the bezel, and work a round using 15° Japanese Charlottes. Sew through the beadwork to exit the round below the one you worked at the start of this step, and work a round of picots with three 15° Czech Charlottes in each stitch (photo h).

[8] Repeat steps 6 and 7 with the remaining bezel-set stones.

Toggle clasp

[1] Sew through the beadwork to exit an end cylinder on an end strip, and work two picots with Czech Charlottes

(figure, a–b). Pick up a Czech Charlotte and a cylinder, sew down through the next two cylinders, add a picot, and sew up through the next cylinder and the cylinder you just sewed down through (b–c). Pick up a Czech Charlotte and a cylinder, and sew through the first cylinder added (c–d and photo i). Working in flat even-count peyote stitch and beginning with the two cylinders just added, make a strip that is two cylinders wide by 10 rows long with five cylinders on each edge.

[2] Repeat step 1 on the other end of the bracelet, making a strip that is two cylinders wide by 18 rows long with nine cylinders on each edge.

[3] Using the thread of the remaining unattached ring, sew through the beadwork to exit a cylinder in the outer round. Work a round with Japanese Charlottes, leaving one cylinder unembellished. Using the unembellished bead, zip up the ring to the 10-row strip made in step 1. Sew through the bead-

For a different look, make the bracelet without the pearl embellishment.

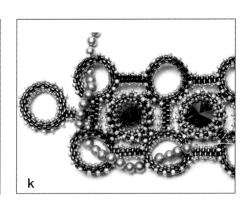

work to exit an end cylinder on the strip, and work picots along the edges with Czech Charlottes. Add picots to the remaining edge of the remaining section of the end strip on the bracelet.

[4] On 1 yd. (.9 m) of Fireline, use cylinders to work a strip of peyote that is 12 rows wide by 12 rows long with six cylinders on each edge. Zip up the ends to form a tube.

[5] Sew through the beadwork to exit a cylinder at the end of the tube. Pick up a 15º, a 4 mm rondelle, and three 15ºs. Skip the three 15ºs, and sew back through the 4 mm. Pick up a 15º, and sew down through the next cylinder and up through the following cylinder (photo j). Pick up a 15º, and sew through the 4 mm, three 15ºs, and back through the 4 mm. Continue in this manner around the end of the tube, and repeat on the other side. End the thread and tail.

[6] Using the thread on the 18-row strip at the end of the bracelet, zip up the strip to the center of the toggle bar.

Add picots to the edges of the strip as in step 3. End all threads.

Pearl embellishment

[1] On 1 yd. (.9 m) of Fireline, attach a stop bead (Basics), leaving a 6-in. (15 cm) tail. String about 15 in. (38 cm) of 3 mm freshwater pearls. Using the strand of pearls, sew up through a ring on the edge of the bracelet from back to front. Continue weaving the pearl strand through the rings around the bracelet in the same manner, from back to front (photo k).

[2] Remove the stop bead, and add or remove pearls as needed. Sew through the first few pearls added, and tie a half-hitch knot. Sew through a few more pearls, and tie a half-hitch knot. Repeat about six times, and end the thread and tail.

[3] Repeat steps 1 and 2 with a second strand of pearls, making sure to keep the second strand around the outer edge of the first strand. ●

DESIGNER'S NOTES:

• Adjust the size of your bracelet by using more rings and 12 mm rivolis or stones. A bracelet made with 21 rings and six stones measures about 7 in. (18 cm). For a 7¾-in. (19.7 cm) bracelet, use 24 rings and seven stones. You may need an extra strand of pearls.

• Use 2 yd. (1.8 m) of Fireline to make the rings that you will use as bezels for the stones.

• Depending on your tension and the manufacturer of your rivolis or stones, when stitching the bezel, you may need to work an extra round with 15º seed beads before switching to 15º Czech Charlottes.

Posit

Nealay used
kyanite marquise
gemstones for his
pendant (bottom).
For testing, the
Bead&Button
editors used
blue sponge
coral (top).

ive SPACES

Use the many spaces in filigree beads to make this dimensional necklace

designed by **Nealay Patel**

All beads have a hole, of course. The lacy filigree spacer beads used in this project have 34 holes each, and they are begging to be put to work. These clever puffs and cages created by stringing beading wire through the filigree holes are the perfect solution. Once you try this project, you may have found a new favorite technique.

stepbystep

Peyote tube beads

[1] On 1 yd. (.9 m) of Fireline or thread, attach a stop bead (Basics, p. 13), leaving a 6-in. (15 cm) tail. Pick up three color A 11º cylinder beads, three color B 11º cylinder beads, five As, three Bs, and three As.
[2] Working in odd-count peyote stitch (Basics), begin at the lower left-hand corner of the **figure** to complete the panel. Zip up (Basics) the edges to form a tube. Remove the stop bead, and end the threads (Basics).
[3] Repeat steps 1 and 2 to make a total of four tube beads.

Pendant

[1] Cut 1 ft. (30 cm) of .018 beading wire, and, leaving a short tail, string the 3 mm crimp bead, the 10 mm wooden bead, and the largest marquise-shaped gemstone. With the long end of the wire, go through the crimp bead and the 10 mm again, leaving a loop of exposed

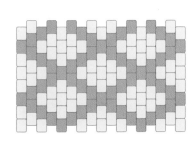

a

FIGURE

materials
necklace 18 in. (46 cm)
- **8** top-drilled marquise-shaped gemstones, various sizes (approximately 8 x 23–12 x 40 mm)
- wooden beads
  10 mm
  6 8 mm
  10 6 mm
- **12** 6 mm filigree beads (item CPB-R60F at abeadstore.com)
- **36–40** 3 x 4 mm gemstone rondelles
- 5 g 11º Japanese cylinder beads in each of **3** colors: A, B, C
- **4** 4 mm round spacers
- clasp
- **4** 4 mm bead caps
- 3 mm crimp bead
- **6** 2 mm crimp beads
- **2** crimp covers (optional)
- Fireline, 6 lb. test or nylon beading thread, size D
- flexible beading wire, .018, .014, and .010
- beading needles, #12
- bead reamer (optional)
- **2** Bead Stoppers or alligator clips
- chainnose pliers (optional)
- crimping pliers
- wire cutters

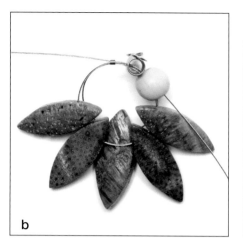

b

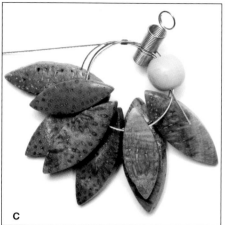

c

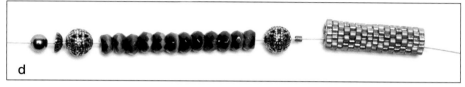

d

e

f

EDITOR'S NOTE:
It can be tricky to pass flexible beading wire through the correct holes of the filigree beads because it sometimes bends inside the bead. If you have trouble, try using a Soft Flex Speeder Beader needle, which is a hollow needle into which you can slip the end of the beading wire. The needle holds the wire stiff, allowing it to pass through the filigree holes easily.

STRING IT INSTEAD
You can make this necklace without any stitching if desired. To do so, replace the peyote tubes with a crimp bead, a section of strung beads, and a crimp bead. After adding the puffs and cages, crimp the crimp beads, and cover them with crimp covers.

For an even easier version, omit the puffs and cages altogether, and string chunky gemstone or wood beads on each side of the pendant.

To make a daintier pendant, like the one shown at the far right, use small petal-shaped glass beads instead of the large marquise-shaped gemstones.

wire (photo a). Attach a Bead Stopper or alligator clip between the crimp bead and the 10 mm to temporarily prevent the crimp bead from sliding into the wooden bead.

[2] String four medium marquise-shaped gemstones, and go through the crimp bead and the 10 mm again, making the loop of wire the same size as the first one (photo b). Repeat with the three smallest marquise-shaped gemstones (photo c).

[3] Remove the Bead Stopper or clip, adjust the wire loops as needed, crimp the crimp bead (Basics), and trim the excess wire. Allow the 10 mm to slide over the crimp to hide it.

Necklace base

[1] On 2 ft. (61 cm) of .014 beading wire, string and center the pendant through the 10 mm.

[2] Later on, you will need to fit nine pieces of beading wire through the end

hole of the second filigree bead strung, so enlarge the end hole of the bead with a bead reamer before stringing it if needed. On one side, string a 4 mm spacer, a 4 mm bead cap, a 6 mm filigree bead, 12–14 3 x 4 mm gemstone rondelles, a filigree bead, a 2 mm crimp bead, and a peyote tube (photo d).

[3] String three repetitions of a filigree bead, a color C 11º cylinder bead, a rondelle, an 8 mm wooden bead, a rondelle, and a C (photo e).

[4] String a filigree bead, a 2 mm crimp bead, a peyote tube, a 4 mm spacer, a bead cap, five 6 mm wooden beads, and a 2 mm crimp bead (photo f). Secure the end with a Bead Stopper or clip.

[5] Repeat steps 2–4 on the other side.

Puffs and cages

[1] Cut 2 ft. (61 cm) of .010 beading wire, and string it through the center of a filigree bead, entering and exiting holes across from each other in the ring

of holes around the center of the filigree bead (photo g). Make sure the wire goes straight through. Repeat three times, using different holes each time, so that you have eight wire ends coming out of the ring of holes around the center of the filigree bead (photo h).

[2] To make a puff, string 40 Cs on a wire, and go through the next filigree bead and the following crimp bead, passing it through a filigree hole near the bottom of the bead and exiting the top hole (photo i). Repeat with the remaining seven wires, passing them through the corresponding filigree holes so as to keep the wires in order.

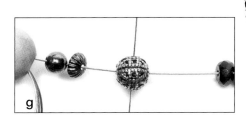

g

h

i

j

[3] Tighten the wires, and crimp the crimp bead. Trim the four shortest wires, then string the remaining four wires through the peyote tube.

[4] String one wire through the end hole of the next filigree bead, exiting a filigree hole in the center round of holes. Repeat with the remaining three wires, spacing them evenly around the bead. There should be one hole between each of the wires.

[5] To make the first cage, on one wire, string 16 Bs, and go through a center-round hole in the next filigree bead, making sure the wire goes straight through. Repeat with the remaining three wires **(photo j)**. Each hole that has

a wire going into it should also have an end coming out of it.

[6] Repeat step 5 twice, but for the last cage, the wires should exit the end hole of the filigree bead instead of a center-round hole.

[7] String the four wires through the next crimp bead, snug up the beads, crimp the crimp bead, and trim the four wire ends.

[8] Repeat steps 1–7 on the other side of the necklace.

Finishing

[1] Test the necklace for fit, and add or remove wooden beads if desired.

[2] On one end, string half of the clasp, go back through the crimp bead, and crimp it. If desired, use chainnose pliers to close a crimp cover over the crimp. Repeat on the other end. **●**

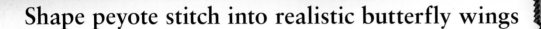

PEYOTE STITCH

Wing it

Shape peyote stitch into realistic butterfly wings

designed by **Antonio Calles**

Improve your peyote stitch skills by making these beautiful butterfly wings. Master the four different turns — odd-count, even-count, increase, and decrease — and you'll soon be a peyote whiz, able to make any shape you desire.

step by step

Large wing

[1] Attach a stop bead (Basics, p. 13) to the center of 1½ yd. (1.4 m) of Fireline or thread.

[2] Work the large wing in peyote stitch (Basics), paying close attention to the turn at the end of each row and referring to **figure 1** to pick up the following 11º seed beads:

Rows 1 and 2: (Outlined in blue in **figure 1**) Two Bs, two As, two Bs, A, three Bs, two Cs, two Bs, two As, two Bs, A, B, three As, B **(a–b)**. Using another needle, pass through every other bead, starting with the last B picked up **(photo a)**. This will help keep your beads in place as you stitch the next row or two.

[3] Work an even-count peyote turn (see turn legend below) to start row 3.

Row 3: B, A, B, two As, four Bs, three As **(b–c)**. Work an even-count turn.

Row 4: B, A, two Bs, A, five Bs, A, B. Work a decrease turn **(c–d** and below**)**.

Row 5: B, two As, B, five As, B, A. Work an increase turn (see below) by picking up a B and an A and sewing through them both again, positioning the two beads next to each other **(d–e)**.

Row 6: A, B, A, B, two As, B, two As, two Bs. Pick up another B, and work an odd-count peyote turn **(e–f** and below**)**.

Row 7: Four Bs, A, two Bs, A, B, two As. Sew through the next A, pick up two Bs, and sew back through the previous A **(f–g)**.

Row 8: A, B, two As, seven Bs. Decrease turn **(g–h)**.

Row 9: Three Cs, B, two Cs, two Bs, two As, B. Work two increase stitches: Pick up two Bs, sew through the first B

again, pick up two Bs, and sew through both Bs again so they sit side by side. Sew through the second B in the first stitch **(h–i)**.

Row 10: C, 10 Bs. Pick up a B, and work an odd-count turn **(i–j)**.

Row 11: Three Bs, C, three Bs, C, four Bs **(j–k)**. Even-count turn.

Row 12: Six Bs. Skip the next two stitches by sewing through four Bs **(k–l)**. Two Bs. Work a decrease turn **(l–m)**.

Row 13: B **(m–n)**. Sew through the next six Bs **(n–o)**. B, three Cs, B. Decrease turn **(o–p)**.

Row 14: Four Bs. Decrease turn **(p–q)**.

Row 15: Three Bs **(q–r)**. End the working thread (Basics).

[4] Remove the stop bead, and thread a needle on the tail. Work a decrease turn **(a–s)**, and complete the wing as follows:

Row 16: B, A, five Bs, two As, B, A. Work an increase turn by picking up two Bs and sewing through them both again **(s–t)**.

Row 17: Three As, two Bs, A, B, C, B, A, B. Decrease turn **(t–u)**.

Row 18: Three Bs, C, two As, three Bs, A. Sew through the next B, and work an odd-count turn **(u–v)**.

Row 19: Three As, B, two As, B, C, two Bs. Decrease turn **(v–w)**.

Row 20: Two Bs, C, three As, two Bs,

Four turns you need to know

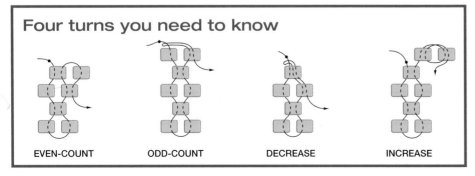

EVEN-COUNT   ODD-COUNT   DECREASE   INCREASE

a

These monarch butterflies look
so realistic, you might expect them
to take wing and flutter away.

materials

pin 4 x 2 in. (10 x 5 cm)
- **2** 8º seed beads (silver-lined)
- 11º seed beads

  3 g color A (orange) (If desired, use a slightly darker shade of orange
  for the large wings and a lighter shade for the smaller wings.)

  5 g color B (black)

  2 g color C (white)

  1 g color D (bronze)
- pin-back finding
- Fireline, 4 lb. test or nylon beading thread
- beading needles, #12

two As. Work an increase turn by
picking up two Bs. Sew through the two
Bs again, then sew through the last A
picked up **(w–x)**.

Row 21: A, B, four As, three Bs.
Decrease turn **(x–y)**.

Row 22: Three Bs, two As, B, A, B, A.
Work two increase stitches using two Bs
for each stitch **(y–z)**. Step up through the
second B of the first increase stitch.

Row 23: Three As, B, three As, two Bs.
Decrease turn **(z–aa)**.

Row 24: Two Bs, three As, two Bs, two
As **(aa–bb)**. Even-count turn.

Row 25: B, two As, B, three As, two Bs.
Decrease turn **(bb–cc)**.

Row 26: Two Bs, three As, B, two As
(cc–dd). Even-count turn.

Row 27: B, A, B, three As, two Bs.
Decrease turn **(dd–ee)**.

Row 28: Two Bs, three As, B, A **(ee–ff)**.
Even-count turn.

Row 29: B, four As, two Bs. Decrease
turn **(ff–gg)**.

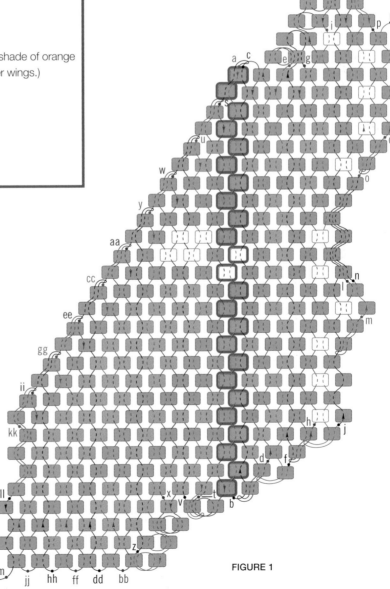

FIGURE 1

31

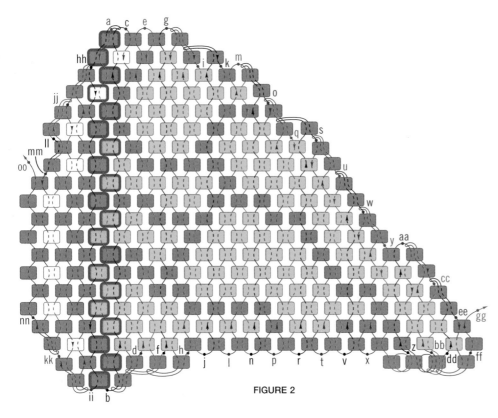

FIGURE 2

Row 30: Two Bs, two As, B, A (gg–hh). Even-count turn.

Row 31: Two Bs, two As, two Bs. Decrease turn (hh–ii).

Row 32: Three Bs, A, B (ii–jj). Even-count turn.

Row 33: Five Bs. Decrease turn (jj–kk).

Row 34: Skip two stitches by sewing back through the next four Bs (kk–ll). Two Bs (ll–mm). End the tail.

[5] Make a second large wing.

Small wing

[1] Attach a stop bead to 1½ yd. (1.4 m) of Fireline or thread, leaving a 12-in. (30 cm) tail.

[2] Work the small wing in peyote stitch as follows, referring to **figure 2**:

Rows 1 and 2: (Outlined in blue in **figure 2**) Three Bs, C, two Bs, A, B, A, B, two As, B, four As, three Bs (a–b). Even-count turn.

Row 3: B, two As, B, A, B, A, two Bs, C (b–c). Even-count turn.

Row 4: Two Bs, A, B, two As, B, two As, B. Decrease turn (c–d).

Row 5: Two As, B, A, two Bs, two As, B (d–e). Even-count turn.

Row 6: B, four As, B, A, B, A, B. Odd-count turn (e–f).

Row 7: Two As, B, two As, B, three As (f–g). Even-count turn.

Row 8: B, four As, three Bs, A, B. Odd-count turn (g–h).

Row 9: Two Bs, A, B, A, B, two As, B. Decrease turn (h–i).

Row 10: Two As, B, A, B, three As (i–j). Even-count turn.

Row 11: Two Bs, two As, three Bs, A, B. Odd-count turn (j–k).

Row 12: Two Bs, A, B, four As (k–l). Even-count turn.

Row 13: Two Bs, two As, B, three As (l–m). Even-count turn.

Row 14: Two Bs, six As (m–n). Even-count turn.

Row 15: Two Bs, two As, B, two As, B. Decrease turn (n–o).

Row 16: B, two As, B, two As, B (o–p). Even-count turn.

Row 17: B, five As, B. Decrease turn (p–q).

Row 18: Two As, B, three As (q–r). Even-count turn.

Row 19: B, two As, two As, B. Odd-count turn (r–s).

Row 20: B, two As, B, two As (s–t). Even-count turn.

Row 21: B, A, B, two As, B. Decrease turn (t–u).

Row 22: B, two As, two Bs (u–v). Even-count turn.

Row 23: B, three As, B. Decrease turn (v–w).

Row 24: B, A, two Bs (w–x). Even-count turn.

Row 25: Two Bs, A, B. Decrease turn (x–y).

Row 26: B, A, B. Work an increase stitch using two Bs (y–z).

Row 27: B, two As (z–aa). Even-count turn.

Row 28: B, two As. Sew through the increase B from the previous turn, pick up a B, and sew through the previous B and the new B (aa–bb).

Row 29: Two As, B. Decrease turn (bb–cc).

Row 30: B, A. Sew through the next B. Odd-count turn (cc–dd).

Row 31: A, B. Decrease turn (dd–ee).

Row 32: Two Bs. Odd-count turn (ee–ff).

Row 33: B (ff–gg).

[3] End the working thread. Remove the stop bead, and thread a needle on the tail. Work a decrease turn (a–hh), and complete the wing as follows:

Row 34: Nine Bs (hh–ii). Even-count turn.

Row 35: B, C, four Bs, two Cs, B. Decrease turn (ii–jj).

Row 36: Eight Bs. Decrease turn (jj–kk).

Row 37: B, four Cs, two Bs. Decrease turn (kk–ll).

Row 38: Skip a stitch by sewing through the next two beads (ll–mm). Five Bs. Decrease turn (mm–nn).

Row 39: Four Bs (nn–oo). End the tail.

[4] Make a second small wing.

Assembly

[1] On 18 in. (46 cm) of thread, work a ladder stitch (Basics) strip three color D 11º seed beads wide, and nine rows long. Repeat to make a second strip, but make it only eight rows long, then work a single D in the center of the ninth row using ladder stitch.

[2] Lay out the ladder stitch strips between the sets of wings (photo b). Align the top of the large wings with the top row of the first strip, and stitch the strip to the wings using a ladder stitch thread path, stitching through the ladder and the edge beads in the wings. Align the second strip between the indentations of the small wings, and stitch them together in the same manner.

[3] Exit the top row of ladder stitch between the two large wings. Pick up an 8º seed bead, a color D 11º, and an 8º,

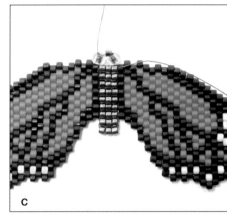

c

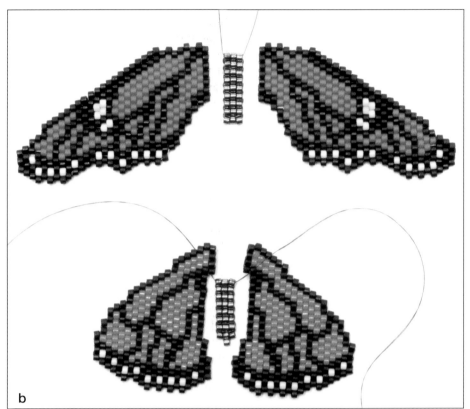

b

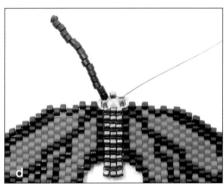

d

e

f

Peyote Stitch

and sew through the first ladder row again, and continue through the first 8º (photo c).

[4] Pick up 16 Bs, skip the last B, and sew back through the remaining Bs, the 8º, the three beads in the ladder, and the other 8º (photo d). Repeat to make the second antenna.

[5] Stitch the large wings to the small wings by first sewing through the last three beads in the ladder stitch strip between the large wings. Sew through the three beads in the top row of the ladder stitch strip between the small

wings (photo e). Retrace the thread path, and tack the two sets of wings together until they're secure.

[6] Position the pin-back finding on the underside of the butterfly (photo f), and tack it down until it is secure by sewing through the holes on the finding and the corresponding beads in the butterfly. End all of the threads. ●

EDITOR'S NOTE:
For a slightly smaller butterfly, try using 11º cylinder beads instead of seed beads. If you really want to challenge yourself, try using 15ºs.

Lively links

Connect ruffled rings to create an organic-looking chain

designed by **Marina Nadke**

Use beads with subtle
color variations or
high-contrast hues to
create impact.

a

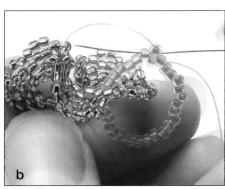

b

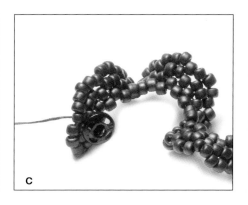

c

materials

necklace 17 in. (43 cm)

- 6–8 g 11º seed beads in each of **7** colors: A, B, C, D, E, F, G
- 4 mm snap fastener
- nylon beading thread, size D
- beading needles, #12

The colors of nature during Indian summer inspired this necklace. Choose your favorite season or theme, and the palette possibilities are endless.

step by step

Ruffled rings

[1] On 1 yd. (.9 m) of thread, pick up 30 color A 11º seed beads, and tie them into a ring with a square knot (Basics, p. 13), leaving a 1-in. (2.5 cm) tail. Sew through the ring again, pulling the knot to hide it in the beadwork. Trim the tail.
[2] Work one round of tubular peyote stitch (Basics). Step up through the first A added in the new round (**figure 1**).
[3] Pick up two As, and sew through the next A in the previous round (**figure 2, a–b**). Continue working a round of two-drop peyote stitch (Basics), sewing through one up-bead and adding two As per stitch, and step up through the first two As (**b–c**).

[4] Work two more rounds of two-drop peyote stitch, sewing through two up-beads and adding two As per stitch, and step up (**figure 3**). End the thread (Basics).
[5] On 1 yd. (.9 m) of thread, pick up 30 color B 11º seed beads. Using a square knot, tie them into a ring through the previous ruffled ring (**photo a**). Sew through the new ring again, pulling the knot to hide it in the beadwork, and trim the tail. Work a round of tubular peyote stitch as in step 2 (**photo b**), rotating the ring as you go. Repeat steps 3–4, rotating the work as you go.
[6] Attach 32 more ruffled rings, as in step 5, cycling through the 11º seed bead colors and ending with color F 11º seed beads.

FIGURE 1

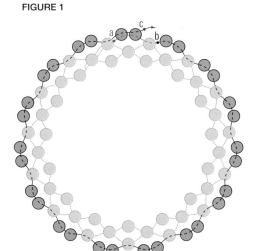

FIGURE 2

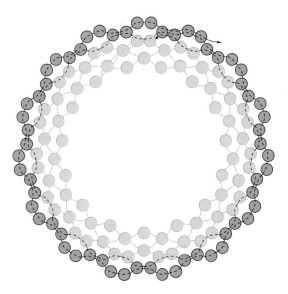

FIGURE 3

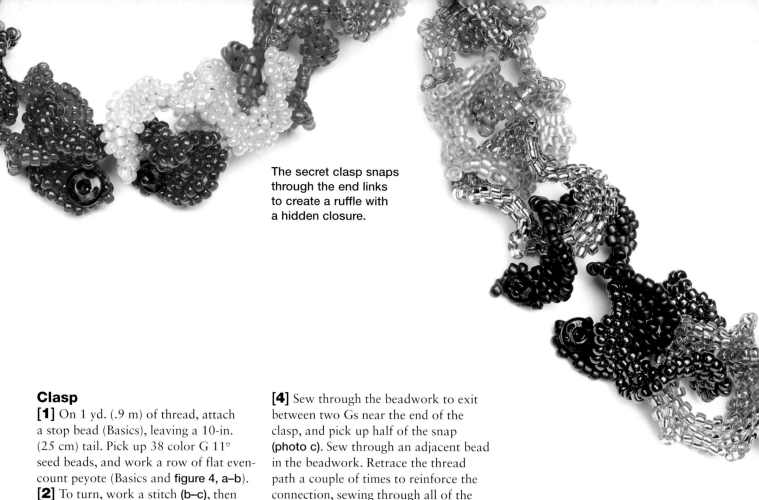

The secret clasp snaps through the end links to create a ruffle with a hidden closure.

Clasp

[1] On 1 yd. (.9 m) of thread, attach a stop bead (Basics), leaving a 10-in. (25 cm) tail. Pick up 38 color G 11º seed beads, and work a row of flat even-count peyote (Basics and **figure 4, a–b**).
[2] To turn, work a stitch (**b–c**), then work a row of two-drop peyote stitch, sewing through one up-bead and adding two Gs per stitch (**c–d**).
[3] To turn, work a stitch, then work a row of two-drop peyote stitch, sewing through two Gs and adding two Gs per stitch (**d–e**). Repeat (**e–f**).

[4] Sew through the beadwork to exit between two Gs near the end of the clasp, and pick up half of the snap (**photo c**). Sew through an adjacent bead in the beadwork. Retrace the thread path a couple of times to reinforce the connection, sewing through all of the open holes of the snap. End the thread.
[5] Remove the stop bead, and thread a needle on the tail. Repeat step 4 with the other half of the snap. ●

FIGURE 4

EDITOR'S NOTES:
• To make a bracelet, make enough links to reach your desired length.
• If your snap is slightly wider than the beadwork, you can work a partial row to hide it. Work a turn and two two-drop stitches on the working end (figure, a–b), and end the thread. Remove the stop bead on the opposite end, and sew through the beadwork to exit two two-drop stitches from the end (x–y). Work two two-drop stitches (y–z), and end the tail.

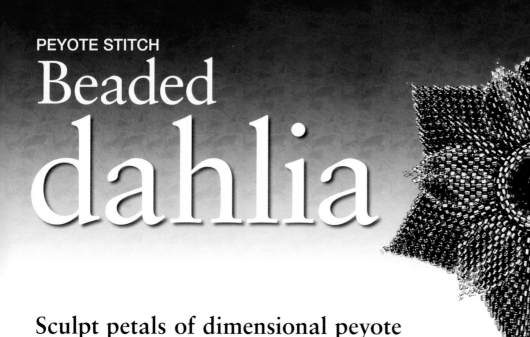

PEYOTE STITCH

Beaded dahlia

Sculpt petals of dimensional peyote to surround a bezel-set rivoli

designed by **Melanie Colburn**

Maintaining proper tension is key when working up the components of these stunning flowers. Pulling tight after each stitch will ensure that the leaves have gentle curves, and the bezel will hold the rivoli securely in place.

materials
brooch 3⅜-in. (8.6 cm) diameter

- 18 mm rivoli
- 5 g 11º cylinder beads
- 4 g 11º seed beads
- 3 g 15º seed beads
- pin-back finding
- Fireline, 6 lb. test
- beading needles, #12

step by step

Rivoli bezel

[1] On 1 yd. (.9 m) of Fireline, pick up 14 15º seed beads, and tie them into a ring with a square knot (Basics, p. 13), leaving a 6-in. (15 cm) tail. Sew through the first 15º again.

[2] Pick up five 15ºs, skip a 15º in the ring, and sew through the next 15º. Repeat six times to complete the round, and step up through the first three 15ºs in the first stitch (**figure 1**).

[3] Pick up five 11º cylinder beads, and sew through the center 15º in the next peak. Repeat six times to complete the

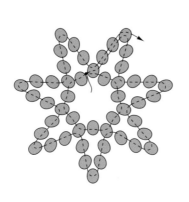

FIGURE 1

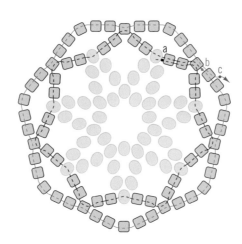

FIGURE 2

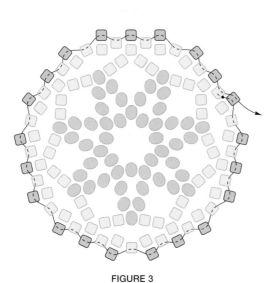

FIGURE 3

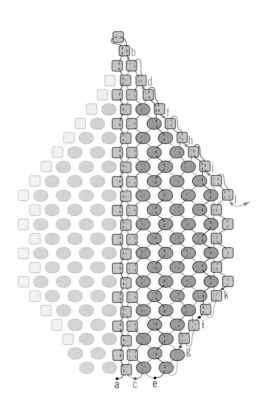

FIGURE 4

round. Step up through the first three cylinders in the first stitch (figure 2, a–b).
[4] Pick up five cylinders, and sew through the center cylinder in the next peak. Repeat six times to complete the round, and step up through the first cylinder in the new round (b–c).
[5] Work one round of tubular peyote stitch (Basics) using cylinders, and step up at the end of the round (figure 3).
[6] Place the rivoli face up in the beadwork, and, holding it in place, work three more rounds of tubular peyote using cylinders, pulling tight so the beads begin to cup around the rivoli.

[7] Work one more round using 15ºs. Sew through the last two rounds to secure the thread, but don't trim the working thread or tail.

Petals
Large petal
[1] Attach a stop bead (Basics) at the center of 1 yd. (.9 m) of Fireline. Pick up 24 cylinders, and slide them up to the stop bead. Skip the last cylinder picked up, and sew back through the next cylinder (figure 4, a–b).
[2] Work in flat peyote stitch (Basics) to complete the row using one cylinder per stitch (b–c).

[3] Continuing in peyote stitch, work the next row using 11º seed beads for 10 stitches, and a cylinder for one stitch. To work a decrease turn, sew back through the last cylinder added (c–d).
[4] Work the next nine rows in decreasing peyote, referring to figure 4:
Row 5: Work one stitch using a cylinder, and nine stitches using 11ºs (d–e).
Row 6: Work nine stitches using 11ºs, and one stitch using a cylinder. Work a decrease turn (e–f).
Row 7: Work one stitch using a cylinder, and eight stitches using 11ºs. Work a decrease turn by sewing back through the last 11º added (f–g).

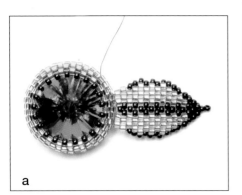

a

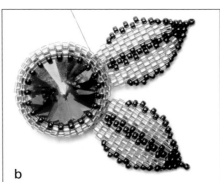

b

c

Use Japanese seed beads for sculptural, three-dimensional petals, or use Czech seed beads for flatter petals.

Row 8: Work one stitch using a cylinder, six stitches using 11°s, and one stitch using a cylinder. Work a decrease turn (g–h).

Row 9: Work one stitch using a cylinder, five stitches using 11°s, and one using a cylinder. Work a decrease turn (h–i).

Row 10: Work one stitch using a cylinder, four stitches using 11°s, and one stitch using a cylinder. Work a decrease turn (i–j).

Row 11: Work five stitches using cylinders. Work a decrease turn (j–k).

Row 12: Work four stitches using cylinders. Work a decrease turn (k–l). End the working thread (Basics).

[5] Remove the stop bead, and repeat rows 4–12 on the other side to complete the second half of the petal.

[6] Make a total of six large petals.

Small petal

[1] Work the small petal in the same manner as the large, with the following bead counts:

Rows 1–3: Pick up 18 15°s. Skip the last 15°, and sew back through the next 15°. Work eight peyote stitches using 15°s.

Row 4: Work seven stitches using cylinders, and one stitch using a 15°. Work a decrease turn.

Row 5: Work one stitch using a 15°, and six stitches using cylinders.

Row 6: Work six stitches using cylinders, and one stitch using a 15°. Work a decrease turn.

Row 7: Work one stitch using a 15°, and five stitches using cylinders. Work a decrease turn.

Row 8: Work one stitch using a 15°, three stitches using cylinders, and one stitch using a 15°. Work a decrease turn.

Row 9: Work four stitches using 15°s. Work a decrease turn.

Row 10: Work three stitches using 15°s. End the working thread and tail.

[2] Remove the stop bead, and work rows 4–10 to complete the second half of the petal.

Assembly

[1] Using the working thread from the rivoli bezel, stitch a small petal to the center outer round of peyote in the bezel by sewing through a cylinder in the bottom row of the petal, then a cylinder in the round of peyote in the bezel. Repeat until the petal is secure (photo a). Skip two beads in the bezel, and stitch the next small petal in place (photo b). Repeat to attach all the small petals.

[2] Sew through the beadwork to exit a cylinder in the next round of peyote in the bezel, behind the small petals. Stitch a large petal in the same manner, centering it between two small petals (photo c). Repeat to attach all the large petals. End the threads.

[3] Add a new thread (Basics) along the outer edge of a large petal. Sew through the beadwork along the edge, and connect the large and small petals so they don't flop forward: Exit a 15° on the edge of a small petal, and sew through a corresponding cylinder on the large petal. Sew through the 15° again. Retrace the thread path, then sew through the beadwork to the opposite edge 15° in the same petal, and repeat. Connect the remaining petals in the same manner.

[4] Position a pin-back finding on the back of the flower, and stitch it into place. End the working thread and tails. ○

PEYOTE STITCH

Learning
curve

**Embellish a peyote
base to create gentle
contours that conceal
a clever closure**

designed by **Aasia Hamid**

Create subtle contrast
between shiny and matte
beads to accent the design
of this curvy cuff.

Give a flat band curves with layers of beads. In this bracelet, hex-cut beads layered on the surface of a peyote band create a rippled shape and leave the perfect opening for a second layer of pearls to accentuate the curves.

step by step

[1] On 2 yd. (1.8 m) of Fireline, pick up six 3 mm cube beads, leaving a 12-in. (30 cm) tail. Working in even-count peyote stitch (Basics, p. 13), make a band 123 rows long, with 62 cubes on each straight edge. End and add thread (Basics) as needed.

[2] Work a decrease turn by sewing under the thread bridge between the last two cubes along an edge, and through the two cubes on the end **(figure 1, a–b)**. Work two stitches **(b–c)**. Work a decrease turn **(c–d)**, and work one stitch **(d–e)**. End the thread.

[3] Using the tail, stitch the male end of the snap to the top surface of the base **(photo a)**, and end the thread.

[4] Add 2 yd. (1.8 m) of Fireline in the beadwork at the decrease end, and exit the first cube in the first full-width row, with the needle pointing toward the beadwork. Pick up two 11º hex-cut seed beads, and sew through the next cube **(figure 2, a–b)**. Pick up two hex-cuts, sew through the next two cubes, then sew through the next edge bead **(b–c)**.

[5] Repeat the bead pattern from step 4 **(c–d)** until you have completed 10 rows of hex-cut embellishment. Zigzag through the next three edge cubes to position the needle to begin the next set of 10 rows of hex-cut embellishments. Repeat for a total of seven sets. End the thread.

[6] Add 2 yd. (1.8 m) of Fireline at the decrease end. Stitch the other end of the snap to the bottom surface of the base, centered under the first set of hex-cut embellishments.

[7] Exit the first two hex-cut beads added in step 4. Pick up a 3 mm pearl, and sew through the next two hex-cut beads. Pick up a pearl and a 15º seed bead, and sew through two cubes on the edge and the first two hex-cut beads in the next row **(figure 3)**. Repeat to add the pearl embellishment to the 10 rows of hex-cut beads. Sew through the cubes to exit the first pair of hex-cut beads in the next set of 10 rows, and repeat the pearl embellishment. Repeat for each set, and end the thread.

[8] Add 2 yd. (1.8 m) of Fireline in the beadwork, exiting an edge cube of the first full-width row at the decrease end. Pick up a 15º, a pearl, and a 15º. Sew under the thread bridge between the first two cubes and back through the last 15º **(figure 4, a–b)**.

[9] Pick up a pearl and a 15º, and sew under the thread bridge between the next two cubes and back through the last 15º **(b–c)**. Repeat to complete the edge, sew through the cubes along the end rows, and continue on the remaining edge.

[10] When you reach the decrease end, add a pearl embellishment to each decrease cube: Pick up a pearl and a 15º, skip the 15º, and sew back through the pearl and the cube your thread exited. Sew through the next three cubes, and repeat **(photo b)**. Add three more pearl embellishments, and end the thread. ○

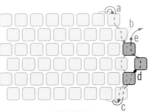

FIGURE 1

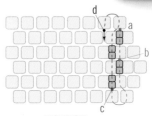

FIGURE 2

FIGURE 3

FIGURE 4

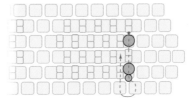

a

b

materials
bracelet 7 in. (18 cm)
- **267** 3 mm pearls
- 15 g 3 mm cube beads
- 10 g 11º hex-cut seed beads
- 3 g 15º seed beads
- 10–15 mm (size 3) snap
- Fireline, 6–10 lb. test
- beading needles, #12

Mirror Mirror

Brightly colored bezels make mirror components splash with summer fun

designed by **CJ Bauschka**

Using seed beads in three or four colors lends both unity and variety to this design.

Catch someone's eye when you wear this colorful set made with mirrors and vibrant seed beads.

stepbystep

Bracelet
Bezel-set mirror components

[1] On 1½–2 yd. (1.4–1.8 m) of Fireline, attach a stop bead (Basics, p. 13) in the center of the thread. Pick up enough color A, B, or C 11º seed beads to wrap loosely around the outside edge of a mirror, making sure to pick up an even number of beads. Sew through the first 11º to form a ring (photo a).

[2] Working in tubular peyote stitch (Basics), work a total of four rounds using 11ºs (photo b).

[3] Work two rounds of tubular peyote stitch using color A, B, or C 15º seed beads, pulling the thread tight as you stitch so the beads begin to form a flat surface (photo c).

[4] Work one or two more rounds of tubular peyote. If your beads are too snug to flatten, work evenly spaced peyote decreases (Basics) in the third or fourth round (photo d).

[5] Place the mirror in the bezel cup. Using the tail, repeat steps 3 and 4.

[6] Sew through the beadwork to exit the second round of 11ºs, pick up a contrasting color 11º seed bead or a 3–4 mm fringe drop, and sew through the next 11º in the round. Repeat around (photo e). Do not end the threads.

[7] Repeat steps 1–6 to stitch bezels around all of the mirrors, changing the bead colors and edging as desired. To add a picot edge, pick up three 15ºs instead of a drop or 11º in step 6.

Toggle clasp

[1] On 1 yd. (.9 m) of Fireline, pick up 38 15ºs, and sew through the first 15º again to form a ring. Working in tubular peyote stitch, work a round with 15ºs and a round with 11ºs (photo f).

[2] Work two rounds with 15ºs, and zip up (Basics) the edges to form a tubular ring. End the threads (Basics).

[3] On 28 in. (71 cm) of Fireline, attach a stop bead, leaving a 6-in. (15 cm) tail. Pick up 16 15ºs, and work in flat even-count peyote stitch (Basics) until you have 10 rows, with five beads along each edge of the strip. Zip up the ends, and exit one end of the tube. Pick up a fringe drop, and sew through the tube to exit the other end. Pick up a drop, and sew back through the tube. Reinforce the thread

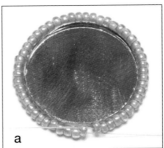
a

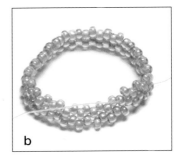
b

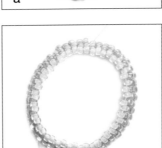
c

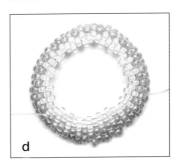
d

e

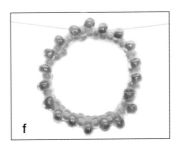
f

materials
both projects
- Fireline, 6 lb. test
- beading needles, #12 and #13

bracelet 8¼ in. (21 cm)
- craft mirrors
  1-in. (25 mm) diameter
  6 ¾-in. (19 mm) diameter
- 3 g 3–4 mm fringe drops
- 4 g 11º seed beads in each of **3** colors: A, B, C
- 3 g 15º seed beads in each of **3** colors: A, B, C

necklace 24 in. (61 cm)
- craft mirrors
  5 1-in. (25 mm) diameter
  8 ¾-in. (19 mm) diameter
  12 ½-in. (13 mm) diameter
- 4 g 3–4 mm fringe drops
- 8 g 11º seed beads in each of **3** colors: A, B, C
- 6 g 15º seed beads in each of **3** colors: A, B, C

Make a necklace to match your bracelet. The sizes of mirrors available may vary from store to store. If you can't find the same sizes listed here, play with the sizes and shapes you can find. Try asymmetrical or layered arrangements.

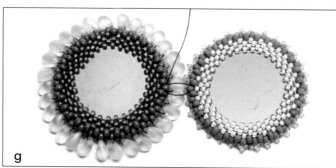

g

path through the drops, and end the thread.

Assembly
[1] Arrange your mirror components on your work surface in the desired order. You'll start with the center component and work your way to the ends as you connect the pieces.
[2] Using the tail on a component, exit an 11º in one of the two center edge rounds, and sew through an 11º in the corresponding round on an adjacent component and the 11º your

thread just exited (photo g). Sew through both beads again. End the thread.
[3] Repeat step 2 to connect the remaining components, taking care to attach them in a straight line.
[4] To attach the clasp, exit an 11º in the embellishment round of an end component, and pick up six 15ºs. Sew through an 11º on the toggle ring, and sew back through the last three 15ºs. Pick up three 15ºs, and sew through the embellishment 11º on the bezel again. Retrace the thread path, and end the thread.
[5] Repeat step 4 on the other end of the bracelet,

but sew through a 15º in the center of the toggle bar. End all remaining threads.

Necklace
[1] Follow the instructions in "Bracelet: Bezel-set mirror components" and "Bracelet: Toggle clasp" to make your necklace components.
[2] Arrange the components on your work surface. To give the necklace a V shape in front, you'll want to connect the components in the center at an angle, rather than in a straight line. Follow the instructions in "Bracelet: Assembly" to finish the necklace. ●

Gala*x*y
BEAD

Peyote components create a beaded bead that is out of this world

designed by **Gill Slone**

The materials list is for the necklace with three beaded beads. To cut down on time and materials, make a necklace with a single focal bead.

Beaders everywhere will think of the sky and the stars and celestial spheres when making Gill's galaxy bead.

Gill added even more sparkle by using crystals at each connection point.

step by step

Components

[1] On 1 yd. (.9 m) of Fireline, attach a stop bead (Basics, p. 13), leaving a 12-in. (30 cm) tail. Pick up an alternating pattern of a color A 11º cylinder bead and nine color B 11º cylinder beads three times. Sew through the first A to form a ring.

[2] Using Bs, work a round of tubular peyote stitch (Basics), and step up through the first B in the new round (figure 1).

[3] Work four stitches using As, then work a decrease by sewing through the next up-bead. Repeat twice, and step up through the first A (figure 2). This round will pull the beadwork into a rounded triangular shape.

[4] Work a round of peyote using color C 15º seed beads, and step up (figure 3).

[5] Sew through the next two beads to exit the center C on one side of the triangle. Pick up a 4 mm bicone crystal, skip three Cs, and sew through the next center C. Repeat twice (figure 4), then retrace the thread path through the beads in the last two rounds, pulling tight to snug up the beads. End the thread (Basics).

[6] Remove the stop bead, and sew through the next outside B. Work four stitches of peyote using color D 15º seed beads. When you reach the corner of the triangle, pick up a D, an A, and a D, and sew through the next B. Repeat twice (figure 5).

[7] Repeat steps 1–6 to make a total of eight components for each beaded bead, but for three of the components, use 2 yd. (1.8 m) of Fireline, leaving a 1-yd. (.9 m) tail. These tails will be used to assemble the beads.

Bead assembly

[1] Arrange four components on your work surface with four corner As

FIGURE 1

FIGURE 3

FIGURE 2

FIGURE 4

materials

necklace with three beaded beads 18 in. (46 cm)

- 4 8 mm bicone crystals
- 8 8 mm accent beads
- 138 4 mm bicone crystals
- 4–5 g 11º cylinder beads in each of 2 colors: A, B
- 3–4 g 15º seed beads in each of 2 colors: C, D
- 16 4 mm daisy spacers
- clasp
- 2 3–4 mm jump rings
- 2 crimp beads
- 2 crimp covers
- 2 Wire Guardians
- Fireline, 6 lb. test
- flexible beading wire, .014
- beading needles, #12
- chainnose pliers
- crimping pliers
- wire cutters

together. Using a 1-yd. (.9 m) tail, sew through to exit the next corner A. Sew through the center corner A in the next three components, then sew through the first A in the first component and the first D. Work five peyote stitches using Ds, and exit the next corner A **(figure 6)**.
[2] Lay the next two components out, and sew through the four corner As. Sew through the next D, and work five peyote stitches using Ds **(figure 7)**. Repeat to connect the last two components.
[3] Sew through the beadwork to exit the last D added, and zip up (Basics) the two adjacent sides **(figure 8)**. Continue

around the bead, either adding a row of Ds and zipping up the sides or just zipping up the sides where the extra row of Ds is already in place, until all the sides are connected. End the threads.
[4] Repeat steps 1–3 to assemble the remaining beaded beads.

Necklace assembly
[1] On 24 in. (61 cm) of beading wire, string a crimp bead, a 4 mm bicone crystal, and a Wire Guardian. Go back through the 4 mm and the crimp bead, and crimp it (Basics). Use chainnose pliers to close a crimp cover over the crimp.

[2] String 13 4 mms and a repeating pattern of an 8 mm accent bead and four 4 mms four times.
[3] String two daisy spacers, an 8 mm bicone crystal, two spacers, a 4 mm, a beaded bead, and a 4 mm. Repeat twice.
[4] String the second side as a mirror image of the first. Finish this end as in step 1.
[5] Open a 4 mm jump ring (Basics), attach half of the clasp to one end of the necklace, and close the jump ring. Repeat on the other end. ●

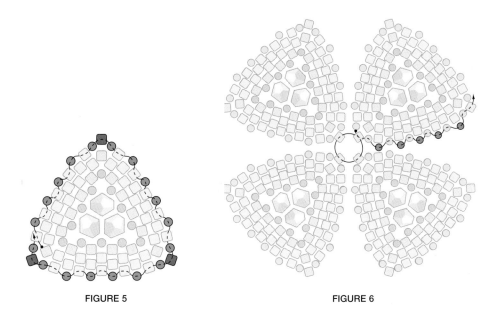

FIGURE 5

FIGURE 6

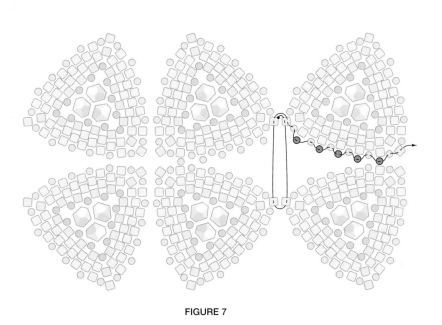

FIGURE 7

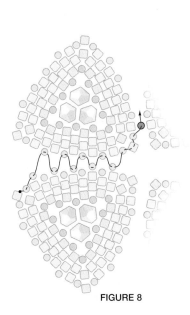

FIGURE 8

Nuts for peyote

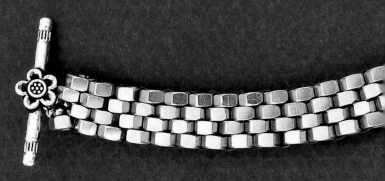

Turn a handful of hardware into a

materials

bracelet 7 in. (18 cm)

- **125–135** 5 x 2 mm stainless steel hex nuts (item FA-268-2829, greenboatstuff.com)
- **6** 11º seed beads
- toggle clasp with perpendicular loops or extra jump rings
- Fireline, 10 lb. test
- beading needles, #10

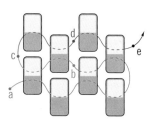

FIGURE

Use tiny stainless steel hex nuts to make a playful and slightly edgy peyote stitch bracelet.

step by step

[1] On 2 yd. (1.8 m) of Fireline, attach a stop bead (Basics, p. 13), leaving a 6-in. (15 cm) tail. Pick up four hex nuts.

[2] Working in flat even-count peyote stitch (Basics), pick up a nut, skip a nut, and sew back through the next nut (figure, a–b). Repeat (b–c).

[3] Pick up a nut, and sew through the next nut in the previous row (c–d). Repeat to complete the row (d–e), keeping your tension as tight as possible. The stitching may feel a bit loose at this point, but don't worry — you'll reinforce the bracelet later to tighten it up.

[4] Continue as in step 3 until the band is about ½ in. (1.3 cm) short of the desired length. Retrace the thread path through the entire band to tighten it up. This may shorten the band a bit, so test the fit, and add rows if necessary. Remove the stop bead, and end the threads (Basics).

[5] Add 12 in. (30 cm) of Fireline (Basics) at one end, and exit between the nuts in the end row. Pick up three 11º seed beads and the toggle loop, and sew through the next two nuts (photo). Retrace the thread path through a few end rows and the toggle loop connection several times, and end the thread. Repeat at the other end with the toggle bar, adding a jump ring or two if needed to allow the toggle bar to pivot. ◉

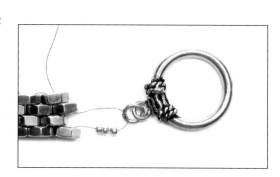

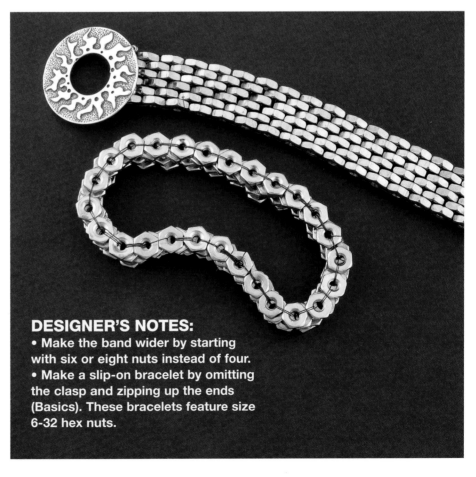

compelling and fun easy-to-stitch bracelet

designed by **Marilyn Mullins**

EDITOR'S NOTE:

Shopping for hex nuts can be confusing because they are sized and classified according to the bolts with which they are used. The nuts Marilyn used are size M3-.5, which indicates a metric size (M) with a 3 mm inner diameter and a 5 mm (or .5 cm) outer diameter. Your local hardware or home-improvement store may not carry this size in the quantity called for, if at all. Standard UTS (Unified Thread Standard) hex nuts are more readily available, but the smallest that can typically be found is 8 x 3 mm (size 6-32), which is what Marilyn used in her bangle-style bracelet (shown at right). In UTS sizes, the first number tells the outer diameter of the thread and the second number tells the number of threads per inch.

DESIGNER'S NOTES:
• Make the band wider by starting with six or eight nuts instead of four.
• Make a slip-on bracelet by omitting the clasp and zipping up the ends (Basics). These bracelets feature size 6-32 hex nuts.

Pretty as a package

Stitch a versatile bow using sculptural peyote

designed by **Ludmila Raitzin**

Use metallic cylinder and hex-cut beads in graduated sizes to create a dynamic bow fit for any special occasion. The shape of the bow is reminiscent of a butterfly, adding a touch of whimsy to an elegant pendant or brooch.

materials
bow 1¾ x 3½ in. (4.4 x 8.9 cm)
- 10º hex-cut seed beads, twisted or plain
  4–6 g color A
  2–4 g color B
- 4–6 g 11º hex-cut seed beads, twisted or plain
- 5–7 g 11º cylinder beads
- 1–2 g 15º seed beads
- Fireline, 6 lb. test
- beading needles, #12

stepbystep

Top ribbons

[1] On 2 yd. (1.8 m) of Fireline, attach a stop bead (Basics, p. 13), leaving a 6-in. (15 cm) tail, and pick up 24 11º cylinder beads. Pick up a cylinder, skip the previous cylinder, and sew through the next cylinder **(figure 1, a–b)**. Continue working in even-count peyote stitch (Basics) to the end of the row **(b–c)**.

[2] Continue working in even- and odd-count peyote stitch (Basics) as follows, keeping your tension relaxed in the first six to seven rows, then tightening your tension for the remaining rows:
Row 4: Work the first four stitches with cylinders and the rest of the row with 11º hex-cut seed beads **(figure 2, a–b)**.
Row 5: Work the first two stitches with 11º hex-cuts, then alternate between a cylinder and an 11º hex-cut for the next

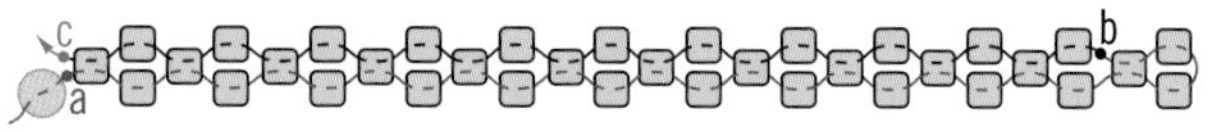

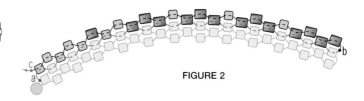

FIGURE 1

FIGURE 2

Wear this bow as a brooch, or attach it to a necklace as a pendant.

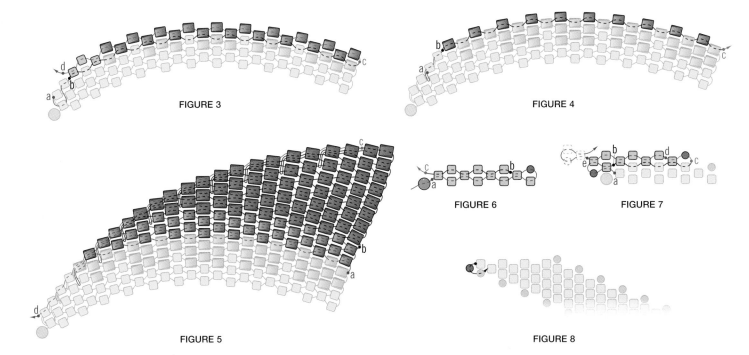

FIGURE 3

FIGURE 4

FIGURE 5

FIGURE 6

FIGURE 7

FIGURE 8

nine stitches, and work the last stitch with a cylinder **(b–c)**.

Row 6: To turn and decrease, sew through the first cylinder added in step 1, under the thread bridge of the last cylinder added, and step up through the last cylinder added **(figure 3, a–b)**. Work the first two stitches with cylinders and the remaining stitches with 11º hex-cuts **(b–c)**.

Row 7: Work the first 10 stitches with 11º hex-cuts and one stitch with a cylinder **(c–d)**.

Row 8: To turn and decrease, sew under the thread bridge between the cylinder your thread exited and the cylinder below it, and sew back through the cylinder your thread just exited and the last cylinder added **(figure 4, a–b)**. Work the row with 11º hex-cuts **(b–c)**.

Rows 9–12: Work the rows with 11º hex-cuts, and decrease at the beginning of each even-numbered row **(figure 5, a–b)**.

Rows 13–27: Work the rows with color A 10º hex-cut seed beads, and decrease at the beginning of each even-numbered row **(b–c)**.

[3] Sew through all the beads along the top diagonal edge **(c–d)**. Remove the stop bead, and end the tail (Basics) but not the working thread.

[4] Repeat steps 1–3 to make a second top ribbon, but work it as a mirror

image of the first. You can do this by working in the opposite direction, or see "Designer's note" (p. 53) for an alternate technique.

Bottom ribbons

[1] On 2 yd. (1.8 m) of Fireline, attach a stop bead, leaving a 6-in. (15 cm) tail, and pick up 26 cylinders. Work in even-count peyote stitch to the end of the row, as in step 1 of "Top ribbons," picking up one cylinder in each stitch.

[2] Continue working in even- and odd-count peyote stitch as follows, keeping your tension relaxed in the first six to seven rows, then tightening your tension for the remaining rows:

Row 4: Work the first eight stitches with cylinders, then alternate between an 11º hex-cut and a cylinder for the remaining stitches in the row.

Row 5: Work the first two stitches with 11º hex-cuts, then alternate between a cylinder and an 11º hex-cut for the remaining stitches in the row.

Row 6: Turn as in row 6 of "Top ribbons" to get into position for the next stitch. Work the first two stitches with cylinders, then alternate between an 11º hex-cut for two stitches and a cylinder for one stitch through the end of the row.

Rows 7–12: Work the rows with 11º hex-cuts, and decrease as in row 8 of

"Top ribbons" at the beginning of each even-numbered row.

Rows 13–15: Work the rows with color B 10º hex-cut seed beads, and decrease at the beginning of each even-numbered row.

Rows 16–29: Work the rows with As, and decrease at the beginning of each even-numbered row.

[3] Repeat step 3 of "Top ribbons."

[4] Repeat steps 1–3 to make a second bottom ribbon, but work it as a mirror image of the first.

Center tie strip

[1] On 2 yd. (1.8 m) of Fireline, attach a stop bead, leaving a 6-in. (15 cm) tail, and pick up eight cylinders and a 15º seed bead. Skip the last two beads picked up, and sew back through the next bead **(figure 6, a–b)**. Work three peyote stitches with cylinders **(b–c)**.

[2] Work an increase stitch: Pick up a cylinder, a 15º, and a cylinder, and sew back through the first cylinder picked up **(figure 7, a–b)**. Work three stitches with cylinders **(b–c)**.

[3] Work a decrease stitch: Pick up a 15º, and sew through the last cylinder added **(c–d)**. Work three stitches with cylinders **(d–e)**.

[4] Repeat steps 2 and 3 17–24 times to create a strip that measures 2⅞ in. (7.3 cm).

FIGURE 9   FIGURE 10

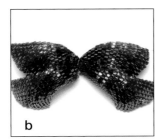

a

b

c

[5] To create a picot at the pointed tip of the strip, sew through the beadwork to exit an end cylinder. Pick up a 15º, and sew through the 15º at the end of the row **(figure 8)**. Remove the stop bead, thread a needle on the tail, and repeat on the remaining end. End the tail, but do not end the working thread.

Assembly and embellishment

[1] With a bottom ribbon overlapping a top ribbon, line up the holes of the two end cylinders of each ribbon. Using any thread, work a square stitch (Basics) thread path to sew an end cylinder of the bottom ribbon to the end cylinder of the top ribbon **(photo a)**. Repeat with the remaining adjacent end cylinders.

[2] Repeat step 1 with the remaining bottom and top ribbons.

[3] Using a square stitch thread path, sew the end cylinders of the top ribbons together **(figure 9, a–b)**. Repeat for the next two cylinders along the diagonal edge of the top ribbons **(b–c)**. Sew through the diagonal edge to exit the end A. Using a second thread, sew through the diagonal edge to exit the end A of the other top ribbon.

[4] Using a remaining thread from a bottom ribbon, work a square stitch thread path to sew the end cylinder of the bottom ribbons together, and repeat for any remaining beads that are touching. Sew through the

beadwork and the diagonal edge of a bottom ribbon to exit the edge end A, and repeat for the remaining bottom ribbon **(photo b)**.

[5] Working with either top or bottom ribbon and with your thread exiting an edge A, pick up three 15ºs, sew down through the next A, and up through the following A **(figure 10)**. Repeat along the edge of the ribbon, and end the thread. Repeat for the remaining ribbons.

[6] Wrap the center tie strip around the center of the bow, and align the edge 15ºs so the ends of the strip overlap the length of the bow's center **(photo c)**. Zip up (Basics) the 15ºs.

[7] Sew through the beadwork to exit a cylinder adjacent to an edge of the bow. Sewing through corresponding beads in the beadwork of both pieces, tack down the center tie strip to the bow. End the thread. ●

DESIGNER'S NOTE:
To make a mirror-image ribbon, work the first six to seven rows exactly as the first ribbon, then push the beadwork in to make the convex beadwork concave. Continue working, keeping the curve intact.

EDITOR'S NOTES:
• To wear the bow as a brooch, sew through the beadwork as you did in step 7 of "Assembly and embellishment" to attach a pin-back finding to the back of the center tie strip.

• To wear the bow as a pendant, leave the center tie strip loose around the back of the bow, allowing space to string a necklace. Cut the desired length of beading wire plus 3–4 in. (7.6–10 cm). Center the bow on the wire through the loop on the back of the center tie strip. On both ends, string a pleasing assortment of beads, leaving 1½–2 in. (3.8–5 cm) at the ends. String a crimp bead and half of a clasp, and go back through the crimp bead again. Crimp the crimp bead (Basics). Repeat for the second half of the clasp.

• If your bows have a more subtle curve than the designer's original, change the alignment in steps 3 and 4 of "Assembly and embellishment": Overlap the pointed tips of the left and right halves of the bow so that about two or three columns align, and sew them together.

Choose a deep, cool color
or vibrant hue for your
fire-polished beads, then
pair it with seed beads
that blend or contrast for
maximum impact.

RIGHT-ANGLE WEAVE

STACKED
sparkle

Lacy picots surround two
rows of fire-polished beads

designed by **Michelle Skobel**

Surround your favorite fire-polished beads with loops of seed beads, then embellish them for a bracelet that makes a sparkling statement with a delicate look. These bracelets work up so fast you'll have time to make them in many different colors.

step by step

[1] On a comfortable length of thread or Fireline, pick up 14 color A 11º seed beads and the loop half of the clasp, leaving a 6-in. (15 cm) tail. Tie the working thread and tail together with a square knot (Basics, p. 13), and sew through the next five As **(figure 1, a–b)**.
[2] Pick up a 4 mm fire-polished bead, two As, and a 4 mm, and sew through the last two As your thread exited, the first 4 mm, and the two As just picked up **(b–c)**.
[3] Repeat step 2, working in right-angle weave (Basics) until the bracelet is ½ in. (1.3 cm) short of the desired length. End and add thread (Basics) as needed.
[4] Pick up 12 As and the other half of the clasp, and sew through the two As your thread exited and the first A of the new loop **(figure 2, a–b)**. Pick up six As, skip the next 4 mm, and sew through the next two As **(b–c)**.
[5] Pick up seven As, skip the next 4 mm, and sew through the next two As **(c–d)**. Repeat **(d–e)** to the end of the bracelet, picking up only six As in the last stitch and sewing through an A in the loop to mirror the other clasp loop.
[6] Sew through the beads in the clasp loop, the two shared As in the first stitch, and the next A **(figure 3, point a)**. Pick up four As, skip the next 4 mm, and sew through the last two As in the next loop, the two center As, and the first two As in the loop on the other side of the bracelet **(a–b)**.

[7] Pick up three As, skip the next 4 mm, and sew through the last two As in the next loop, the two center As, and the next two As on the other side **(b–c)**. Repeat to the other end. Sew through the clasp loop on the other end, and exit a center A in the first three-A set on one edge **(figure 4, point a)**.
[8] Pick up three As, sew through the A your thread exited again, and continue through the next A **(a–b)**. Pick up an A, and sew through the next two As **(b–c)**. Repeat along the edge, sew through the clasp loop, and repeat along the other edge.
[9] Sew through the beadwork to exit the third bead in the first picot on one edge, with your needle pointing away from the bracelet **(figure 5, point a)**. Pick up three color B 11º seed beads, and sew down through the nearest A in the next picot, the A at the base of the picot, and the next picot A **(a–b)**. Repeat **(b–c)** along the edge, and sew through the beadwork to repeat along the other edge. End the thread and tail. ●

EDITOR'S NOTE:
As you stitch, make sure each segment is loose enough to lie flat. If you pull the beads tight with each stitch, you'll end up with a ruffled effect on the edges.

materials
bracelet 7 in. (18 cm)
- **54** 4 mm fire-polished beads
- **6 g** 11º Japanese seed beads, color A
- **3 g** 11º seed beads, color B
- clasp
- nylon beading thread, size D, or Fireline, 6 lb. test
- beading needles, #12

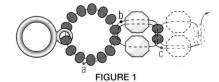

FIGURE 1

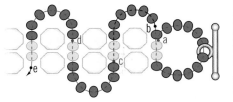

FIGURE 2

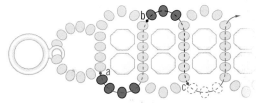

FIGURE 3

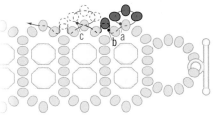

FIGURE 4

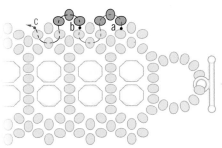

FIGURE 5

Metal rings linked by seed beads mimic traditional chain mail, a style Cindy has dubbed BeadMaille™.

Chain of rings

Use seed beads in right-angle weave to create a stitched variation of a European chain mail pattern

designed by **Cindy Thomas Pankopf**

Right-Angle Weave

Small decorative rings and chains of seed beads come together for a necklace that unites two techniques. Linking the rings through the loops of right-angle weave creates a look that mimics traditional chain mail patterns but includes the color and texture of seed beads.

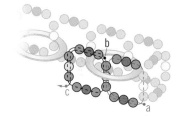

FIGURE 1

stepbystep

Row 1

[1] On a comfortable length of Fireline, pick up a color A 11º seed bead, a color B 11º seed bead, two As, a color C 11º seed bead, and an A. Repeat the six-bead pattern, and pick up a 9 mm ring. Tie the beads into a ring with a square knot (Basics, p. 13), leaving a 10-in. (25 cm) tail. Sew through the first six beads again (**figure 1, a–b**).

[2] Pick up an A, a B, two As, a C, two As, a B, and an A, and sew through the 9 mm and the last three beads in the previous stitch again (**b–c**). Continue through the first six beads picked up in this step (**c–d**).

[3] Following the established color pattern, pick up nine 11ºs and a 9 mm. Working in right-angle weave (Basics), sew through the end three 11ºs in the previous stitch and the first six beads just added. Repeat step 2 (**d–e**).

[4] Repeat step 3 until your chain has 36 9 mms, ending and adding thread (Basics) as needed.

[5] Work one stitch of right-angle weave following the established color pattern, but do not add a 9 mm.

Row 2

[1] Pick up nine 11ºs following the established color pattern, and sew through the last 9 mm added in the previous row, the last three 11ºs in the previous stitch, and the first six 11ºs just added (**figure 2, a–b**).

[2] Pick up nine 11ºs, and sew through the same 9 mm, the last three 11ºs in the previous stitch, and the first six 11ºs just added (**b–c**).

[3] Continue working in right-angle weave, sewing through the 9 mms added in the previous row as in steps 1 and 2, until you have stitched the second row through a total of 11 9 mms.

[4] Begin adding 9 mms to the second row: Pick up nine 11ºs in the

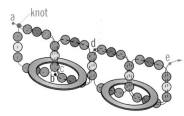

FIGURE 2

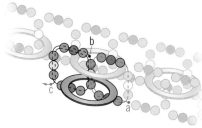

FIGURE 3

established color pattern and a 9 mm, and sew through the next 9 mm in the previous row and the last three 11ºs in the previous stitch. Continue through the first six 11ºs added in this step and the two 9 mms (**figure 3, a–b**). Pick up

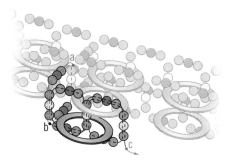

FIGURE 4

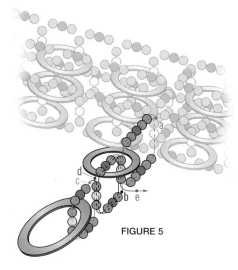

FIGURE 5

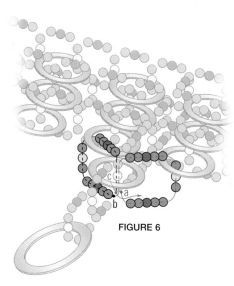

FIGURE 6

FIGURE 7

nine 11ºs in the established pattern, and work a stitch, sewing through both 9 mms **(b–c)**.

[5] Repeat step 4 to add a total of 14 9 mms in the second row. Depending on how you stitch, the new 9 mms may sit above or below the 9 mms added in the first row, but they must be consistent.

[6] Work the remainder of the row as in steps 1 and 2 without adding new 9 mms.

[7] Join the ends of the first and second row with a regular stitch, as you did at the other end: Pick up an A, a B, and an A, and sew through the three edge 11ºs in the first stitch of the first row. Pick up an A, a B, and an A, and sew through the three end 11ºs at the end of the second row. End the thread.

Row 3

[1] On a comfortable length of Fireline, pick up an A, a B, two As, a C, two As, a B, and an A, and sew through the three 11ºs that are shared by the stitches between the second and third 9 mm in the second row. Tie the working thread and tail together with a surgeon's knot (Basics), and sew through the first six 11ºs added in this step **(figure 4, a–b)**.

[2] Work as in step 4 of "Row 2" **(b–c)** to add a total of 10 9 mms to the third row. Connect the third row to the second as in step 1: Pick up an A, a B, and an A, and sew through the A, C, and A connecting the corresponding stitching in row 2. Pick up an A, a B, and an A, and sew through the beads your thread exited in the third row.

Center dangle

[1] Sew through the beadwork to exit the A, C, and A between the fifth and sixth 9 mm in the third row. Pick up two As, a B, three As, a C, three As,

a B, two As, and a 9 mm. Sew through the A, C, and A your thread exited and the first eight 11ºs added in this step **(figure 5, a–b)**.

[2] Work a nine-bead stitch following the established color pattern **(b–c)**. Work another stitch, picking up the 12 x 18 mm oval **(c–d)**. Sew back through the beadwork to exit the A, C, and A in the single 9 mm **(d–e)**.

[3] Pick up two As, a B, three As, a C, three As, a B, and two As, and sew through one of the two nearest 9 mms in the third row and through the three 11ºs your thread exited at the start of this step **(figure 6, a–b)**. Repeat with the other 9 mm **(b–c)**. End the thread.

Clasp

[1] Using the tail at one end of the necklace, pick up two As, a B, two As, the loop of half of the clasp, two As, a B, and two As. Sew through the three 11ºs at the end of the first row **(figure 7)**. Retrace the thread path, and end the thread.

[2] Add 12 in. (30 cm) of thread to the other end of the necklace. Repeat step 1 to attach the other half of the clasp. ●

materials

necklace 17 in. (43 cm)

- 12 x 18 mm OD decorative metal oval
- **61** 9 mm outside-diameter (OD) decorative metal rings
- 11º seed beads
  10 g color A
  5 g each of **2** colors: B, C
- clasp
- Fireline, 6 lb. test
- beading needles, #10 or #12

A hammered clasp matches the finish of the 9 mm rings.

RIGHT-ANGLE WEAVE

Waves
of symmetry

Playful scallops encircle your wrist

designed by **Cindy Caraway**

Try combining different brands or types of seed beads to play with the shapes in this bracelet.

FIGURE 1

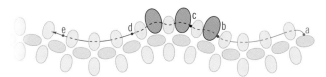

FIGURE 2

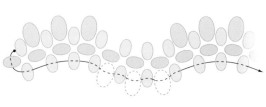

FIGURE 3

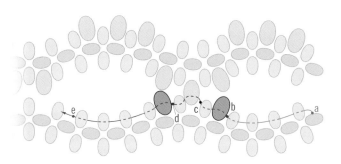

FIGURE 4

An embellishment of 8° seed beads joins and shapes simple bands of right-angle weave into waves of color. Each row is constructed and joined the same way, so you can make bracelets as wide or narrow as you'd like.

materials
bracelet 7 in. (18 cm)
- 6–8 mm accent bead
- 3 g 8° seed beads
- 4 g 11° seed beads in each of
  2 colors: A, B
- nylon beading thread
- beading needles, #12

step by step

[1] On a comfortable length of thread, pick up a color A 11° seed bead, a color B 11° seed bead, an A, and a B, leaving a 10-in. (25 cm) tail. Sew through the four beads again to form a ring, and continue through the next A and B **(figure 1, a–b)**.

[2] Pick up an A, a B, and an A, and sew through the B your thread exited at the start of this step **(b–c)**. Continue through the next A and B **(c–d)**.

[3] Repeat step 2 to continue in right-angle weave (Basics, p. 13), until the strip has 73 As along one edge, or a multiple of six plus one. Keep in mind that the

bracelet will shrink a bit as you work the edge embellishments, so you should create an initial strip about 20 percent longer than your desired finished length.

[4] Exiting the last B, sew through the next four As along the top of the row **(figure 2, a–b)**. Pull the thread snug so the As sit side by side.

[5] Pick up an 8° seed bead, and sew through the next A **(b–c)**. Repeat twice **(c–d)**, then continue through the next three As **(d–e)**. Pull snug. Repeat to the end of the strip, ending with three 8°s.

[6] Sew through the B at the end of the strip, and continue through the first four As on the other side **(figure 3)**. Work the second side as in step 5,

taking care to alternate the placement of the 8°s with the 8°s on the other side of the band. Do not end the thread.

[7] Repeat steps 1–3 to create a second right-angle weave strip with the same number of stitches as the first.

[8] Exit the last B, and sew through the next four As along the top of the strip, pulling the thread snug **(figure 4, a–b)**.

[9] Pick up an 8°, and sew through the next A **(b–c)**. Align the new strip with the embellished strip, and sew through the corresponding 8° on the lower edge

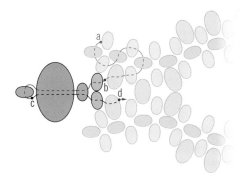

FIGURE 5

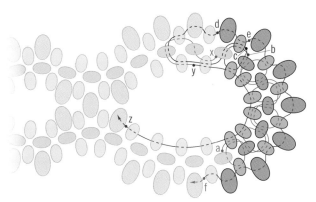

FIGURE 6

DESIGNER'S NOTE:
To make your bracelet wider, stitch additional waves by repeating steps 7–10.

of the embellished strip and the next A on the new strip **(c–d)**. Pick up an 8º, and sew through the next four As on the new strip **(d–e)**. Repeat for the length of the strip.

[10] Embellish the lower edge as in step 6. Do not end the threads or tails.

[11] One end of the bracelet ends with five 8ºs in the center, while the other end has six 8ºs on the outer edges. At the joined end of the bracelet, use a tail to sew through the beadwork and exit an 8º at the end of the bracelet **(figure 5, a–b)**. Pick up an A, a B, a 6–8 mm accent bead, and a B **(b–c)**. Skip the last B, and sew back through the 6–8 mm and B, pick up an A, and sew through the other end 8º **(c–d)**. Flip the beadwork, and use the other tail to sew the same thread path through the beads. End both tails (Basics).

[12] At the other end of the bracelet, using a working thread, exit an end B, and work five right-angle weave stitches

off the center strip, following the original color pattern **(figure 6, a–b)**. Pick up an A, sew through the B at the end of the other strip, pick up an A, and sew through the last B added **(b–c)**. Sew through the beadwork to exit the last 8º on the outside of the embellished strip, and sew through the next A **(c–d)**.

[13] Pick up an 8º, and sew through the next A **(d–e)**. Repeat around the outside of the strip until you meet the embellishment on the other edge **(e–f)**, and end the thread.

[14] With the other working thread, sew through the beadwork to exit one of the inner-edge As in the initial strip **(x–y)**. Sew through all the As on the inner edge of the loop **(y–z)**, leaving enough slack so the beadwork is flexible enough to fit around the clasp bead, and end the thread. ●

You can choose just about any type of 6–8 mm bead for a great-looking closure.

Shimmering snowflakes

Use this easy technique
to create an elegant chain of
crystal snowflakes that drapes
dramatically around your neck

designed by **April Bradley**

Enjoy the icy look of snowflakes
year-round with crystals.

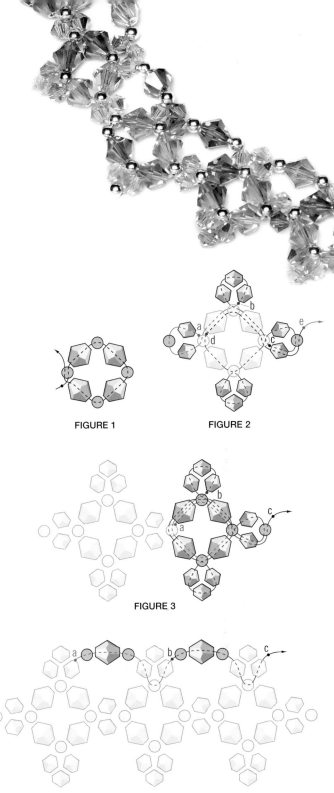

Form and function go hand-in-hand in this pretty necklace. Picots at the corners of right-angle weave units add delicate detail while also providing useful connection points.

step by step

[1] On 2 yd. (1.8 m) of Fireline, pick up a repeating pattern of a 3 mm silver bead and a 6 mm bicone crystal four times. Tie the beads into a ring with a square knot (Basics, p. 13), and sew through the next 3 mm in the ring **(figure 1)**.

[2] To add picots to the 3 mms around the ring, pick up a 4 mm bicone crystal, a 3 mm, and a 4 mm. Sew through the 3 mm your thread exited at the start of this step, and through the next 6 mm and 3 mm in the ring **(figure 2, a–b)**.

[3] Pick up three 4 mms, and sew through the 3 mm your thread exited at the start of this step. Sew through the next 6 mm and 3 mm in the ring **(b–c)**.

[4] Repeat steps 2 and 3 **(c–d)**, then sew through the next four beads and the next 4 mm and 3 mm **(d–e)**.

[5] Pick up a repeating pattern of a 6 mm and a 3 mm three times, then pick up a 6 mm. Sew through the 3 mm your thread exited at the start of this step and the next 6 mm and 3 mm **(figure 3, a–b)**.

[6] Work picots off the 3 mms in the new ring **(b–c)**.

[7] Repeat steps 5 and 6 until you have 22 6 mm units. End the threads (Basics).

[8] Add 30 in. (76 cm) of thread (Basics) on one end of the necklace, leaving a 6-in. (15 cm) tail and exiting the inside top 4 mm **(figure 4, point a)**.

[9] Pick up a 3 mm, a 6 mm, and a 3 mm. Sew through the next 4 mm, 3 mm, and 4 mm at the top of the next 6 mm unit **(a–b)**. Repeat **(b–c)** until you reach the other end of the necklace. End the threads.

[10] Cut a 3-in. (7.6 cm) piece of 22-gauge wire. Make the first half of a wrapped loop (Basics), and slide the loop through the end 3 mm on one end of the necklace. Complete the wraps **(photo a)**. Make the first half of a wrapped loop above the wraps, attach one half of the clasp, and complete the wraps.

[11] Repeat step 10 on the other end of the necklace **(photo b)**. ◉

materials
necklace 18 in. (46 cm)
- bicone crystals
  109 6 mm
  178 4 mm
- **132** 3 mm silver beads
- clasp
- 6 in. (15 cm) 22-gauge wire
- Fireline, 6 lb. or 8 lb. test
- beading needles, #12
- chainnose pliers
- roundnose pliers
- wire cutters

FIGURE 1

FIGURE 2

FIGURE 3

FIGURE 4

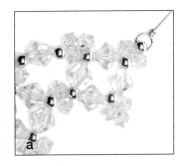

a

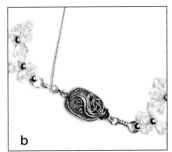

b

RIGHT-ANGLE WEAVE

Pearls and pagodas

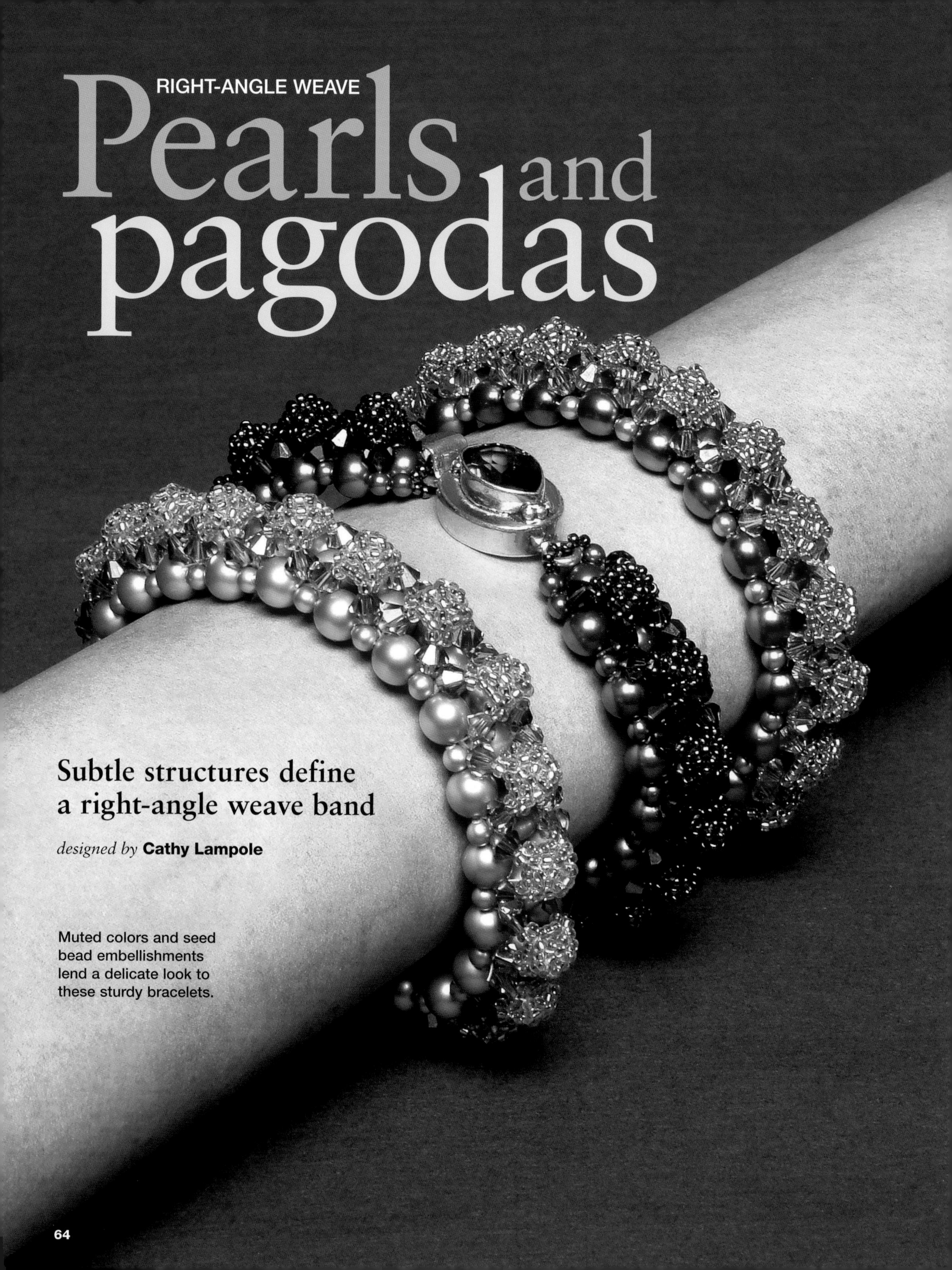

Subtle structures define a right-angle weave band

designed by **Cathy Lampole**

Muted colors and seed
bead embellishments
lend a delicate look to
these sturdy bracelets.

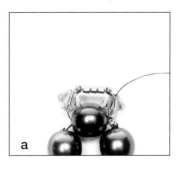
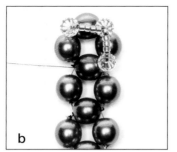
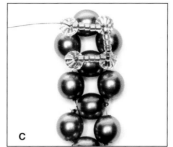
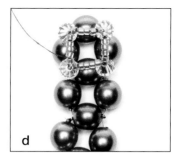

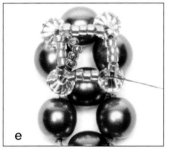

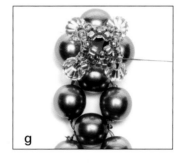

Right-angle weave provides all sorts of opportunities for embellishments. Take full advantage of that in this bracelet by building up from the base row and filling all the spaces in between!

step by step

[1] On 3 yd. (2.7 m) of thread, leave a 6-in. (15 cm) tail, and use 6 mm pearls to make a right-angle weave strip (Basics, p. 13) that is 19 stitches long.

[2] With the thread exiting the end 6 mm in the last stitch, pick up a 4 mm bicone crystal, five 15° seed beads, and a 4 mm. Sew through the end 6 mm and the first 4 mm again **(photo a)**.

[3] Working in right-angle weave, pick up five 15°s and a 4 mm, and sew through the next 6 mm in the stitch, the 4 mm your thread just exited, the five 15°s and 4 mm just added, and the next 6 mm in the stitch **(photo b)**.

[4] Pick up a 4 mm and five 15°s. Sew through the previous 4 mm and 6 mm, through the next 6 mm in the stitch, and through the adjacent 4 mm that was added in step 2 **(photo c)**.

[5] Pick up five 15°s, and sew through the 4 mm added in the previous stitch, the 6 mm below the 15°s just added, the next 4 mm, and the first four 15°s of the set just added **(photo d)**.

[6] Pick up five 15°s, and sew through the last three 15°s your thread exited at the start of this step and the center three 15°s in the next stitch **(photo e)**.

[7] Pick up four 15°s, and sew through the end 15° in the previous stitch, the center three 15°s your thread just exited, and the center three 15°s in the next stitch. Repeat.

[8] Sew through the end 15° in the first stitch, pick up three 15°s, and sew through the end 15° in the last stitch and the three center 15°s your thread just exited. Step up through the first three 15°s in the new stitch **(photo f)**.

[9] Pick up a 15°, and sew through the center 15° in the next stitch. Repeat three more times **(photo g)**. Retrace the thread path through the top ring of 15°s, and sew through the beadwork to exit the 6 mm connecting the next right-angle weave stitch.

[10] To work each subsequent "pagoda," exit the connecting 6 mm, and repeat steps 2–9, ending and adding thread (Basics) as needed. End with at least 1 yd. (.9 m) of thread.

[11] To attach the clasp, exit an end 6 mm. Pick up two 3 mm pearls, three 15°s, half of the clasp, and three 15°s. Sew back through the two 3 mms and the end 6 mm **(photo h)**. Pick up two 3 mms and three 15°s, sew through the same half of the clasp, and pick up three 15°s. Sew back through the two 3 mms, retrace the thread path several times, and exit an edge 6 mm next to the end 6 mm.

[12] Pick up a 3 mm, and sew through the next 6 mm on the same edge **(photo i)**. Repeat along this edge until you reach the last 6 mm. Sew through the end 6 mm, and repeat step 11 to attach the other half of the clasp on this end. Then continue adding 3 mms along the remaining edge. End the threads. ⊙

materials

bracelet 7½ in. (19.1 cm)
- 58 6 mm pearls
- 44 3 mm pearls
- 76 4 mm bicone crystals
- 5–7 g 15° Japanese seed beads
- clasp
- nylon beading thread, size D
- beading needles, #12

Make the strips of herringbone along the edges of the base a contrasting finish to really highlight the design.

Layered LOOPS

Repeat a simple technique to produce an intriguing bracelet

designed by **Smadar Grossman**

A herringbone band provides the foundation for strips of seed beads that curve delicately as they are stitched in place. The look resembles basket weaving while creating spaces to showcase tiny glass drops.

step by step

Base

[1] On a comfortable length of Fireline, use color A 11º seed beads, and work a row of ladder stitch (Basics, p. 13) 76 beads long, leaving a 12-in. (30 cm) tail. Add or omit beads to achieve the desired length, making sure you end with an even number of beads.

[2] Working in herringbone stitch (Basics) and using As, stitch a total of 13 rows, ending and adding thread (Basics) as needed. If your working thread is shorter than 30 in. (76 cm), end it and add a new thread.

[3] Work a ladder stitch thread path through the last row, and position the working thread and tail at opposite ends.

[4] Exit the fifth bead in an end stack. Sew through the loop of one half of the clasp and back into the end stack of As, exiting the A that lines up with the next loop of the clasp. Repeat to attach the other clasp loop. Retrace the thread path several times to secure the connection. End the working thread. Repeat on the other end using the tail.

materials

bracelet 6½ in. (16.5 cm)

- **38** 3 mm drop beads
- 11º seed beads
  - 25–30 g color A
  - 2 g color B
- 4–5 g 15º seed beads
- two-strand sliding tube clasp
- Fireline, 4 lb. test
- beading needles, #12

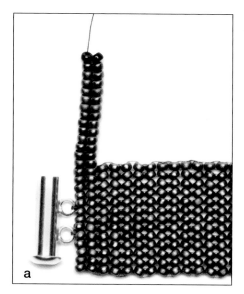

a

b

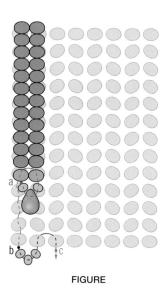

FIGURE

a

b   c

Embellishment

[1] Add a new thread, and exit the first A on one edge of the base.

[2] Pick up two As, and sew through the next A in the edge row, the first A in the row, and the first new A.

[3] Pick up two As, and sew through the second A in the previous stitch, the first A in the previous stitch, and the first A in the new stitch. Repeat for a total of 12 stitches, then work one stitch using color B 11º seed beads **(photo a)**.

[4] Bend the strip over so the Bs align with the two As in the fourth row from the opposite edge, and sew

through the two As and the two Bs **(photo b)**.

[5] Pick up a 15º seed bead, a drop bead, and a 15º. Sew through the two Bs again and the next four As in the first stack on the base **(figure, a–b)**. Pick up three 15ºs, and sew through the next two As in the row **(b–c)**.

[6] Repeat steps 2–5 until you reach the other end of the bracelet, ending and adding thread as needed. ●

DESIGNER'S NOTE:

For a chunkier version of this bracelet, use size 8º seed beads in place of the 11ºs, 11ºs in place of the 15ºs, 4 mm drops in place of the 3 mm drops, and a three-strand tube clasp in place of the two-strand

clasp. Stitch 10 rows of herringbone for the base, and for steps 2 and 3, work nine stitches with As and one stitch with Bs. In step 4 of "Embellishment," sew through the As in the third row instead of the fourth row.

TUBULAR HERRINGBONE STITCH

Flame tree flowers

Turn to nature for botanical inspiration

designed by **Judith Golan**

Stitched with 11° cylinder beads (far left), each blossom measures about 1 x ¾ in. (2.5 x 1.9 cm). Stitched with 15°s (left), each comes in at ⅞ x ⅝ in. (2.2 x 1.6 cm).

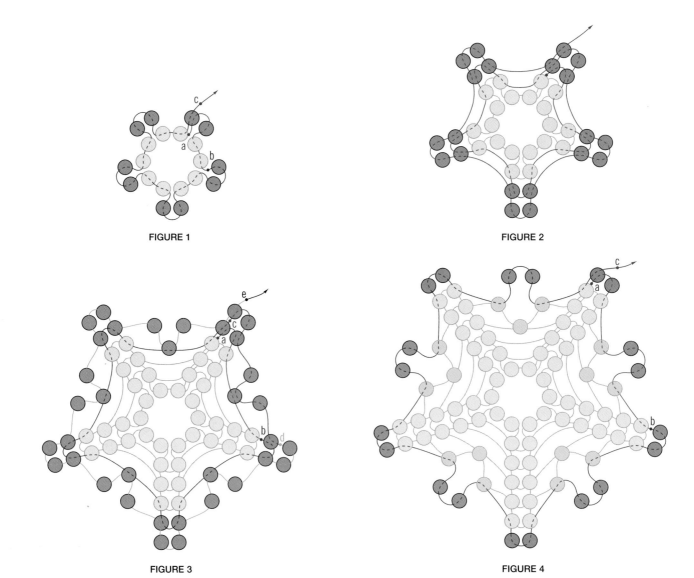

FIGURE 1

FIGURE 2

FIGURE 3

FIGURE 4

materials

pair of earrings

- **2** 6º seed beads or 4 mm beads
- **11**º cylinder beads or 15º seed beads

  5 g color A

  3 g color B

  2 g color C
- **10** or more color D seed beads in assorted sizes for stamen (optional)
- pair of earring findings
- Fireline, 6 lb. test
- beading needles, #12, #13, or #15

Each spring, the Australian flame tree (*Brachychiton acerifolius*) covers itself in brilliant red bell-shaped flowers. Use herringbone stitch to create your own tiny bells. Stitch them in the authentic red, or get creative and experiment with multiple colors.

step by step

The following instructions are for the three-color version of the flower, with fuchsia used for color A, violet for color B, and orchid for color C. The red version uses opaque red luster for color A and transparent red AB for colors B and C.

[1] On 1½ yd. (1.4 m) of Fireline, pick up 10 color A 11º cylinder beads or 15º seed beads, leaving a 10-in. (25 cm) tail. Sew through all the beads again to form a ring, and sew through the first bead once more. This is round 1.

[2] Work in tubular herringbone stitch (Basics, p. 13) as follows:

Round 2: Pick up two As, and sew through the next two As in the ring **(figure 1, a–b)**. Repeat four times, and step up through the first A added in this round **(b–c)**.

Rounds 3 and 4: Work two rounds of five stitches per round using two As per stitch **(figure 2)**.

Round 5: Pick up two As, and sew down through the next A. Pick up a B, and sew up through the next A **(figure 3, a–b)**. Repeat four times, and step up **(b–c)**.

a

b

c

d

e

f

Though you have to peek inside the beaded buds to see them, the stamens add a charming touch to these earrings.

EDITOR'S NOTE:
Choose beading needles based on the beads' size. Use #12 if you're stitching with 11° cylinders. Select #13 or #15 if you're stitching with 15°s.

Round 6: Pick up two As, and sew down through the next A. Pick up a B, and sew through the next B. Pick up a B, and sew through the next A **(c–d)**. Repeat four times, and step up **(d–e)**.
Round 7: Pick up two As, and sew through the next A and B. Pick up two Bs, and sew through the next B and A **(figure 4, a–b)**. Repeat four times, and step up **(b–c)**.
Rounds 8 and 9: Work two rounds with an alternating pattern of a stitch with two As and a stitch with two Bs five times. Pull tight so the beadwork curves.
Rounds 10 and 11: Pick up two As, and sew down through the next A. Pick up a C, and sew up through the next B **(photo a)**. Pick up two Bs, and sew down through the next B. Pick up a C, and sew up through the next A. Repeat four

times, and step up. Work another round.
Round 12: Work as in rounds 10 and 11, but pick up two Cs between the stitches instead of one **(photo b)**.
Rounds 13 and 14: Work two rounds as in rounds 10 and 11, positioning the Cs as in rounds 10 and 11.
Round 15: Work a stitch with two As, skip the next C, and sew up through the following B. Work a stitch with two Bs, skip the next C, and sew up through the following A. Repeat around, and step up. Pull tight after each stitch so the beadwork begins to curve inward.
Round 16: Work 10 stitches with two As per stitch.
Round 17: Pick up one A per stitch to create a picot at the end of each herringbone column. Step up through the first picot A **(photo c)**.

Round 18: Pick up two As, and sew through the next picot A and the following three As to exit the following picot A **(photo d)**. Repeat four times, and step up through the first A added in this round.
Round 19: Pick up an A, a C, and an A, and sew through the next six As **(photo e)**. Repeat four times, and end the thread (Basics).

[3] With the tail, pick up a 6° seed bead or 4 mm bead, six As, and the loop of an earring finding. Sew back through the 6° or 4 mm, and sew through a bead opposite where your thread exited at the start of this step **(photo f)**. Retrace the thread path a few times.
[4] If desired, add a stamen: Sew through the 6° or 4 mm so your needle exits inside the flower. Pick up five or more color D seed beads. Skip the last one, and sew back through the rest of the Ds and the 6° or 4 mm. Sew through the hanging loop again, and end the thread.
[5] Repeat steps 1–4 to make a second earring. ○

Bonus Earrings

Dripping with an abundance of copper-coated leaves, this lovely lariat is the perfect autumn accessory.

Fall fascination

Copper-dipped leaves contribute an authentic fall motif to this vine-like lariat

designed by **Babette Borsani**

Free-form fringe clusters disguise a branching herringbone rope — a stylishly practical way to taper the thickness of this lush lariat.

step by step

Lariat

Herringbone rope

[1] On a comfortable length of thread, use 8º seed beads to work a row of ladder stitch (Basics, p. 13) eight beads long, leaving a 6-in. (15 cm) tail. Join the ends of the ladder to form a ring (Basics), and exit the first bead.
[2] Working in tubular herringbone stitch (Basics), stitch five rounds using 8ºs.
[3] Continue stitching rounds using 6º

seed beads, 8ºs, and 11º seed beads to create a bumpy texture in the rope **(photo a)**. End and add thread (Basics) as needed.
[4] When the herringbone rope is about 7 in. (18 cm) long, reduce the four-stitch rope to a three-stitch rope: Begin by adding two beads for the first stitch. Skip two columns, and sew up through the top 8º in the following stack **(photo b)**. Work two more stitches to complete the round. You will return to the two columns you

skipped to stitch a branch after you have completed the herringbone rope.
[5] Continue stitching three-stitch rounds for 3–5 in. (7.6–13 cm). Reduce the three-stitch rope to a two-stitch rope as in step 4.
[6] Continue stitching two-stitch rounds for another 9 in. (23 cm).
[7] Repeat steps 3–6 to complete the other half of the herringbone rope.

Branches

[1] Add a new thread near a point where you reduced the beadwork from four stitches to three, and exit a bead in the skipped stitch. This stitch will be referred to as the base stitch.
[2] Pick up four 8ºs, and sew through both beads of the base stitch to form a ring **(photo c)**, then sew through the first bead just added. This ring will be the basis for a new herringbone tube.
[3] Pick up two 8ºs, and sew through the next two beads in the ring **(photo d)**. This is the first herringbone stitch in the

a

b

c

d

EDITOR'S NOTE:
For a budget-friendly option to copper-coated leaves, try using leaf dangles made from shells, as shown at right. Other options include resin leaves, Czech pressed-glass leaves, and base metal charms or stampings.

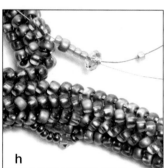

branch. Pick up two 8ºs, and sew through the fourth bead in the ring and the first bead in the base stitch **(photo e)**. Pick up two 8ºs, and sew through the next bead in the base stitch and the top two beads in the first herringbone stitch **(photo f)**.

[4] Working off the beads added in step 3, continue in herringbone for the desired number of rounds. If you want, taper the branch by replacing the 8ºs with 11ºs, and then the 11ºs with 15º seed beads for four or five rounds.

[5] Sew back to the reduction point, and secure the unattached part of the first round of the branch to the rope.

[6] Repeat steps 1–5 at the remaining reduction points.

Embellishments
Enhance the ends of the rope and branches, the column reduction points, and any other desired spots using one or more of the following embellishments.

Surface embellishment
Pick up a combination of five to nine seed beads and crystals, and sew through a bead in the herringbone rope to create a ridge **(photo g)**. Repeat as desired, altering bead counts to your liking.

Fringe
Pick up a combination of seed beads, rondelles, pearls, or bicones, ending with one or three B 11ºs. Skip the B 11ºs, and sew back through the rest of the fringe beads and into the rope **(photo h)**. Repeat as desired, altering bead counts to your liking.

Leaf-shaped fringe
[1] Pick up four to 15 A 11ºs and 11 B 11ºs, skip the end B 11º, and sew back through the second-to-last B 11º **(figure 1, a–b)**. Pick up nine B 11ºs, and sew back through the last two A 11ºs picked up in this stitch **(b–c)**.

[2] Pick up two A 11ºs and 11 B 11ºs, skip the end B 11º, and sew back through the second-to-last B 11º. Pick up nine B 11ºs, and sew back through the two A 11ºs picked up in this stitch and the next two A 11ºs in the stem **(c–d)**.

[3] Repeat step 2 to fill the stem with leaves **(d–e)**, substituting a 3 or 4 mm bicone crystal as the next-to-last bead, if desired, and altering bead counts to your liking.

Tendril
Pick up a repeating pattern of a 15º and a B 11º until you have the desired length, and end with a 15º. Skip the end 15º, and sew back through only the 11ºs **(figure 2)**. Tighten the thread to make the tendril curl **(photo i)**. Sew into the herringbone rope, and tie a half-hitch knot (Basics).

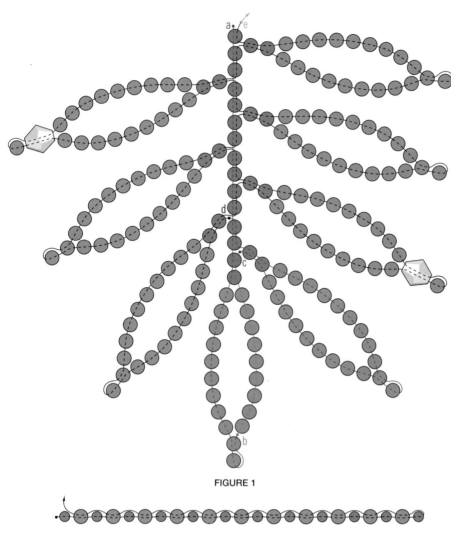

FIGURE 1

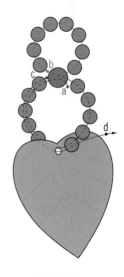

FIGURE 2

materials

both projects

- nylon beading thread, size D
- beading needles, #12

lariat 46 in. (1.2 m)

- **28–35** 25–51 mm one-hole copper-coated leaves (Shipwreck Beads, shipwreckbeads.com)
- **2–3** 16-in. (41 cm) strands 5–7 mm pearls
- **30–35** 6 mm crystal rondelles
- **70–85** 3–6 mm bicone crystals
- **10–15 g** 6º seed beads
- **75–90 g** 8º seed beads
- 11º seed beads
  5–10 g color A
  5–10 g color B
- **3–5 g** 15º seed beads

pair of earrings

- **2** 25–30 mm one-hole copper-coated leaves
- **2** 3–4 mm crystals
- **2** 8º seed beads
- **1 g** 11º seed beads, color A or B
- **1 g** 15º seed beads
- **2** 4 mm jump rings
- pair of earring findings
- **2** pairs of pliers

Pearl "berry" cluster

[1] Pick up five to 10 8ºs, two or three 15ºs, a pearl, and two or three 15ºs, and sew back through the last 8º **(photo j)**.
[2] Pick up two or three 15ºs, a pearl, and two or three 15ºs, and sew back through the next 8º. Repeat to add one or more loops to each 8º in the stem, altering bead counts to your liking.

Leaf dangle fringe

Pick up: two to four 8ºs, five to nine A 11ºs, leaf, rondelle, five to nine A 11ºs. Sew back through the 8ºs **(photo k)**. Sew into the branch, and exit another column. Repeat as desired to add more leaves, altering bead counts as desired.

Earrings

[1] On 1 yd. (.9 m) of thread, pick up an 8º seed bead, five 11º seed beads, a leaf, and five 11ºs. Sew through the 8º to form a loop **(figure 3, a–b)**.

[2] Pick up eight 11ºs, and sew through the 8º again to form a loop above the first loop **(b–c)**. Sew through the beads of the lower loop to exit an 11º on the front of the leaf **(c–d)**.
[3] Working as in "Embellishments: Tendril," pick up a repeating pattern of an 11º and a 15º seed bead 11 times, then sew back through the 11ºs. Pull tight to make the strand curl. Sew through the next 11º on the front of the leaf.
[4] Repeat step 3 twice, substituting a 3 mm or 4 mm crystal for the last 11º on one of the tendrils, if desired.
[5] Sew through the 8º and the loop of 11ºs above it, and end the threads (Basics).
[6] Open a 4 mm jump ring (Basics), attach the top loop of 11ºs and the loop of an earring finding, and close the jump ring.
[7] Make a second earring. o

FIGURE 3

Sunflower

A cluster of crystals sets the stage
for a blossom of fanciful fringe.

power

A flourish of fringe in a contrasting color demands attention

designed by **Merle Berelowitz**

Catch the sunlight with the sparkle of crystals and the shine of seed beads when you combine simple herringbone stitch with basic — and not so basic — bead-embroidered fringe to make a cuff with powerful impact.

stepbystep

Base

[1] Wrap the Ultrasuede around the cuff blank, and cut a piece that will cover the blank front and back, end to end. Spread E6000 adhesive on the inside of the cuff blank, and center the Ultrasuede along the inside of the cuff blank. Allow 12 hours for the glue to dry.

[2] Fold the ends of the Ultrasuede over the outside of the cuff, and trim them so they lie flush next to each other. Sew the edges together using whip stitch (Basics, p. 13, and **photo a**).

[3] On a comfortable length of Fireline or Power Pro, use 10º cylinder beads to make an even-count ladder (Basics) wide enough to span the width of the cuff blank (about 22 cylinders). Work in herringbone stitch (Basics) until the beadwork covers the blank (about

82 rows), ending and adding thread (Basics) as needed. Align the strip along the outside of the fabric-covered cuff blank, making sure the strip is the correct length, and add or remove rows as needed.

[4] If desired, place a strip of double-sided tape down the center of the cuff, and position the herringbone strip on it. Sew through the edge row of the strip, and stitch the strip to the Ultrasuede by sewing through the Ultrasuede (**photo b**), then through the next few beads on the edge of the strip. Repeat around the cuff until the strip is secure. End the thread.

Flower

[1] Using a compass or circular template, trace a circle with a 1¹⁄₁₆-in. (2.7 cm) radius on a piece of Lacy's Stiff Stuff beading foundation. Make a circle within the first circle with a ¾-in.

(1.9 cm) radius. Cut around the edge of the larger circle (**photo c**).

[2] Using a permanent marker close to the color of your margaritas, color the inner circle (**photo d**).

materials

cuff bracelet
- **38** 6 mm margaritas
- approximately **200** 3 mm bicone crystals
- 20 g 10º cylinder beads
- 30 g 11º seed beads
- 5 g 15º seed beads
- 2-in. (5 cm) brass bracelet cuff blank
- Fireline, 6 lb. or 8 lb. test, or Power Pro, 10 lb. test
- beading needles, #10 or #12
- compass to make a circle, or a 2⅛-in. (5.4 cm) diameter and 1½-in. (3.8 cm) diameter circular template
- double-sided tape (optional)
- E6000 adhesive
- Lacy's Stiff Stuff beading foundation
- permanent marker
- Ultrasuede

Herringbone Stitch

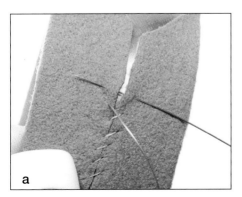

a

b

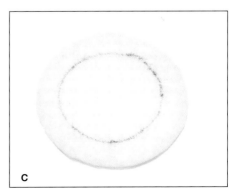

c

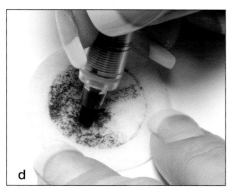

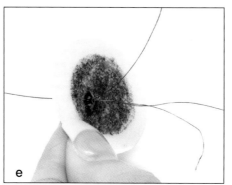

[3] To embellish the center of the flower, tie an overhand knot (Basics) at the end of 1 yd. (.9 m) of thread. Sew through the foundation from back to front, exiting near the edge of the colored circle. Pick up a 6 mm margarita and a 15º seed bead. Skip the 15º, and sew back through the 6 mm and the foundation **(photo e)**. Repeat to fill in the colored circle with 6 mms, placing them close to each other.

[4] To make the flower petals, use a comfortable length of thread, and exit close to the outside edge of the colored circle. Pick up five 11º seed beads, a 3 mm crystal, and a 15º. Skip the 15º, and sew back through the 3 mm and the next 11º. Pick up three 11ºs, skip three 11ºs, and sew through the next 11º. Sew back through the foundation **(photo f)**. Come up through the foundation close to the first petal. Repeat around the circle.

[5] For each petal in the second round, pick up seven 11ºs, a 3 mm, and a 15º. Skip the 15º, and sew back through the 3 mm and the next 11º. Pick up five 11ºs, skip five 11ºs, and sew through the next 11º. Sew back through the foundation and up through the foundation close to the previous petal. Repeat around the circle.

[6] Continue adding rounds of petals until the outer circle is filled, increasing

the number of 11ºs picked up before the 3 mm by two in each round, and matching the second half of the petal to the first **(photo g)**.

[7] Exit the foundation near the outer circle of petals. Pick up two 11ºs, and sew down through the foundation. Come up right next to where you sewed through the foundation. Sew through the last bead added **(photo h)**. Continue in brick stitch (Basics) along the outside edge of the circle.

[8] If desired, cut a circle of Ultrasuede to fit the back of the embellished circle. Glue it to the back of the foundation, and let it dry.

[9] Center the flower on the herringbone strip, and secure it by sewing through beads in the brick stitch edge and corresponding beads in the herringbone strip **(photo i)**. Repeat around the flower, and end the thread. ○

EDITOR'S NOTE:
To make a daintier bracelet, use a smaller cuff, stitch a narrower strip of herringbone, and embellish a smaller circle of beading foundation.

TUBULAR HERRINGBONE STITCH / FRINGE

Draped
expectations

Connect herringbone scallops and add fringe for an elegant necklace

designed by **Melissa Grakowsky**

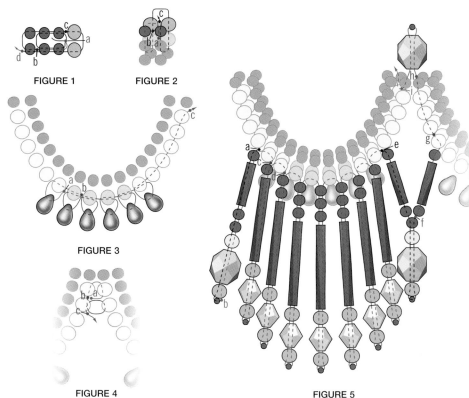

FIGURE 1

FIGURE 2

FIGURE 3

FIGURE 4

FIGURE 5

materials

necklace 13 in. (33 cm)

- **91** 15 mm bugle beads
- **26** 6 mm bugle beads
- **91** 4 mm bicone crystals
- **28** 4 mm fire-polished beads
- **140** 3 mm magatama or fringe drops
- **8–10 g** 8º seed beads in each of 2 colors: A, B
- **8–10 g** 11º seed beads
- **1–2 g** 15º seed beads
- Fireline, 6 lb. test
- beading needles, #12

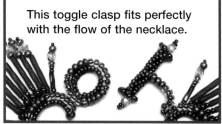

This toggle clasp fits perfectly with the flow of the necklace.

This necklace took careful planning to create, but it is deceptively simple to work up. Once you get the hang of your tension — tight scallops and relaxed fringe — the units come together with ease.

step by step

Scallops

[1] On 1 yd. (.9 m) of Fireline, pick up four 11º seed beads, and tie them into a ring with a square knot (Basics, p. 13), leaving a 10-in. (25 cm) tail. Sew through the first two 11ºs again (**figure 1, a–b**).
[2] Pick up two 11ºs, and sew through the next two 11ºs in the ring (**b–c**). Pick up two color A 8º seed beads, sew through the next two 11ºs, and step up through the first 11º in this round (**c–d**).
[3] Pick up two 11ºs, and sew through the next 11º and up through the next A (**figure 2, a–b**). Pick up two As, and sew down through the next A and up through the next two 11ºs (**b–c**). Working in tubular herringbone (Basics), repeat until you have six rounds with As. Work four rounds substituting color B 8º seed beads for the As, six rounds with As, and a round with 11ºs only.

[4] Sew through each column, and pull the Fireline taut to reinforce the curvature of the scallop. Sew through the beadwork to exit an A adjacent to a B, pick up a 3 mm magatama or fringe drop, and sew through the A again and the next B (**figure 3, a–b**). Working in square stitch (Basics), add five more 3 mms, and sew through the remaining As in the column to exit the A adjacent to the 11º (**b–c**). Do not end the working thread or tail.
[5] Repeat steps 1–4 to make 13 scallops.

Assembly

[1] Thread a needle on the tail of a scallop, and sew through the beadwork to exit the first A. Using a square stitch thread path, sew through the corresponding A in the next scallop, and continue through the A your thread exited in the previous scallop (**figure 4, a–b**). Sew through the next A, and use a square stitch thread path to connect the corresponding A in the adjacent scallop

(**b–c**). Sew through the beadwork to exit an A on the back side of the scallop, and repeat to connect the top two As of each column. End the tail (Basics).
[2] With the remaining thread, sew through the beadwork to exit the fourth A on the back side (**figure 5, point a**). Pick up an 11º, a 6 mm bugle bead, two 11ºs, an A, a 4 mm fire-polished bead, a B, and a 15º seed bead (**a–b**). Skip the 15º, sew back through all the beads just added, and continue through the next A (**b–c**).
[3] To add the next fringe, pick up an 11º, a 15 mm bugle bead, a B, a 4 mm bicone crystal, a B, and a 15º. Skip the 15º, sew back through all the beads just added, and continue through the next 8º (**c–d**). Repeat six times with the following changes: Pick up two 11ºs for the second fringe, three 11ºs for the third through fifth fringes, two 11ºs for the sixth fringe, and one 11º for the seventh fringe (**d–e**).
[4] Pick up an 11º, a 6 mm, two 11ºs, an A, a fire-polished, a B, and a 15º. Skip the 15º, and sew back through the B, fire-polished, A, and an 11º (**e–f**). Pick up an 11º, a 6 mm, and an 11º, and sew through the fourth A in the next unit (**f–g**).

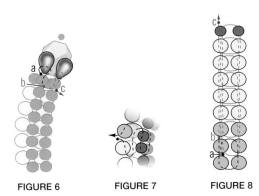

FIGURE 6   FIGURE 7   FIGURE 8

EDITOR'S NOTES:
• At 13 in. (33 cm), this necklace fits only the smallest necks. To make your choker a little longer, add more scallops. Each scallop will add about ⅞ in. (2.2 cm).
• You can substitute 12 mm bugles for the 15 mm bugles, which are slightly easier to find and won't change the look of the necklace too much.
• The toggle bar fits through the loop snugly. To give it a little more room, stitch two more rounds in the loop and two more rounds on the toggle bar connector.

a

b

c

[5] Sew through the remaining beads in the column to exit an end 11º (g–h). Pick up a fire-polished and a 15º, skip the 15º, sew back through the fire-polished, and continue through the 11º in the previous scallop (h–i). Sew up through the adjacent 11º at the end of the column of 8ºs, and sew through the fire-polished, 15º, fire-polished, and corresponding 11º in the next scallop.
[6] Sew up through an 11º at the end of an inner column of 11ºs, pick up a 3 mm, and sew back down through the 11º (figure 6, a–b). Sew up through the 11º at the end of the next inner column, and repeat (b–c). Sew through the beadwork to exit an 11º at the end of an inner column in the previous unit, and add two more 3 mms as before. End the thread.
[7] Repeat step 1 to connect the remaining scallops, and repeat steps 3–6 to add fringe and embellishments.

Clasp
Loop
[1] On 1 yd. (.9 m) of Fireline, pick up two 11ºs and two As, and tie them into a ring with a square knot, leaving a 6-in. (15 cm) tail. Sew through the first 11º again. Work six rounds of tubular herringbone as in "Scallops," following the established pattern until you have seven rounds with As.

[2] Work four rounds substituting Bs for the As, seven rounds with As, and four rounds with Bs.
[3] To form the curved beadwork into a ring, work a herringbone thread path connecting the last beads added to the first beads added in step 1 (figure 7).
[4] Use a square stitch thread path to connect the As of two rounds of the loop to an end scallop, as in step 1 of "Assembly." Sew through the beadwork to exit an edge 11º of an inner column at the end of the scallop. Pick up a 3 mm, sew back through the 11º, and exit the adjacent 11º. Repeat to add a second 3 mm, and end the thread.

Toggle bar
[1] On 1½ yd. (1.4 m) of Fireline, attach a stop bead (Basics), leaving a 10-in. (25 cm) tail. Pick up 14 11ºs. Work a total of 10 rows of flat even-count peyote stitch (Basics) to make a panel that is 14 11ºs wide with five 11ºs on each straight edge. Remove the stop bead, and zip up (Basics) the panel to make a tube.
[2] Sew through the beadwork to exit an edge 11º. Pick up a fire-polished and three 15ºs. Sew back through the fire-polished and an 11º opposite the one your thread exited (photo a). Sew up through an adjacent 11º, through all

of the beads just added, and the 11º opposite the one your thread exited.
[3] Sew up through an adjacent 11º, pick up a 3 mm, and sew back through the 11º your thread exited (photo b). Repeat around the edge to add five 3 mms.
[4] Thread a needle on the tail, and repeat steps 2 and 3 on the remaining end of the toggle bar. End the tail.
[5] With the working thread, sew through the beadwork to exit a center 11º on the toggle bar. Pick up two As, and sew through an adjacent 11º (photo c). Sew through all the beads again to reinforce the connection, and exit an A.
[6] Pick up two As, and sew down through the adjacent A and up through the A your thread exited and the first A added (figure 8, a–b). Repeat with another pair of As, five pairs of Bs, and a pair of 11ºs (b–c).
[7] Use a square stitch thread path to connect two rows of the toggle bar's connector to an end scallop, as in step 1 of "Assembly." Sew through the beadwork to exit an edge 11º of an inner column at the end of the scallop. Pick up a 3 mm, sew back through the 11º, and exit the adjacent 11º. Repeat to add a second 3 mm, and end the thread. ◉

Herringbone Stitch

Coming around

Basic brick stitch bands
get thrown for a loop

designed by **Dina Broyde**

Maintaining even tension is easier to accomplish on
the first looped band. When you start the first looped
band, try not to pull too tight as you stitch. It isn't
possible to work the second looped band as tightly
because of the intertwined design.

Increasing bead sizes in each row of brick stitch transforms straight lines into a bracelet full of motion, and intertwined bands create an interesting intersection.

stepbystep

Base
[1] On 3 yd. (2.7 m) of thread, pick up an 11º cylinder bead, two 11º seed beads, and a cylinder, leaving a 10-in. (25 cm) tail. Sew through all four beads again, snugging the beads into two stacks of two beads (figure 1, a–b).
[2] Working in ladder stitch (Basics, p. 13), pick up a cylinder and an 11º, and sew through the previous two beads and the two new beads (b–c). Pick up an 11º and a cylinder, and sew through the previous two beads and the two new beads (c–d). Repeat for a total of 81 stitches.
[3] Fold the ladder in half, lining up the first and last cylinders end to end (photo a). Sew through the ladders, using a ladder stitch thread path (figure 2), until you have a 1-in. (2.5 cm) opening at the center of the curved end of the base. Sew back through the ladder to exit an end 11º.
[4] Work a row of brick stitch (Basics) off the thread bridges between the 11ºs, using triangle beads (figure 3). Note: Because the triangle beads nestle together, you will have to add two triangle beads to some of the thread bridges. As you work subsequent rows, you may skip thread bridges because the bigger beads take up more room along the row.
[5] Continuing in brick stitch, use 8º seed beads to work a row of brick stitch off of the triangles, work a row of 3 mm fire-polished beads off the row of 8ºs, and work a row of 3 mm cube beads off the row of fire-polished beads.
[6] To work a decorative picot row, exit an end cube, and pick up three 15º seed

beads. Sew back through the cube your thread just exited, and continue through the next cube in the row (figure 4). Repeat to complete the row, then sew through the beadwork to exit a 3 mm fire-polished bead with the needle pointing toward the ladder rows.
[7] With a new thread, repeat steps 1 and 2. Slide the new ladder through the opening of the first band (photo b). Repeat steps 3–6, but exit an end 11º in the ladder row instead of a fire-polished bead at the end of step 6.

Clasp
[1] To make the toggle bar: On 1 yd. (.9 m) of thread, pick up a cylinder, an 11º, a triangle, an 8º, a fire-polished bead, two cubes, a fire-polished bead, an 8º, a triangle, an 11º, and a cylinder. Work eight rows of flat even-count peyote stitch (Basics), using the corresponding beads (figure 5).
[2] Roll the strip into a tube, and zip up (Basics) the ends. End the working thread and tail (Basics).
[3] Using the tail from the base that is exiting the 11º, pick up four cylinders, and sew through a cube of the toggle bar (photo c). Sew through the beadwork to exit the adjacent cube. Pick up four cylinders, and sew through the opposite 11º in the base. Retrace the thread path, and end the thread.

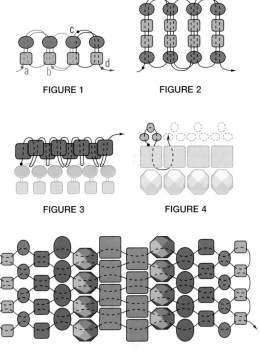

FIGURE 1   FIGURE 2

FIGURE 3   FIGURE 4

FIGURE 5

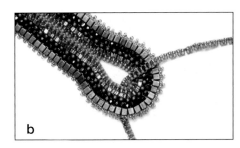

b

c

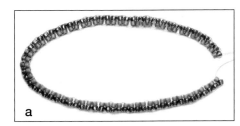

a

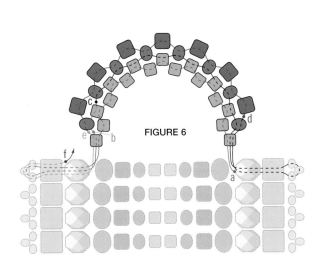

FIGURE 6

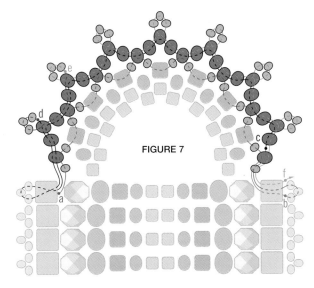

FIGURE 7

[4] To make a loop, use the remaining working thread on the opposite end of the base, and pick up 17 cylinders. Sew through the opposite fire-polished bead (**photo d**). Sew through the beadwork to exit the last cylinder picked up (**figure 6, a–b**). Pick up an 11º, skip a cylinder, and sew through the next cylinder (**photo e and b–c**). Continue in peyote stitch to complete the row. Sew through the beadwork to exit the last 11º picked up (**c–d**).

[5] Work a row of peyote off the row of 11ºs, using triangles (**d–e**). Sew through the beadwork to exit the end cube (**e–f**).

[6] Work the next row by picking up a 15º, an 11º, and a 15º for each stitch (**figure 7, a–b**). Sew through the beadwork to exit the last 11º picked up (**b–c**).

[7] Work the next row by picking up three 11ºs per stitch. Sew through the beadwork to exit the last center 11º picked up (**c–d**).

[8] Pick up three 15ºs, and sew through the center 11º again. Sew through the next four 11ºs (**d–e**). Repeat to add three 15ºs to each center 11º (**e–f**). End the thread. ○

EDITOR'S NOTE:
To change the length of the bracelet, work more or fewer stitches in the ladder in step 2. There are about 13 stitches per inch in the ladder.

d

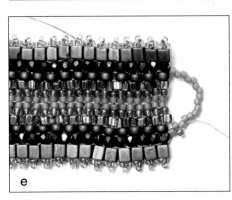

e

materials
bracelet 7 in. (18 cm)
- **148–158** 3 mm fire-polished beads
- 5–7 g 3 mm cube beads
- 4–5 g 8º seed beads
- 4–5 g 10º triangle beads
- 3–4 g 11º cylinder beads
- 3–4 g 11º seed beads
- 3–4 g 15º seed beads
- nylon beading thread, size D
- beading needles, #12

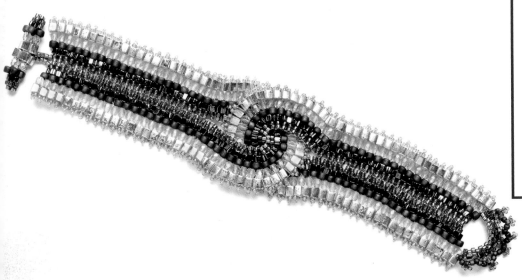

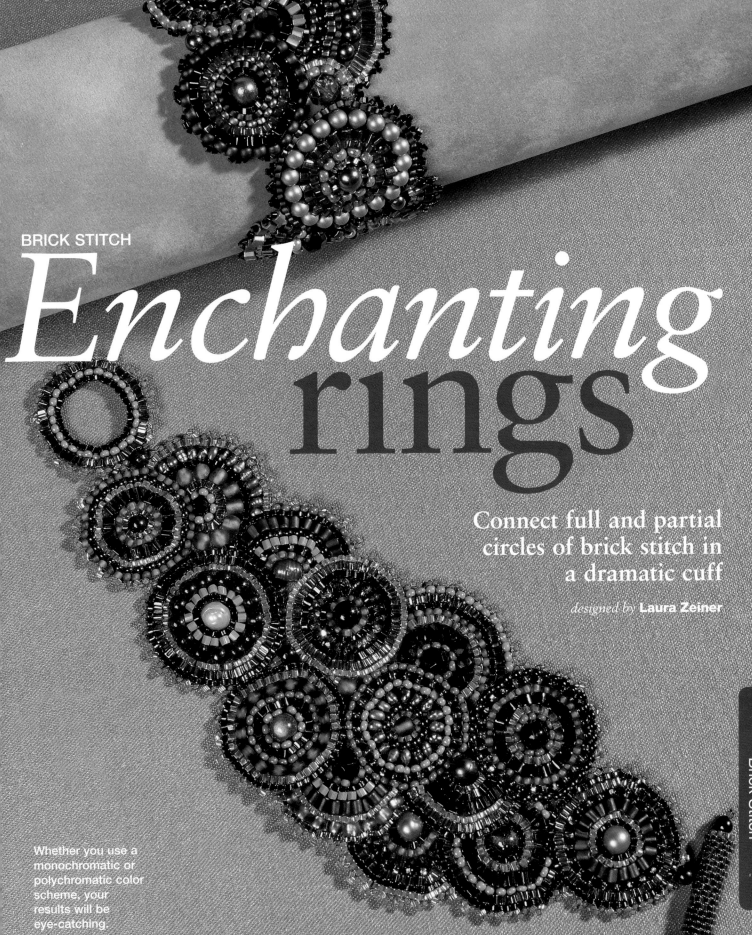

BRICK STITCH

Enchanting
rings

Connect full and partial
circles of brick stitch in
a dramatic cuff

designed by **Laura Zeiner**

Whether you use a
monochromatic or
polychromatic color
scheme, your
results will be
eye-catching.

This bead-stash-busting project will have you going in circles as you make lively rings radiating from center beads. The circles are all created in the same manner, but you'll switch the style and size of the beads to make every one different from the next.

stepbystep

Full circles

[1] On 2 yd. (1.8 m) of thread, pick up a 4 mm or 6 mm round bead, leaving a 6-in. (15 cm) tail. Sew through the bead again in the same direction, making a thread bridge around the bead. Repeat, then position the thread bridges opposite each other (**figure 1**).

[2] Pick up two cylinder beads, sew under a thread bridge, and back through the second cylinder (**figure 2**). Continue in circular brick stitch (Basics, p. 13), picking up one cylinder per stitch, sewing under the thread bridge, then sewing back through the cylinder (**figure 3**). Repeat to complete the round. Sew through the first cylinder, under the thread bridge, and back through the first cylinder (**figure 4**).

[3] Pick up two 11º seed beads, and sew under the thread bridge between the next two cylinders in the previous round, and back through the second 11º. Continue in brick stitch to complete the round using 11ºs, and sew through the first 11º, under the thread bridge, and back through the last 11º.

[4] Repeat step 3 using a different style of bead for each of six rounds, or until you achieve the desired number of rounds. If you switch from a larger bead to a smaller one in the next round, you may need to add two beads to a single thread bridge to ensure the beads sit right next to each other and the circle lies flat. If you add a much larger bead in the new round, you may need to skip

a thread bridge. End the tail (Basics) but not the working thread.

[5] Repeat steps 1–4 to make seven brick stitch circles, substituting different beads for each round.

Connections

[1] Lay out the circles in a pleasing arrangement.

[2] With the thread exiting a bead in the outer round of one circle, sew through an edge bead in another circle. Zigzag through several beads in the two outer rounds to connect the two circles (**figure 5**), and end the thread.

[3] Connect the remaining circles as in step 2, but offset some of them so they do not lie in a completely straight line. This will create spaces to fill with partial components.

Partial components
Semicircles

[1] Add a new 2-yd. (1.8 m) thread (Basics) in a circle, and exit a bead in the outer round. Pick up a 4 mm or 6 mm round bead, and sew through it in the same direction. Repeat, creating two thread bridges around the bead. Sew through two beads in the outer round of the circle (**figure 6**). Pick up a seed bead, and sew under the thread bridge and back through the seed bead.

[2] Work rows of brick stitch, but when you reach the outer round of an adjacent circle, sew through two beads along the outer round and back through the end bead in the new row.

[3] Continue adding rows of beads until you reach the desired number of rows, then end the thread.

Semicircle connectors

[1] Add a new thread in a circle, and exit a bead in the outer round near the connection point to the next component.

[2] Pick up a 4 mm or 6 mm bead and sew through it again, making a thread bridge around the bead. Sew through two corresponding beads in the outer round of the next component, back through the 4 mm or 6 mm, and through two beads of the first component (**figure 7**).

[3] Sew through the 4 mm or 6 mm bead again, and through two beads on the outer round of the other component. Pick up a seed bead, and sew under the thread bridge and back through the new seed bead (**figure 8**). Complete the row, sewing through beads in the outer round of the adjacent components to turn (**figure 9**).

[4] Add 4 mm or 6 mm beads between circles to fill in any spaces that are too small for a semicircle.

materials

bracelet 7 in. (18 cm)
- assortment of round or faceted beads, bicone crystals, or pearls
  7–15 6 mm
  30–75 4 mm
- assortment of seed beads, cylinder beads, cubes, triangles, hex-cuts, or other seed beads, 6–10 g in each of sizes 6º–15º
- nylon beading thread, size D
- beading needles, #12

FIGURE 1

FIGURE 2

FIGURE 3

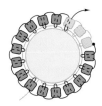

FIGURE 4

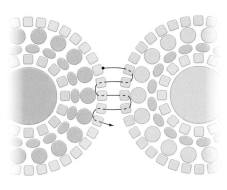

FIGURE 5

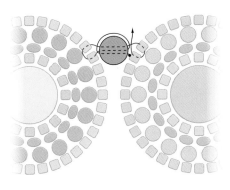

FIGURE 6

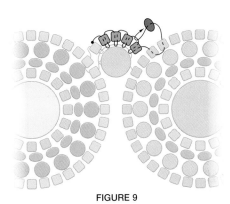

FIGURE 7

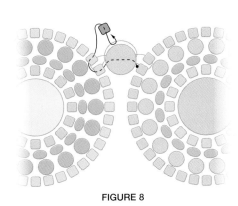

FIGURE 8

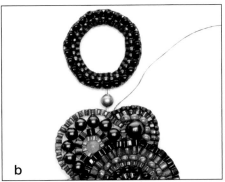

FIGURE 9

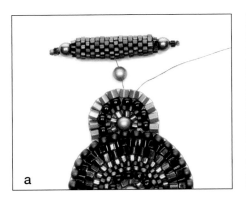

a

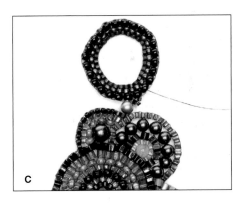

b

c

Clasp

Toggle bar

[1] On 1 yd. (.9 m) of thread, pick up 16 cylinder beads, and work 16 rows of even-count peyote stitch (Basics), leaving a 10-in. (25 cm) tail. There should be eight cylinders along each straight edge.

[2] Zip up the end rows (Basics) to make a tube, and exit an end cylinder on the end opposite the tail.

[3] Using 15º seed beads, work a round of brick stitch off of the thread bridges between the cylinders. Repeat on the other end using the tail. End the tail.

[4] On the working thread, pick up a 4 mm and three 15ºs. Skip the 15ºs, and sew back through the 4 mm, creating a picot with the 15ºs. Sew through the toggle bar, and repeat on the other end. Retrace the thread path several times, and exit between two cylinders in the center of the toggle bar.

[5] Pick up a 4 mm, sew through a bead in the outer round of an end circle, and sew back through the next bead in the round **(photo a)**. Retrace the thread path to secure the join, and end the thread.

Toggle loop

[1] On 2 yd. (1.8 m) of thread, work in ladder stitch (Basics) to make a strip of 30 cylinders. Join the ends to form a ring (Basics).

[2] Work two rounds of circular brick stitch using any beads desired, and exit a bead in the outer round.

[3] Pick up a 4 mm, and sew through a bead in the outer round at the end opposite the toggle bar and back through the next bead **(photo b)**. Retrace the thread path to secure the join, and exit the next bead in the outer round of the toggle loop.

[4] Pick up three 15ºs, and sew through the next two beads in the outer round, making a picot **(photo c)**. Repeat around the edge of the toggle loop, then sew through the 4 mm and repeat around the outer edge of the bracelet, adding picots to all the exposed outer rounds. End the thread. ●

These shimmering stars are perfect for pendants, ornaments, or a pair of earrings.

MODIFIED ST. PETERSBURG CHAIN

Starry night

Cube beads create a sparkling star that catches the light

designed by **Virginia Jensen**

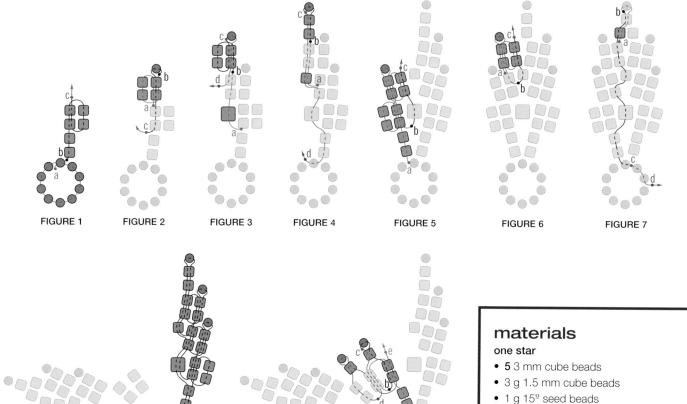

FIGURE 1   FIGURE 2   FIGURE 3   FIGURE 4   FIGURE 5   FIGURE 6   FIGURE 7

FIGURE 8

FIGURE 9

materials

one star

- **5** 3 mm cube beads
- 3 g 1.5 mm cube beads
- 1 g 15º seed beads
- nylon beading thread
- beading needles, #12

New sizes of cube beads allow for more combinations than ever before. This star uses elements of St. Petersburg chain to pull together two sizes of cube beads into a ring of stepped points.

step by step

[1] On 1 yd. (.9 m) of thread, pick up 10 15º seed beads, leaving a 6-in. (15 cm) tail, and sew through the first 15º again to form a ring (**figure 1, a–b**).
[2] Pick up six 1.5 mm cube beads, and sew through the third and fourth 1.5 mms again to form a square (**b–c**).
[3] Pick up four 1.5 mms, and sew through the first two 1.5 mms again to form a square (**figure 2, a–b**). Pick up a 15º, and sew down through the next four 1.5 mms (**b–c**).
[4] Pick up a 3 mm cube bead, and sew up through the last two 1.5 mms added (**figure 3, a–b**).

[5] Pick up four 1.5 mms, and sew through the first two 1.5 mms again to form a square (**b–c**). Pick up a 15º, and sew down through the next three 1.5 mms (**c–d**).
[6] Pick up a 1.5 mm, and sew up through the last two 1.5 mms added (**figure 4, a–b**). Pick up two 1.5 mms and a 15º (**b–c**), turn, and sew down through the next five 1.5 mms, the bottom 1.5 mm in the next column, the 3 mm, the first two 1.5 mms picked up in step 1, and the 15º your thread exited on the original ring (**c–d**).
[7] Repeat steps 2 and 3 to start the second half of the star point (**figure 5, a–b**). Sew through the 3 mm added to the

first half of the point, and sew through the last two 1.5 mms added (**b–c**).
[8] Repeat step 5 (**figure 6, a–b**), and sew through the offset 1.5 mm added to the first half of the point in step 6 and the last two 1.5 mms added (**b–c**).
[9] Pick up a 1.5 mm, and sew through the 1.5 mm and 15º at the tip of the star point (**figure 7, a–b**). Turn, and sew back through the next six 1.5 mms, the 3 mm, the second and first bead added in step 7, and the 15º your thread exited in the ring (**b–c**). Continue through the next two 15ºs (**c–d**).
[10] Repeat steps 2–6 to complete the first half of the next star point (**figure 8**).
[11] To start the second half of the new star point and link it to the adjacent point, pick up four 1.5 mms, and sew down through the two outer 1.5 mms on the adjacent point (**figure 9, a–b**). Sew up through the last two 1.5 mms just added, and pick up a 1.5 mm and

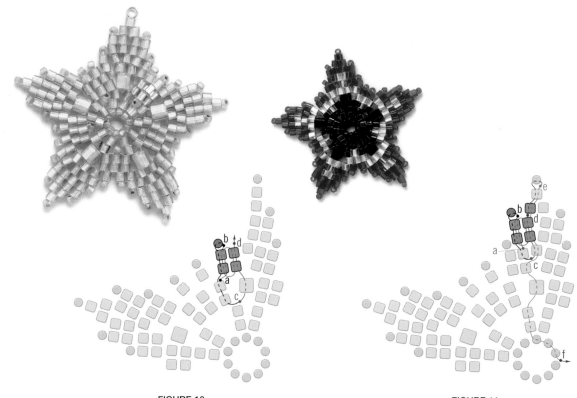

FIGURE 10

FIGURE 11

DESIGNER'S NOTES:
• This project also can be made using 4 mm
and 2 mm cube beads with 11° seed beads.
• To add a hanging loop to one point,
substitute a 3 mm jump ring for the end
15° in step 6.

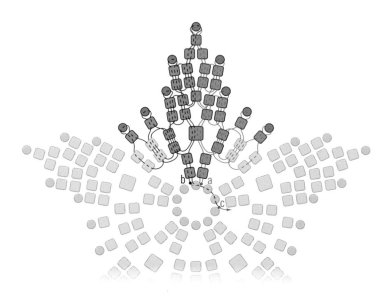

FIGURE 12

a 15° (b–c). Turn, sew back through the
1.5 mm, and continue through the two
1.5 mms in the shared column (c–d).
Sew up through the two 1.5 mms in
the next column, pick up a 1.5 mm and
a 15°, and sew down through the new
1.5 mm and two shared 1.5 mms, and
up through the top two 1.5 mms in the
new column (d–e).

[12] Pick up four 1.5 mms, and sew
through the first two 1.5 mms again
(figure 10, a–b). Pick up a 15°, turn,
and sew down through the next four

1.5 mms (b–c). Sew up through the
3 mm in the first half of the star point
and the last two 1.5 mms added (c–d).
[13] Pick up four 1.5 mms, and sew
through the first two 1.5 mms again to
form a square (figure 11, a–b). Pick up a
15°, and sew down through the next
three 1.5 mms (b–c). Sew through the
offset 1.5 mm added to the first half of
the point and the last two 1.5 mms
added (c–d). Pick up a 1.5 mm, and sew
through the 1.5 mm and 15° at the tip
of the star point (d–e). Turn, and sew

back through the next six 1.5 mms, the
3 mm, and the next two 1.5 mms and
three 15°s (e–f).
[14] Repeat steps 10–13 twice to work
the next two star points.
[15] To connect the final star point to
the two adjacent points, repeat step 11,
then work steps 3–6 to complete the
first half of the final point (figure 12,
a–b). Repeat steps 11–13 to finish the
second half of the star point (b–c),
and end the working thread and tail
(Basics, p. 13). ●

Regal rivolis

Flash your rivolis by enclosing them in netting instead of a traditional peyote stitch bezel

designed by **Donna Pagano Denny**

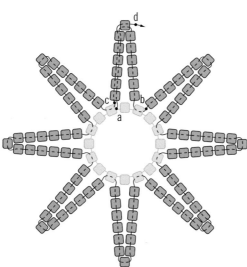

FIGURE 1

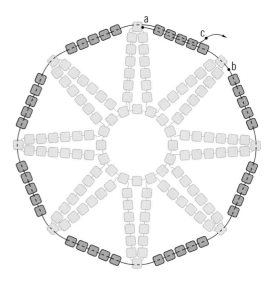

FIGURE 2

materials

bracelet 8 in. (20 cm)
- **3** Swarovski 18 mm square fancy stones or rivolis
- **4** Swarovski 14 mm rivolis
- **10** Swarovski 4 mm bicone crystals
- **4 g** 11º Japanese cylinder beads, color A
- **1 g** 15º Japanese seed beads, color B
- Fireline, 6 lb. test
- beading needles, #12

Whether linked in a bracelet or dangling from your ears, these components are sure to attract attention.

stepbystep

Fancy stone bezel

[1] On 1 yd. (.9 m) of Fireline, pick up 16 color A 11º cylinder beads. Tie the As into a ring with a square knot (Basics, p. 13), leaving a 10-in. (25 cm) tail. Sew through the next cylinder in the ring.
[2] Pick up 13 As, skip an A in the ring, and sew through the next A (figure 1, a–b). Repeat around the ring (b–c). Step up through the first seven As in the first stitch (c–d).
[3] Pick up five As, and sew through the center A in the next point (figure 2, a–b). Repeat around the ring, then sew through the first four As in the first stitch (b–c).
[4] Place an 18 mm fancy stone or rivoli in the bezel. Pick up a color B 15º seed bead, skip three As, and sew through the next three As (photo a). Repeat around the ring. Sew through all the As and Bs encircling the top of the rivoli, pulling tight to form a ring. Do not end the working thread or tails.
[5] Repeat steps 1–4 to enclose a total of three 18 mm fancy stones or rivolis in netted bezels.

Small stone bezel

[1] On 1 yd. (.9 m) of Fireline, pick up 12 As. Tie the As into a ring with a square knot, leaving a 10-in. (25 cm) tail. Sew through the next A in the ring.
[2] Pick up nine As, skip an A in the ring, and sew through the next A. Repeat around the ring. Step up through the first five As in the first stitch.
[3] Pick up five As, and sew through the center A in the next point. Repeat around the ring, then sew through the first four As in the first stitch.
[4] Place a 14 mm rivoli in the bezel. Pick up a B, skip three As, and sew through the next three As. Repeat around the ring. Sew through all the beads encircling the top of the rivoli, pulling tight to form a ring. Do not end the working thread or tail.
[5] Repeat steps 1–4 to enclose a total of four 14 mm rivolis in netted bezels.

Clasp
Toggle ring

[1] On 2 yd. (1.8 m) of Fireline, center 34 Bs, and tie them into a ring with a square knot.

[2] Work a round of tubular peyote stitch (Basics) using Bs, and step up through the first B in the new round.
[3] Work two rounds of peyote using As.
[4] Work one round using two Bs per stitch, and step up through the first two Bs in the new round.
[5] Work one round using As, sewing through the two Bs in the previous round as if they were one.
[6] Using the tail, work steps 3 and 4. Zip up the two end rounds (Basics). End one thread (Basics).

Toggle bar

[1] On 1 yd. (.9 m) of Fireline, pick up 20 As, leaving a 10-in. (25 cm) tail.
[2] Work a total of 12 rows of flat even-count peyote stitch (Basics) using As.

EDITOR'S NOTE:
For earrings, reduce the size of all the beads used. Follow the instructions for the small stone, and substitute 12 mm rivolis for 14 mm rivolis, 15º seed beads for 11º cylinder beads, and 15º Charlottes for 15º seed beads. Make two components, and attach an earring finding with a seed bead loop.

92

a

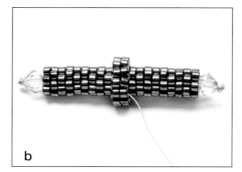

b

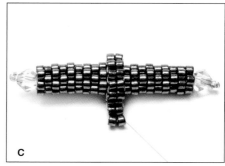

d

e

f

g

h

[3] Roll the strip into a tube, and zip up the end rows.

[4] Sew through the center of the tube, and pick up a 4 mm bicone crystal and a B. Sew back through the crystal, and exit the other end of the tube. Repeat. Reinforce the thread path several times, and end the working thread and tail.

[5] On 24 in. (61 cm) of Fireline, pick up four As, and sew through them again in the same direction. Working in ladder stitch (Basics), make a strip of bead-work two beads wide and 13 rows long.

[6] Wrap the strip around the center of the toggle bar, and stitch the first and last rows together to form a ring **(photo b)**. Stitch the ring to the peyote tube to secure it in place. Exit any bead in the ring.

[7] Work two two-bead ladder stitches off the ring **(photo c)** using As.

Assembly

[1] Using a tail from a small stone bezel, sew through the beadwork to exit the fourth A in one of the netted stitches on the back of the rivoli. Pick up three Bs, a 4 mm, and three Bs. Sew through the corresponding A in the next netted stitch **(photo d)**.

[2] Pick up two Bs, and sew through the center B, 4 mm, and B added in the previous step. Pick up two Bs, and sew through the A your thread exited in step 1. Sew through the first three Bs, 4 mm, and B again **(photo e)**.

[3] To connect the small stone to a large stone, pick up two Bs, and sew through the sixth A in a netted stitch on the back of the large stone. Pick up two Bs, and sew back through the B, 4 mm, and B in the connector **(photo f)**. Repeat, sewing through the corresponding A in the next netted stitch. End the thread.

[4] Connect the remaining stones as in steps 1–3, alternating the large and small stones.

[5] To connect the toggle ring to an end small stone, repeat steps 1 and 2. Pick up three As, and sew through an A, two Bs, and an A in the center round of the ring. Pick up three As, and sew through the B, 4 mm, and B again **(photo g)**. Retrace the thread path, and end the thread.

[6] To connect the toggle bar to the other end stone, repeat steps 1 and 2, and end the thread. Using the thread from the toggle bar, pick up three As and three Bs. Sew through the B, 4 mm, and B in the end connector. Pick up three Bs and three As, and sew through the two As at the end of the toggle bar **(photo h)**. Retrace the thread path, and end the thread. ◉

MODIFIED NETTING

Bejeweled bridge

Crystal accents pull netting into a shapely band

designed by **Kim Spooner**

Metallic beads give the appearance of fine jewelry, while sparkling crystals shine through a bezel setting.

This clever technique allows you to give netting a more rigid structure. Once you embellish the top surface of the band, the arch sits comfortably on your wrist.

stepbystep

Base

[1] On a comfortable length of Fireline, attach a color B 11º seed bead as a stop bead (Basics, p. 13), leaving a 10-in. (25 cm) tail.

[2] Pick up a repeating pattern of two color A 11º seed beads and a B four times.

[3] Pick up a color C 15º seed bead, and sew back through the last B picked up (figure 1, a–b).

[4] Pick up two As, a B, and two As. Sew through the middle B in the previous row (b–c). Pick up two As, a B, and two As, skip five beads in the previous row, and sew through the next B (c–d).

[5] Pick up a C, and sew back through the previous B (d–e).

[6] Pick up three As, a B, and a C. Sew back through the B (figure 2, a–b). Pick up two As, and sew through the next B in the previous row (b–c).

[7] Pick up two As, a B, and two As. Skip five beads in the previous row, and sew through the next B (figure 3, a–b).

[8] Pick up two As, a B, and a C. Sew back through the B (b–c). Pick up three As, sew through the B and C in the previous point, and sew back through the B (c–d). Continue through the three new As, the B, and the C in the new point, and back through the B (d–e). From this point on, make sure when you

add the three As along the edges of the netted band that they stay to the back surface of the band. To do this, make sure your thread is exiting to the back of the band when you exit the Bs, and sew into the Bs from the back of the band.

[9] Repeat steps 4–8, but in step 5, sew through the C next to the B instead of picking up a new one (figure 4). Continue until you have 22 points along each edge of the band, ending on step 4.

[10] Work a center end stitch, referring to figure 5, and end the working thread (Basics). Repeat with the tail.

Embellishments

[1] Add 1 yd. (.9 m) of Fireline (Basics), exiting the ninth center B in the netted base (figure 6, point a).

[2] Pick up a 5 mm crystal, and sew through the next center B, back through the crystal, and continue through the B

94

FIGURE 1   FIGURE 2   FIGURE 3   FIGURE 4

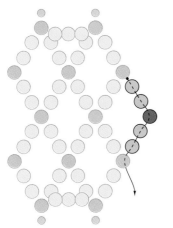

FIGURE 5

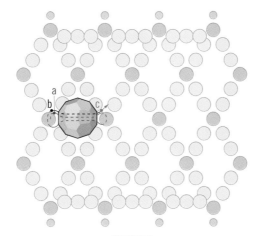

FIGURE 6

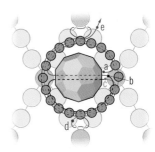

FIGURE 7

materials

bracelet 7 in. (18 cm)

- **11** Swarovski article 5100 5 mm round crystals
- 11º seed beads
  5 g color A
  3 g color B
- **3–4 g 15º seed beads, color C**
- clasp
- **2 jump rings**
- Fireline, 6 lb. test
- beading needles, #12
- **2 pairs of chainnose pliers**

your thread exited at the start of this step (a–b). Sew through the crystal again (b–c).

[3] Pick up nine Cs, and sew through the crystal again, positioning the Cs along the outer edge of the crystal (figure 7, a–b). Repeat (b–c).

[4] Sew through the nine Cs just added, pick up a C, and sew through the next nine Cs. Pick up a C, and sew through the next five Cs (c–d).

[5] Sew under the threads in the base between the B and the two As to anchor this side of the ring to the base. Sew

through the fifth C again, and on through the next 10 Cs. Sew under the threads in the base between the B and the two As, and through the 10th C again (d–e). Sew through the next five Cs.

[6] Sew through the B in the base, the last C, and the B in the base again.

[7] Repeat steps 2–6 to add a total of 11 crystals. End the thread.

[8] Open a jump ring (Basics), and attach half of the clasp to an end netted stitch. Close the jump ring. Repeat on the other end. ◉

EDITOR'S NOTE:

To change the length of the bracelet, add or omit two rows of netting at a time so you end up with an odd number of stitches.

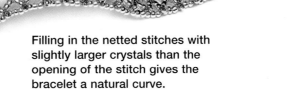

Filling in the netted stitches with slightly larger crystals than the opening of the stitch gives the bracelet a natural curve.

NETTING
Bedecked boughs

Encircle a glass globe with sparkling components

designed by **Lora Groszkiewicz**

Suspend delicately netted components from a peyote stitch ring. Use this technique to spruce up opaque ornaments with contrasting beads and crystals. It's the perfect way to liven up the holidays.

step by step

Peyote ring
[1] On 1 yd. (.9 m) of Fireline, pick up a color B 11º cylinder bead, four color A 11º cylinder beads, and a B. Working in flat even-count peyote stitch (Basics, p. 13), follow the established pattern using As and Bs until the strip has 36 beads along each edge (**figure 1**).

[2] Wrap the strip around the neck of the ornament to test the fit, and add or remove rows as necessary. The red ornament cover above has five crystal star components spaced evenly around a ring that has 35 beads along the edge, with three beads between each connection. The blue ornament cover (p. 98) has six crystal star components spaced evenly around a ring

that has 36 beads along the edge, with two beads between each connection.
[3] Zip up (Basics) the ends of the strip to form a ring, and secure the working thread with a few half-hitch knots (Basics), but do not trim. Set the ring aside.

Crystal components
[1] On 1 yd. (.9 m) of Fireline, pick up 12 As.

materials
one ornament
- 8¾-in. (22.2 cm) circumference glass ornament
- **162** 4 mm bicone crystals
- 11º Japanese cylinder beads
  10 g color A
  5 g color B
- 2 g 15º Japanese seed beads
- Fireline, 4 or 6 lb. test
- nylon beading thread, size B or D
- beading needles, #12

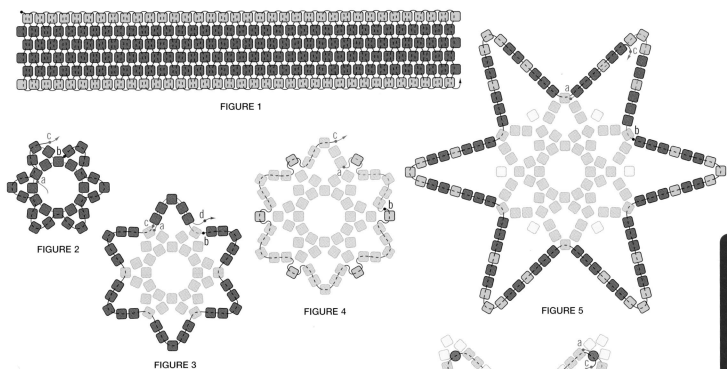

FIGURE 1

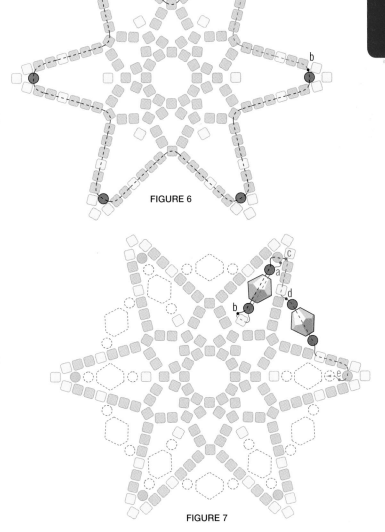

FIGURE 2

FIGURE 3

FIGURE 4

FIGURE 5

FIGURE 6

FIGURE 7

Tie the As into a ring with a square knot (Basics), leaving an 8-in. (20 cm) tail. Sew through the next A in the ring.
[2] Pick up three As, skip an A in the ring, and sew through the next A (**figure 2, a–b**). Repeat around the ring, and step up through the first two As in the new round (**b–c**).
[3] Pick up five As, and sew through the next center A in the previous round (**figure 3, a–b**). Repeat to complete the round (**b–c**). Sew through the five As in the first stitch (**c–d**).
[4] Pick up a B, and sew through the five As in the next stitch of the previous round (**figure 4, a–b**). Repeat to complete the round, but in the last repeat, sew through only three As in the previous round instead of five (**b–c**).
[5] Pick up three As, a B, two As, three Bs, two As, a B, and three As. Sew through the next center A in the previous round (**figure 5, a–b**). Repeat to complete the round, and step up through the first three As, B, and two As in the first stitch of the new round (**b–c**).

[6] Pick up a 15º seed bead, skip the next three Bs, and sew through the next 13 cylinders (**figure 6, a–b**). Repeat to complete the round, and exit the first 15º added (**b–c**).
[7] Pick up a 15º, a 4 mm bicone crystal, and a 15º, and sew through the B at the opposite end of the point (**figure 7, a–b**). Sew back through the 15º, 4 mm, and the next two 15ºs (**b–c**). Sew through the next two As and the next B (**c–d**).
[8] Pick up a 15º, a 4 mm, and a 15º, and sew through the next B, two As, and the next 15º (**d–e**).
[9] Repeat steps 7 and 8 to complete the round. Secure the working thread with a few half-hitch knots, and exit a B at the tip of a point, but do not trim.
[10] Repeat steps 1–9 to make six (or the desired number) crystal star components.

Assembly
[1] Lay out all the crystal star components evenly

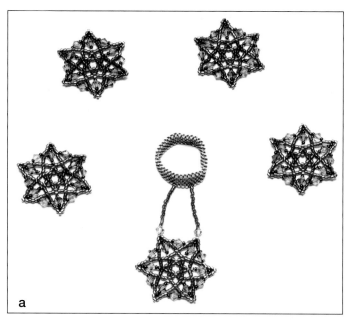

a

b

c

EDITOR'S NOTES:
• If you want to use a different size ornament, alter the number of crystal components you stitch.
• When stitching the peyote ring, try to make the number of beads along the edge divisible by the number of components you make. That way it's easier to place them evenly around the ring.

around the peyote ring. Determine how many beads to skip between each connection.

[2] Using the tail on the peyote ring, exit an edge B. Pick up 16 As and a 4 mm, and sew through the tip B on a point of a crystal component. Sew back through the 4 mm and 16 As, then through the edge B on the peyote ring. Zigzag through the next two Bs along the edge of the peyote ring, then exit the next B. Pick up 16 As and a 4 mm. Sew through the tip B of the next point on the same crystal component. Sew back

through the 4 mm and 16 As, then through the next three edge Bs. End the thread (photo a and Basics). Add a new thread (Basics) in the peyote ring, and connect the remaining components to the ring. End the thread.

[3] Use a tail on one crystal component to connect it to the next component: Exit the tip B on a side point. Pick up a 15º, a 4 mm, and a 15º (or just a 4 mm if the spacing between the components is too close for three beads), and sew through the corresponding B on the next component (photo b). Sew back through the 15º, 4 mm, and 15º, and into the crystal component, and end the thread. Repeat to connect all the crystal components together.

[4] Add a 2-yd. (1.8 m) length of beading thread to a

crystal component, and exit the first B of the three Bs on a bottom point. Pick up 10 As or Bs, a 4 mm, 12 As or Bs, a 4 mm, and an A or B. Skip the last A or B, and sew back through the fringe beads and the B your thread exited at the start of this step, and continue through the next B in the point. Repeat to make a second fringe, but use eight As or Bs, a 4 mm, 16 As or Bs, a 4 mm, and an A or B. Work the third fringe the same as the first. Sew through the beadwork to exit the first B on the next point of the same crystal component (photo c). Repeat to add fringe to the remaining points, ending and adding thread as needed. End the threads. ●

NETTING / STRINGING

Crystal-caged pearls

Beaded beads make a great focal point for a monochromatic necklace.

Highlight two styles of beaded beads in an asymmetrical necklace

designed by **Cathy Lampole**

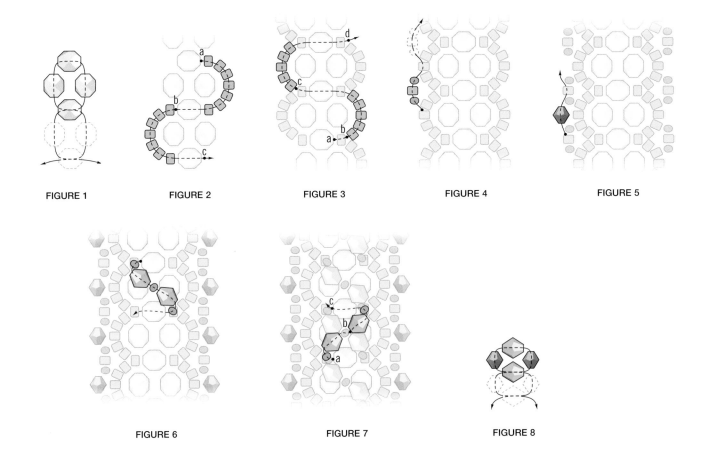

FIGURE 1   FIGURE 2   FIGURE 3   FIGURE 4   FIGURE 5

FIGURE 6   FIGURE 7   FIGURE 8

Catch a glimpse of pearly luster within a woven coat of crystals and seed beads. The combination of glow and sparkle is perfect for an elegant necklace.

step by step

materials

necklace 20 in. (51 cm)

- 3 14 mm pearls
- 8 10 mm round crystals
- 2 10 mm accent beads
- 40 8 mm pearls
- 78 4 mm bicone crystals
- 52 4 mm fire-polished beads
- 60 3 mm bicone crystals
- 3 g 11º Japanese cylinder beads
- 2 g 15º seed beads
- 2 3 mm spacers
- clasp
- 2 crimp beads
- 2 crimp covers
- nylon beading thread or Fireline, 6 lb. test
- flexible beading wire, .015
- beading needles, #12
- chainnose pliers
- crimping pliers
- wire cutters

Large beaded bead

[1] Thread a needle on each end of 1½ yd. (1.4 m) of thread, and center a 4 mm fire-polished bead. With each needle, pick up a fire-polished. With one needle, pick up a fire-polished, and cross the other needle through it **(figure 1)**.

[2] Continue in crossweave technique (Basics, p. 13) until you have seven beads along each edge of the strip and eight in the center. With each needle, pick up a fire-polished, and cross the

needles through the first fire-polished to form a ring.

[3] With one needle, pick up seven cylinder beads, and sew through the next parallel fire-polished, skipping an edge fire-polished and forming an arc around it **(figure 2, a–b)**. Repeat **(b–c)** around the ring, so that the arcs alternate on each side of the ring. Sew through the first cylinder added in this step **(figure 3, a–b)**, pick up five cylinders, and, working in the opposite direction, sew through the last cylinder in the next group on the same side of the ring, the next fire-polished, and the next cylinder **(b–c)**.

Repeat **(c–d)** around the ring, and exit the center cylinder of an arc.

[4] Pick up a 15º seed bead, a cylinder, and a 15º, and sew through the center cylinder of the next arc **(figure 4)**. Repeat around the ring, and exit the first cylinder added in this step. With the other needle, sew through the beadwork to exit the center cylinder of an arc on the other side of the ring, and repeat.

[5] Working one side of the ring at a time, pick up a 3 mm bicone crystal, and sew through the next cylinder added in the previous round **(figure 5)**. Repeat around the ring, and pull the beads snug. Sew through all the beads in the last round again. Insert the 14 mm pearl so the hole is centered in the opening, and repeat this step on the

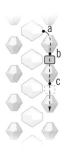

FIGURE 9

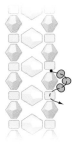

FIGURE 10

FIGURE 11

FIGURE 12

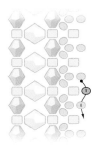

FIGURE 13

other side of the ring with the other needle, enclosing the pearl.

[6] With one needle, sew through the beadwork to exit a center fire-polished. Pick up a 15°, a 4 mm bicone crystal, a 15°, a 4 mm bicone, and a 15°. Cross over the center round at a diagonal, and sew through the next parallel fire-polished **(figure 6)**. Repeat around the ring, and end the thread (Basics).

[7] Using the remaining thread, sew through the beadwork to exit a center fire-polished. Pick up a 15° and a 4 mm bicone, and sew through the center 15° of the adjacent stitch **(figure 7, a–b)**. Pick up a 4 mm bicone and a 15°, and sew through the next parallel fire-polished **(b–c)**. Repeat around the ring, and end the thread.

[8] Repeat steps 1–7 to make a second large beaded bead.

Small beaded bead

[1] Thread a needle on each end of 1½ yd. (1.4 m) of thread, and center a 4 mm bicone. With each needle,

pick up a 3 mm bicone. With one needle, pick up a 4 mm bicone, and cross the other needle through it **(figure 8)**. Continue in crossweave technique, following the established pattern, until you have 13 3 mms along each edge and 14 4 mm bicones in the center. With each needle, pick up a 3 mm, and cross the needles through the first 4 mm bicone to form a ring.

[2] Working with one needle at a time, sew through an edge 3 mm **(figure 9, a–b)**. Pick up a cylinder, and sew through the next 3 mm **(b–c)**. Repeat around the ring, and exit the first cylinder added. Repeat on the other side with the other needle.

[3] With one needle, pick up three 15°s, and sew through the next cylinder **(figure 10)**. Repeat around the ring, and step up to exit the center 15° of the first arc.

[4] Pick up a cylinder, and sew through the next center 15° **(figure 11)**. Repeat around the ring, pulling the beads snug, and exit the first cylinder added in this round.

[5] Pick up a 15°, and sew through the next cylinder **(figure 12)**. Repeat around the ring, and exit the first 15° added in this round.

[6] Pick up a 15°, and sew through the next 15° in the previous round **(figure 13)**. Repeat around the ring, and end the thread.

[7] Insert the 14 mm pearl so the hole is centered in the opening, and repeat steps 3–6 to finish the other side of the bead.

Necklace

[1] Cut 26 in. (66 cm) of beading wire, and center eight 10 mm round crystals. On each end, string a 10 mm accent bead.

[2] On one end, string an 8 mm pearl, a large beaded bead, an 8 mm, the small beaded bead, an 8 mm, a large beaded bead, and 14 8 mms. On the other end, string 23 8 mms.

[3] On each end, string a crimp bead, two 4 mm bicones, a 3 mm spacer, and half of the clasp. Go back through the spacers,

4 mm bicones, and crimp beads. Test the fit, and add or remove beads as necessary. Crimp the crimp beads (Basics), and trim the wires. Close a crimp cover over each crimp bead with chainnose pliers. ●

Intersecting elements

Clever use of rose monteés allows for multiple thread paths and lots of embellishment

designed by **Jenny Van**

materials

bracelet 7¼ in. (18.4 cm)

- **12** 6 mm round crystals
- **11** 6 mm rose monteés
- bicone crystals
  - **22** 5 mm
  - **44** 4 mm
- 3 g 11º seed beads
- clasp
- French bullion wire
- **2** crimp beads
- **2** crimp covers
- Fireline, 6 or 8 lb. test
- flexible beading wire, .012
- beading needles, #12
- tape or Bead Stopper
- chainnose pliers
- crimping pliers
- wire cutters

Rose monteés come in a limited number of colors, so choose them first, then select the rest of the beads.

Rose monteés have two intersecting channels on the back. When you string the rose monteés, the channel the beading wire passes through is referred to as the center channel, and the channel that you will be stitching through is referred to as the side channel. As you begin stitching, the rose monteés may turn over — make sure they are all facing up when you cross through them.

step by step

[1] On 12 in. (30 cm) of beading wire, string a crimp bead, ½ in. (1.3 cm) of French bullion wire, and half of the clasp. Go back through the crimp bead **(photo a)**, and crimp it

(Basics, p. 13). Trim the short wire tail.
[2] String a 5 mm bicone crystal. String a repeating pattern of a 6 mm round crystal and a 6 mm rose monteé **(photo b)** 11 times, then string a 6 mm round and a 5 mm bicone. Temporarily

secure the end of the wire with tape or a Bead Stopper.
[3] Thread a needle on each end of 2 yd. (1.8 m) of Fireline. Center the thread in the side channel of the first rose monteé on one end of the bracelet.

[4] With one needle, pick up an 11º seed bead, a 4 mm bicone crystal, an 11º, a 5 mm, an 11º, a 4 mm, and an 11º. Repeat with the other needle, and cross the needles through the side channel of the next rose monteé (photo c).

[5] Repeat step 4 until you cross the needles through the last rose monteé.

[6] Pick up three 11ºs, a 4 mm, and three 11ºs. Sew back through the end 6 mm round crystal and the center channel of the rose monteé your thread exited at the start of this step. Repeat with the other needle (photo d).

[7] With one needle, pick up five 11ºs, and sew back through the 5 mm of a previous side loop (photo e). Pick up two 11ºs, and sew through the center 11º of the five just picked up (photo f). Pick up two 11ºs, and sew through the next center channel (photo g). Repeat with the other needle.

[8] Repeat step 7 until you sew through the last rose monteé.

[9] Repeat step 6, and end the threads (Basics).

[10] Remove the tape or Bead Stopper, and string a crimp bead, ½ in. (1.3 cm) of French bullion wire, and the other half of the clasp. Go back through the crimp bead, crimp it, and trim the remaining wire. Use chainnose pliers to close crimp covers over the crimps. ●

EDITOR'S NOTES:

• If desired, use smaller beads, substituting 4 mm rose monteés for the 6 mms, 3 mm bicones for the 4 mms, 4 mm bicones for the 5 mms, and 15º seed beads for the 11ºs. Just remember you'll need more of each bead.
• If you want a longer bracelet, but don't have more rose monteés, add one or more extra 4 mm bicone crystals to each end of the bracelet to make up the length.

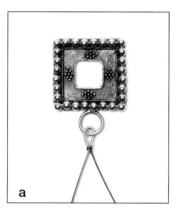

a

b

c

d

e

f

g

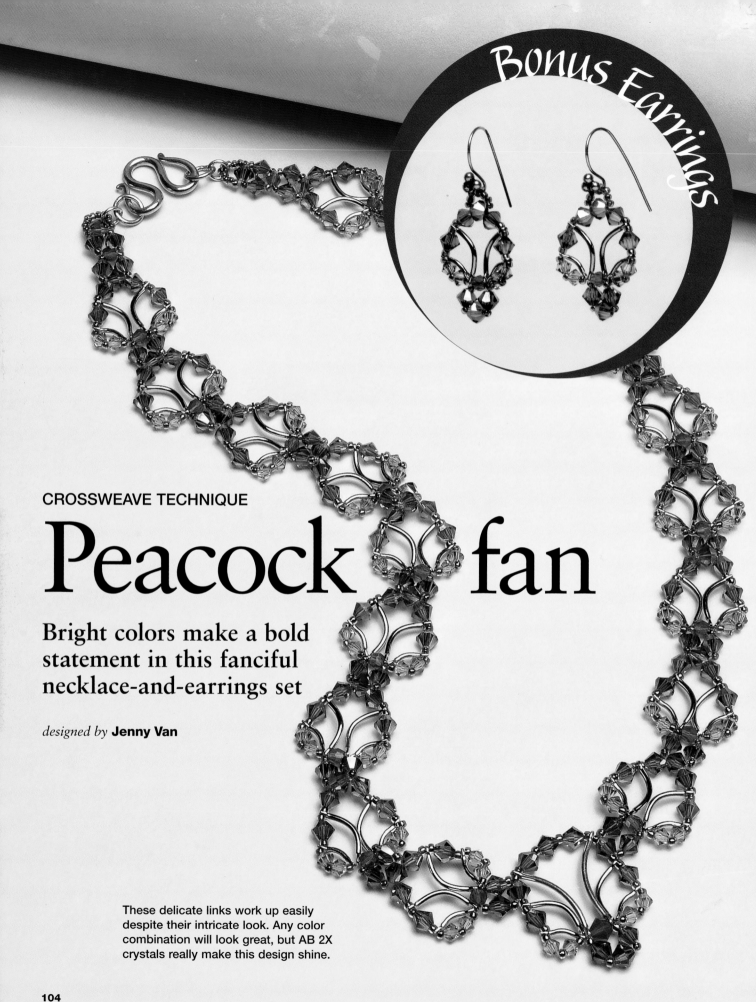

CROSSWEAVE TECHNIQUE

Peacock fan

Bright colors make a bold statement in this fanciful necklace-and-earrings set

designed by **Jenny Van**

These delicate links work up easily despite their intricate look. Any color combination will look great, but AB 2X crystals really make this design shine.

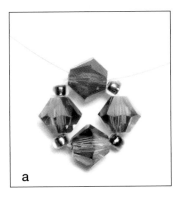

a

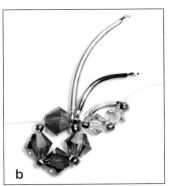

b

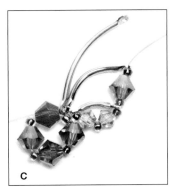

c

d

e

f

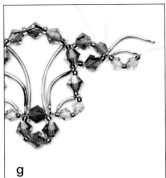

g

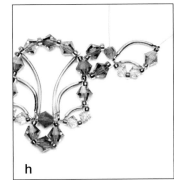

h

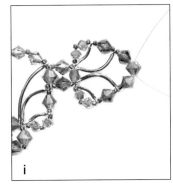

i

materials

both projects

- Fireline, 6 or 8 lb. test
- beading needles, #12
- 2 pairs of pliers
- wire cutters

necklace 19 in. (48 cm)

- 4 mm bicone crystals
  70 color A
  76 color B
- 4 mm round or bicone crystal, color C
- **76** 3 mm bicone crystals, color D
- **20** 3 mm round crystals, color C
- 4–5 g 15º seed beads
- curved bar links (sold as chain, jjbead.com)
  2 14 mm
  38 9 mm
  38 7 mm
- clasp
- **2** 4 mm jump rings

pair of earrings

- **8** 4 mm bicone crystals, in each of **2** colors: A, B
- **8** 3 mm bicone crystals, color D
- **2** 3 mm round crystals, color C
- **40** 15º seed beads
- curved bar links
  4 9 mm
  4 7 mm
- pair of earring findings

Crossweave Technique

Use unexpected materials for a new look. In this necklace, pieces of curved bar chain create beautiful lines within fan-shaped motifs.

stepbystep

Cut apart the chain links before beginning.

Necklace

[1] Thread a needle on each end of 4 ft. (1.2 m) of Fireline. On the threads, center a color C 4 mm round or bicone crystal, a 15º seed bead, a color A 4 mm bicone crystal, a 15º, an A, a 15º, an A, and a 15º. Sew through the C 4 mm to form a ring **(photo a)**.

[2] With one needle, pick up a 14 mm link, a 9 mm link, a 7 mm link, a 15º, a color D 3 mm bicone crystal, a 15º, a D, and a 15º. Sew through the remaining hole of the 7 mm link **(photo b)**. Pick up a 15º, a color B 4 mm bicone crystal, and a 15º. Sew through the remaining hole of the 9 mm link **(photo c)**. Pick up a 15º, an A, and a 15º, and sew through the remaining hole of the 14 mm link **(photo d)**. Repeat this step with the other needle.

[3] With one needle, pick up a 15º, a B, a 15º, an A, a 15º, a B, and a 15º, and sew through the next 14 mm link, 15º, and A **(photo e)**. With the other needle, sew through the beadwork to exit the same A in the opposite direction.
[4] With one needle, pick up a 15º, an A, and a 15º. Repeat with the other needle. With one needle, pick up a color C 3 mm round crystal, and cross the other needle through it **(photo f)**.

[5] With one needle, pick up a 9 mm link, a 7 mm link, a 15º, a D, a 15º, a D, and a 15º, and sew through the remaining hole of the 7 mm link **(photo g)**. Pick up a 15º, a B, and a 15º, and sew through the remaining hole of the 9 mm link **(photo h)**. Pick up a 15º and a B. Repeat the entire step with the other needle.
[6] With one needle, pick up an A, and cross the other needle through it **(photo i)**.

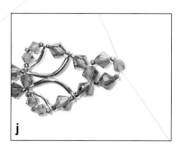

j

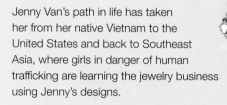

[7] Repeat steps 4 (photo j), 5, and 6 until you have a total of nine small units on one side of the necklace (not including the center unit made in steps 1–3).
[8] With one needle, pick up a 15º, an A, and a 15º. Repeat with the other needle. With one needle, pick up a C 3 mm, and cross the other needle through it. With one needle, pick up a 15º, an A, and a 15º. Repeat with the other needle. With one needle, pick up an A, and cross the other needle through it. With one needle, pick up 10 15ºs, and cross the other needle through them. Retrace the thread path through the 15ºs to reinforce the loop, retrace the thread path through the last few units, and end the threads (Basics, p. 13).
[9] Thread a needle on each end of 4 ft. (1.2 m) of Fireline, and center it in the side A opposite the first half of the necklace. Repeat steps 4–8 to complete the second side of the necklace.
[10] Open a jump ring (Basics), attach half of the clasp and a loop of 15ºs on one end of the necklace, and close the jump ring. Repeat on the other end.

EDITOR'S NOTE: Stitch up a band of small units for a bracelet to complete this sparkling set.

Earrings

[1] Thread a needle on each end of 2 ft. (61 cm) of Fireline. Center a color C 3 mm round crystal, a 15º seed bead, a color A 4 mm bicone crystal, a 15º, an A, a 15º, an A, and a 15º. Sew through the C 3 mm to form a ring.
[2] With one needle, pick up a 9 mm link, a 7 mm link, a 15º, a color D 3 mm bicone crystal, a 15º, a D, and a 15º. Sew through the remaining hole of the 7 mm link. Pick up a 15º, a color B 4 mm bicone crystal, and a 15º. Sew through the remaining hole of the 9 mm link. Pick up a 15º and a B. Repeat the entire step with the other needle.
[3] With one needle, pick up an A, and cross the other needle through it.
[4] With one needle, pick up eight 15ºs, and cross the other needle through them. Continue with one needle through the A, and end the thread (Basics). Repeat with the other needle.
[5] Open the loop of an earring finding (Basics), attach it to the seed bead loop, and close the loop.
[6] Repeat steps 1–5 to make a second earring. ●

MAKING A DIFFERENCE

Jenny Van's path in life has taken her from her native Vietnam to the United States and back to Southeast Asia, where girls in danger of human trafficking are learning the jewelry business using Jenny's designs.

A jewelry designer and owner of JJBead shop in Huntington Beach, Calif., Jenny came to the U.S. as a university student. After she graduated and began working in biochemistry, her coworkers loved her jewelry so much that Jenny began her own jewelry business in 2004.

In June 2009, Lisa Nguyen, host of the Vietnamese TV variety show Asia Entertainment Inc., asked Jenny if she would design jewelry to help girls in Cambodia. Jenny didn't hesitate, and quickly got to work creating more than a dozen high-end pieces for sale to the public, with the proceeds slated for Senhoa, a nonprofit agency that supports victims of human trafficking.

Lisa launched Senhoa in January 2010 as an offshoot of the Washington, D.C., organization VOICE, for which she had previously worked. Senhoa's administrative office is in Huntington Beach and its focus is on Cambodia, where the nonprofit supports a shelter for girls, a preschool, a community center, and vocational training programs. Jenny is now creative director for Senhoa Jewelry and her designs are sold at senhoa.org.

Lisa asked Jenny to use the theme of the phoenix, the mythical bird that rose from the ashes, for her latest Senhoa designs. The 13-piece collection celebrates endurance, survival, and rebirth. Jenny selected Swarovski Elements beads and opals as the primary beads for the pieces. "The jewelry is very high end, very 'wow' — you won't fly away when you wear it!" Jenny says.

"There is a perfect harmony between strength and elegance in Jenny's designs," Lisa says. "Her pieces are striking and bold while capturing the essence of femininity."

Jenny also taped a teaching DVD that the girls in Cambodia use to make the jewelry. Thirty-five girls have participated in the workshops so far. And, as this article went to press, Lisa was raising funds for Jenny to teach a workshop in Cambodia. "It's great for me to lend a hand," Jenny says. "I lived in a poor country and I've had so many opportunities here that I'm happy to help these girls. We have a lot of girls in need but we don't have enough money to rescue all the girls, so we try to do our best."

Senhoa also teaches the girls language, math, and life skills; how to use computers; money management; health; and self-sufficiency. For more information about Senhoa, contact Lisa at info@senhoa.org. – *Ann Dee Allen*

CROSSWEAVE TECHNIQUE

Sparkling spikes

Goth and glamour unite in a fun and fashionable bracelet

designed by **Samantha Mitchell**

materials

bracelet 7½ in. (19.1 cm)
- **8** 10 x 6 mm crystal pendants
- **90** 4 mm bicone crystals
- **81** 3 mm bicone crystals
- **2–3 g** 15º seed beads
- clasp
- **2** jump rings
- **2** crimp beads
- flexible beading wire, .010–.012
- tape or Bead Stoppers
- **2** pairs of pliers
- crimping pliers
- wire cutters

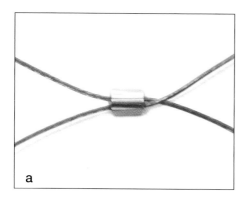

a

b

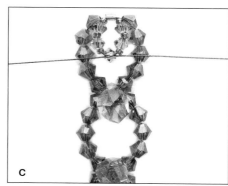

c

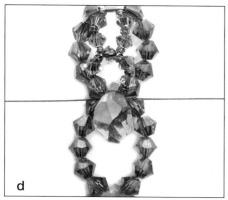

d

e

Crystal pendants are often suspended from fringe or incorporated into flowers as petals. In this easy crossweave design, however, they are nestled between two rows of bicone crystals, creating a glittering ring of spikes around your wrist.

step by step

[1] Cut two 1-yd. (.9 m) pieces of beading wire. Center a crimp bead over both wires, and crimp it (Basics, p. 13). Separate the strands, creating a pair of wires on each side of the crimp bead **(photo a)**.

[2] On one wire from each side of the crimp bead, string five 4 mm bicone crystals. On one wire end, string a crystal pendant, and cross the other wire end through it **(photo b)**.

[3] Repeat step 2 until you reach your desired length, then string five 4 mms on each wire end. On one wire end, string a crimp bead, and cross the other wire through it, but do not crimp it. Temporarily secure the first pair of wires with tape or a Bead Stopper.

[4] On each remaining wire, string a 15º seed bead, a 3 mm bicone crystal, a 15º, a 3 mm, and a 15º. On one wire end, string a 3 mm, and cross the other wire end through it **(photo c)**. On each wire end, string a 15º, a 3 mm, a 15º,

a 3 mm, and a 15º. Cross the ends through the next pendant **(photo d)**.

[5] Repeat step 4 until you reach the last pendant. Repeat once more, but cross the ends through the crimp bead instead of a pendant.

[6] Snug up all the wires, and crimp the crimp beads. Trim the tails.

[7] Open a jump ring (Basics), attach half of the clasp and the loop of 4 mms and 3 mms next to a crimp bead **(photo e)**, and close the jump ring. Repeat on the other end. •

DESIGN NOTE:
Substitute round crystals in place of the pendants for a more two-dimensional take on this bracelet.

BEAD EMBROIDERY / FRINGE

Moonlit
garden

designed by **Melissa Grakowsky**

**Embroider
an elegant
necklace for
evening wear**

Crystals catch the light in this
dazzling design, drawing the
eye to a rich focal flower.

Bead Embroidery

109

materials

both projects
- Fireline, 6 lb. test or nylon beading thread, size D
- beading needles, #12
- E6000 adhesive

necklace 18 in. (46 cm)
- **9** 14 x 16 mm glass leaf beads or other shape
- **14** mm dentelle
- **19** 8 mm round Czech glass or fire-polished beads
- **13** 4 x 6 mm fringe drop beads
- **411** 4 mm bicone crystals in a mix of **3** colors: C, D, E
- **45–55** 3 mm magatamas
- 11º seed beads
  3–5 g color A
  2–3 g color B
- **1–3** g 11º cylinder beads
- **1** g 13º Czech Charlottes
- **1** g 15º seed beads
- **5** x 5-in. (13 x 13 cm) piece of beading foundation
- **5** x 5-in. (13 x 13 cm) piece of Ultrasuede

pair of earrings
- **2** 14 x 16 mm glass leaf beads or other shape
- **4** 8 mm round Czech glass or fire-polished beads
- **38** 4 mm crystals in a mix of **3** colors: C, D, E
- **35–45** 3 mm magatamas
- **1–2** g 11º seed beads in each of **2** colors: A, B
- **2** 3–4 mm soldered jump rings
- pair of earring findings
- **2** x 2-in. (5 x 5 cm) piece of beading foundation
- **2** x 2-in. (5 x 5 cm) piece of Ultrasuede
- **2** pairs of pliers

Drape a path of twinkling light from two embroidered side components for extra panache. Make a pair of earrings out of single components to match your necklace.

step by step

Necklace
Focal flower

[1] Trace an outline of the dentelle onto a piece of beading foundation, leaving about 1¼ in. (3.2 cm) around all sides.

[2] Tie an overhand knot (Basics, p. 13) at the end of 3 yd. (2.7 m) of Fireline or thread, and sew up through the back of the foundation along the outline. Using an even number of 11º cylinder beads, work a round of beaded backstitch (Basics) around the outline.

[3] Using cylinders, work four rounds of peyote stitch (Basics) off of the beaded backstitch round to create a bezel, and place the dentelle inside it. Work a round with 15º seed beads and a round with 13º Czech Charlottes, pulling the beads taut to keep the dentelle encased.

[4] Sew through the beadwork to exit a cylinder in a middle round of the bezel, and pick up an 8 mm round Czech glass or fire-polished bead. Working with the hole of the 8 mm perpendicular to the bezel, sew down through the foundation, back up, back through the 8 mm, and through the next few cylinders in the bezel **(photo a)**. Repeat to add a total of 10

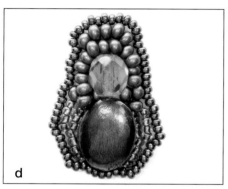

FIGURE 1

FIGURE 2

or 11 8 mms around the bezel, making sure they are evenly spaced.

[5] Sew through the beadwork to exit an 8 mm next to the bezel. Pick up two 3 mm magatamas, and sew through an adjacent 8 mm, the 8 mm your thread just exited, the pair of 3 mms, and the adjacent 8 mm again **(figure 1, a–b)**. A lot of thread will show between the 8 mms, but it will be hidden later. Sew through the following 8 mm, and pick up two 3 mms. Sew back through the previous 8 mm and the following 8 mm **(b–c)**. Continue around, adding two 3 mms next to the bezel between pairs of 8 mms.

[6] Sew through the beadwork to exit the first 3 mm of a pair of 3 mms. Pick up a 4 x 6 mm fringe drop, and sew through the next two 3 mms **(photo b)**. Repeat around to add a 4 x 6 mm between every other pair of 3 mms.

[7] Sew through the beadwork to exit a 4 x 6 mm. Pick up a color C 4 mm bicone crystal, and sew through the next 4 x 6 mm. Repeat around to add a 4 mm between each pair of 4 x 6 mms. End the thread (Basics).

Embellishment

[1] Tie an overhand knot at the end of a comfortable length of Fireline or thread, and sew up through the back of

the foundation next to an 8 mm. Using color A 11º seed beads, work a round of beaded backstitch close to the 8 mms, concealing the thread between 8 mms added in step 4 of "Focal flower."

[2] Exit close to the edge of the As, pick up a 14 x 16 mm glass leaf or other shape, and sew down through the foundation. Working in beaded backstitch, work a round of As around the leaf. Exit between the leaf and the focal flower, and work in beaded backstitch to add three 3 mms. Repeat with a second leaf adjacent to the first, and add a 4 x 6 mm between the two groups of 3 mms **(photo c)**.

[3] Repeat step 2 on the other side of the flower to create a mirror image. End the thread.

[4] Trim the beading foundation close to the beadwork, taking care not to cut the thread. Cut a piece of Ultrasuede to match the beading foundation, and glue them together. Let the glue dry.

[5] Tie an overhand knot at the end of 2 ft. (61 cm) of Fireline or thread. Sewing between the beading foundation and Ultrasuede, bring the needle up through the top of the beading foundation close to the edge, hiding the knot between the two pieces. Pick up two color B 11º seed beads, and sew down through the beading foundation

and Ultrasuede and back up through the last B added **(figure 2, a–b)**. Working in modified brick stitch (Basics), pick up a B, and sew down through the beading foundation and Ultrasuede and back up through the B **(b–c)**. Repeat around the focal piece, and end the thread.

Accent medallions

[1] Tie an overhand knot at the end of a comfortable length of Fireline or thread, and sew up through the back of a piece of beading foundation. Working in beaded backstitch, attach an 8 mm and a 14 x 16 mm. Continue in beaded backstitch to surround the 8 mm and top of the 14 x 16 mm with a pleasing arrangement of 3 mms. Surround the bottom of the 14 x 16 mm with Bs. Work a round of As to encircle the beadwork, and trim the beading foundation close to the edge, taking care not to cut the thread **(photo d)**.

[2] Cut a piece of Ultrasuede to match the beading foundation, glue them together, and let the glue dry. Using Bs, work a round of modified brick stitch around the edge, as in step 5 of "Embellishment." End the thread.

[3] Repeat steps 1 and 2 to make a second accent medallion.

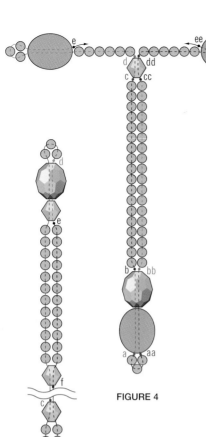

FIGURE 4

e

f

Swags

To connect the focal flower to the accent medallions, sew through an edge bead of an embroidered piece, pick up seed beads and 4 mm crystals (photo e) as explained below to create a balanced drape, and sew through an edge bead of the next embroidered piece. End and add Fireline or thread (Basics) as needed, and make the swag a mirror image on each side.

For the designer's necklace, the swag and bead counts are as follows:

Between the two bottom 14 x 16 mms of the focal flower: a B, 19 4 mms, and a B in the top swag; a B, 24 4 mms, and a B in the second; a B, 29 4 mms, and a B in the third; and a B, 16 4 mms, an 8 mm, 16 4 mms, and a B in the fourth.

From an accent medallion to the space between two 14 x 16 mms: six 4 mms in the top swag; seven 4 mms in the second; eight 4 mms in the next three; and two Bs and eight 4 mms in the sixth.

From an accent medallion to the bottom corner of the focal flower: a B and 20 4 mms in the top swag; a B and 23 4 mms in the second; and 27 4 mms in the third. All the swags in the third group should overlap the swags connecting the 14 x 16 mms of the focal flower.

Finishing

[1] On 1½ yd. (1.4 m) of Fireline, sew through an edge bead at the top of an accent medallion, and pick up a B; 11 4 mms in a mixture of colors C, D, and E; an A; and an 8 mm (figure 3, a–b).

EDITOR'S NOTES:
• You may need to adjust your bead counts to fit your design.
• To make a simplified version of this necklace, skip the accent medallions and swag, but lengthen the sides, or work an extra two to three repeats in step 1 of "Finishing."

FIGURE 3

FIGURE 5   FIGURE 6

Pick up a repeating pattern of 12 As and a C (b–c) five times, then an 8 mm and three As (c–d). Skip the three As, and sew back through the 8 mm and C (d–e).

[2] Pick up 12 As, and sew through the next C (e–f). Repeat four times, sewing through the 8 mm in the fourth repeat (f–g).

[3] Pick up an A, 11 4 mms, and a B, and sew through an edge B on the accent medallion (g–h). Sew through the next edge B, pick up a B, 11 4 mms, and an A, and sew through the 8 mm (h–i). Retrace the thread path to reinforce the beadwork, and end the thread.

[4] Repeat steps 1–3 on the remaining side.

[5] To create the connecting clasp component, center three As on 1 yd. (.9 m) of Fireline or thread. Over both ends, string a 14 x 16 mm and an 8 mm (figure 4, a–b and aa–bb). On each end, pick up 18 As (b–c and bb–cc). Over both ends, string a 4 mm (c–d and cc–dd). On each end, pick up six As, a 14 x 16 mm, and three As, and sew back through the 14 x 16 mm (d–e and dd–ee). Retrace the thread path to reinforce the beadwork, and end each thread. To clasp the necklace, slide each top 14 x 16 mm through an end loop of the necklace (photo f).

Earrings

[1] Work steps 1 and 2 of "Accent medallions."

[2] To add fringe, sew through a bottom edge B, and pick up a B; the desired number of colors C, D, and E 4 mms; and a B. Skip the B, and sew back through the 4 mms, B, and edge B. Sew through the next edge B (figure 5), and repeat. Add five fringes with three 4 mms in the outer fringes, four 4 mms in the second and fourth fringes, and five 4 mms in the middle fringe.

[3] Sew through a top edge B, and pick up a B, an 8 mm, six Bs, and a 3–4 mm soldered jump ring. Skip the last five Bs, and sew through the next B, 8 mm, B, and edge B (figure 6). Retrace the thread path to reinforce the connection, and end the thread (Basics).

[4] Open the loop of an earring finding (Basics), attach the soldered jump ring, and close the loop.

[5] Make a second earring. ○

Arctic cuff

Create a story in a bead-embroidered cuff

designed by **Heidi Kummli**

A plastic toy animal plus carved and cast sea creatures make for a cohesive cuff.

a

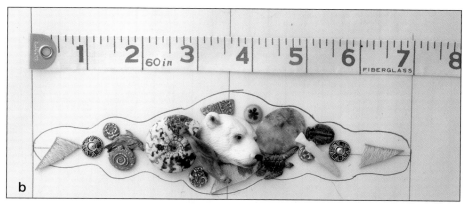

b

c

d

materials

bracelet 7 in. (18 cm)

- plastic toy animal
- **18–25** 6–25 mm assorted cabochons, stones, buttons, metal pieces, and animal shapes
- 1–2 g 2 mm bugle beads
- 2–3 g 9º three-cut seed beads
- 15º seed beads
  5–10 g color A
  1–2 g in each of **3** colors: B, C, D
- 2-strand slide clasp
- nylon beading thread, size B
- beading needles, #12
- Aleene's Thick Designer Tacky Glue
- bottle or drinking glass
- 7 x 3-in. (18 x 7.6 cm) piece of cardboard
- 2 x 2-in. (5 x 5 cm) fur or leather scrap (optional)
- jeweler's saw with blade for cutting plastic
- paper for pattern
- ruler
- sandpaper, 60 grit
- scissors
- small drill
- toothpicks
- two-part epoxy glue
- 8 x 8-in. (20 x 20 cm) piece of Ultrasuede

Most of Heidi's work includes animals and nature, and she's always looking out for interesting and unusual components to use in her designs. Gem and mineral shows are great places to start, but you can find elements to include in your beadwork anywhere — even in the toy aisle. With a little bead embroidery and a dash of imagination, you can put your own treasures to good use when you create a story with beads.

step by step

Bracelet base

[1] Holding the plastic animal firmly on your work surface, saw the head off at an angle **(photo a)**. Drill a few small holes about 1/16–1/8 in. (2–3 mm) from the edge, and sand the back of the head to remove the rough edges.

[2] On a piece of paper, draw a straight line that is 7 in. (18 cm) long, or the desired bracelet length. Draw a perpendicular line through the center. Lay out your components, placing the animal head on the center line and arranging the remaining elements around it. If you are using scraps of fur or leather, cut them to the desired shapes. Draw around your design to make a template **(photo b)**. If you have a digital camera, take a photo so you can remember the placement of your components.

[3] Cut out your template, and trace it onto a piece of Ultrasuede. Mark the center lines **(photo c)**.

[4] Mix a pea-sized amount of epoxy glue, and use a toothpick to spread it on the back of the head. Glue the head to the center of the Ultrasuede. Allow the glue to dry. Using a comfortable length of thread, tie an overhand knot (Basics, p. 13) at the end of the thread. Sewing up through the back of the Ultrasuede, tack the head to the Ultrasuede, sewing through the drilled holes **(photo d)**.

[5] Using color A 15º seed beads, work a round of beaded backstitch (Basics) around the head. Sew through all the beads again to snug them up against the head.

[6] Mix another small amount of epoxy, and glue your two largest cabochons to the Ultrasuede. Using 15ºs or 9º three-cut seed beads, work a

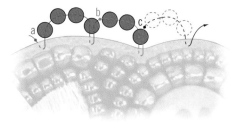

FIGURE

round of beaded backstitch around one or both of them **(photo e)**, and sew through all the beads again to snug them to the components, as in step 5.

[7] Continue gluing one or two components to the Ultrasuede, working from the center toward the edges, and working one or two rounds of beaded backstitch around each component as you go **(photo f)**. End and add thread (Basics) as needed. Leave enough room between components to work beaded backstitch between them, and keep your beadwork inside the lines of the pattern. Sand the backs of your components as needed to create a good bond to the Ultrasuede. If you are using scraps of fur or leather, use Aleene's Thick Designer Tacky Glue to glue them to the Ultrasuede, allow it to dry, and tack down the edges. Layer components as desired, gluing where possible and tacking them to the Ultrasuede through the beadwork **(photo g)**.

[8] Fill in spaces between the components with beaded backstitch using 2 mm bugle beads, 9°s, and 15°s in colors A, B, C, and D **(photo h)**. Wrap the embellished Ultrasuede around a bottle or drinking glass **(photo i)**. This

will show you how it will look on your wrist and may reveal more places to embellish. Fill in the vacant areas with more seed beads and/or layered components **(photo j)**, and end the thread.

Assembly

[1] Trim the Ultrasuede about 1/16–1/8 in. (2–3 mm) from the edge of your beadwork, taking care not to cut any threads.

[2] Trace the Ultrasuede onto the cardboard. Cut about 1/8–3/16 in. (3–5 mm) inside the lines so the cardboard will be slightly smaller than the beadwork.

[3] Trace the embellished Ultrasuede onto the remaining Ultrasuede, and trim it so they are both the same size **(photo k)**.

[4] Bend the cardboard around the bottle or glass so it curves **(photo l)**. Using Aleene's Thick Designer Tacky Glue, glue both pieces of Ultrasuede to the cardboard, leaving the edges unglued. Making sure the cardboard maintains its bend, let the glue dry.

[5] Sew the clasp to the back side of the beadwork or to the cardboard **(photo m)**, and end the thread. Glue the edges of the Ultrasuede together, and trim any excess Ultrasuede to make sure the back

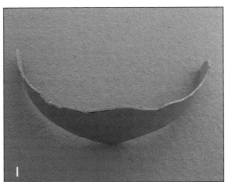

DESIGNER'S NOTES:
• Keep a few extra components on hand, as you may find that brainstorming your design works better as you go.
• Heidi likes to use the cardboard from the back of memo pads or notebooks; it's thick enough to be sturdy yet thin enough to cut with scissors.

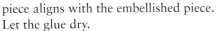

piece aligns with the embellished piece. Let the glue dry.

[6] Cut a 2-ft. (61 cm) piece of thread, and tie an overhand knot at the end. Sew between the front and back pieces of Ultrasuede, and bring the needle up through the top of the embellished Ultrasuede, hiding the knot between the two pieces. Pick up four As, slide them close to the Ultrasuede, and sew through both layers of Ultrasuede.

Sew back through the last A added **(figure, a–b)**. Pick up three As, slide them close to the last A, and sew through the layers of Ultrasuede. Sew back through the last A added **(b–c)**. Repeat around the edge **(photo n)**. When you reach the last stitch, pick up enough beads to fit between the last A added and the first A added, and sew down through the first A. End the thread. **○**

Use components that complement the animal you are highlighting in your piece.

Bead Embroidery

Stitch a classic beaded bead,
then embellish it to create
four looks

designed by **Kathryn Bowman**

Bonus Earrings

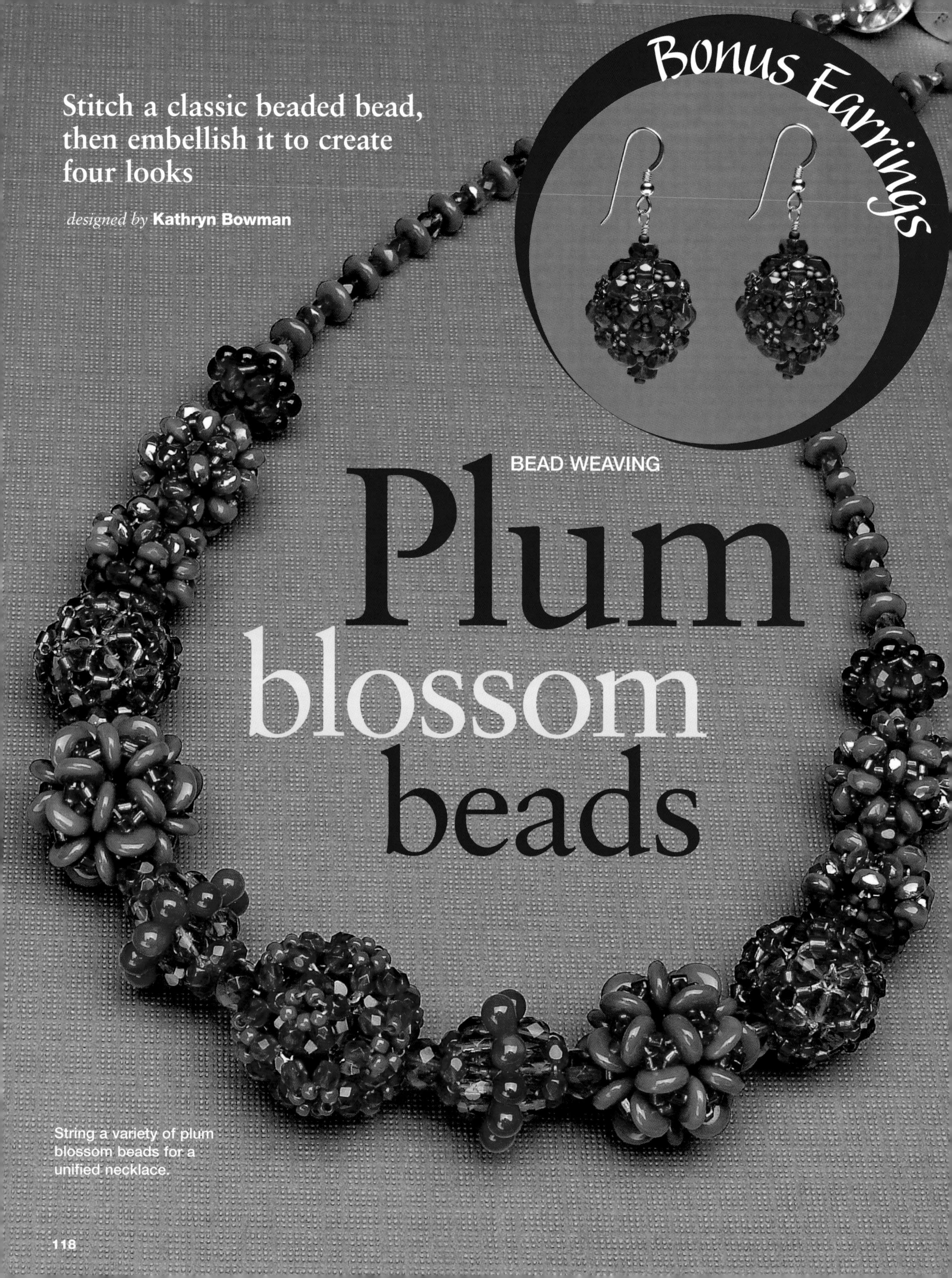

BEAD WEAVING

Plum
blossom
beads

String a variety of plum
blossom beads for a
unified necklace.

FIGURE 1

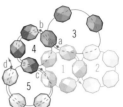

FIGURE 2

FIGURE 3

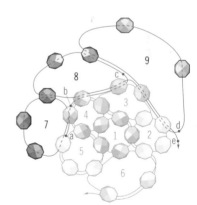

FIGURE 5

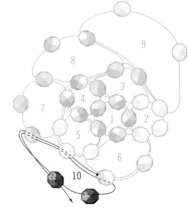

FIGURE 6

FIGURE 4

This beaded bead offers four design options for embellishment: basic plum blossom bead, plum blossom with seeds, embellished plum blossom, and double-embellished plum blossom. Play with bead shapes and sizes to create an endless variety. Then, make your beads into a simple strung necklace or earrings. Where you take this design is up to you.

step by step

Beaded beads
Basic plum blossom

The illustrations show a different color 4 mm fire-polished bead for each stitch to help you keep track of the stitches. It may be helpful to make a test bead in this manner. To make your own beaded beads, use 4 mms in a single color.

[1] Place your beads in rows as in **figure 1**. Each row contains the beads needed to complete a stitch, and they are arranged in the order they should be worked, from top to bottom. This will help you keep track of each stitch.

[2] On 1 yd. (.9 m) of monofilament, center five 4 mm fire-polished beads, and cross the tail through the last 4 mm picked up to form ring 1 **(figure 2, a–aa)**. Color one end of the thread red and the other end black.

[3] To make ring 2, use the red thread to pick up four 4 mms, and sew through the 4 mm your thread exited and the next 4 mm in ring 1 **(a–b)**.

[4] To make ring 3, use the red thread to pick up three 4 mms, and sew through the adjacent 4 mm in ring 2, the 4 mm your thread exited at the start of this step, and the first 4 mm picked up **(figure 3, a–b)**.

[5] To make ring 4, use the red thread to pick up three 4 mms, and sew through the next 4 mm in ring 1, the 4 mm your thread exited in ring 3, and the 4 mms just picked up **(b–c)**.

[6] To make ring 5, use the red thread to sew through the next 4 mm in ring 1, pick up three 4 mms, and sew through the last 4 mm picked up in ring 4 and the next four 4 mms **(c–d)**.

[7] To make ring 6, use the black thread to sew through the next 4 mm in ring 2, and pick up two 4 mms. Sew through the adjacent 4 mm in ring 5, the next 4 mm in ring 1, the 4 mm your thread exited in ring 2, and the two 4 mms just picked up **(figure 4)**.

[8] To make ring 7, use the red thread to sew through the next 4 mm in ring 4, and pick up three 4 mms. Sew through the adjacent 4 mm in ring 5 and the 4 mm your thread exited in ring 4 **(figure 5, a–b)**.

[9] To make ring 8, use the red thread to sew through the next 4 mm in ring 4 and the adjacent 4 mm in ring 3 **(b–c)**. Pick up two 4 mms, and sew through the adjacent 4 mm in ring 7, the last two 4 mms your thread exited, the next 4 mm in ring 3, and the adjacent 4 mm in ring 2 **(c–d)**.

[10] To make ring 9, use the red thread to pick up two 4 mms, and sew through the first 4 mm picked up in ring 8, the next 4 mm in ring 3, and the 4 mm in ring 2 your thread exited **(d–e)**.

[11] To make ring 10, use the black thread to sew through the next 4 mm in ring 5 and the adjacent 4 mm in ring 7. Pick up two 4 mms, and sew through the 4 mm your thread exited in ring 6, the 4 mm in ring 5, the 4 mm in ring 7, and the first 4 mm picked up **(figure 6)**.

[12] Rings 11 and 12 will be completed with the remaining bead. Look at the opening in your beadwork. You will see that it has eight 4 mms — two pairs that are up high and two pairs that angle down. With the black thread coming out between two high beads, pick up a 4 mm, cross over the opening, and sew through the corresponding high bead of the other pair (figure 7, a–b). This will turn the large opening into two rings. Sew through the beads of each ring to stabilize them (b–c), and end the threads (Basics, p. 13).

Plum blossom with seeds
These instructions call for 4 mm fire-polished beads, but you may substitute Czech glass disks or fringe drops if desired.
[1] Place your beads in rows as in **figure 8**. This will help you keep track of each stitch. The seed beads at the bottom of the figure show the beads used to fill in the gaps between the stitches.
[2] On 1 yd. (.9 m) of monofilament, pick up an alternating pattern of a 4 mm fire-polished bead and an 11º seed bead five times. Sew through the first 4 mm picked up, and center the beads to make ring 1 (figure 9, a–b). Color one end of the thread read and the other end black. On the red thread, pick up an alternating pattern of an 11º and a 4 mm four times, and pick up an 11º. To make ring 2, sew through the 4 mm your thread exited in ring 1 and the next two beads in ring 1 (b–c).
[3] To make ring 3, use the red thread to pick up an alternating pattern of an 11º and a 4 mm three times, and pick up an 11º. Sew through the adjacent 4 mm in ring 2, pick up an 11º, and sew through the next 4 mm your thread exited in ring 1 and the first 11º and 4 mm picked up in ring 3 (c–d).
[4] Continue following the steps to make a "Basic plum blossom," but pick up an 11º between each pair of 4 mms as in steps 1–3 above, making sure to add an 11º between the 4 mms of adjoining rings.

Embellished plum blossom
[1] Follow the steps to make a "Basic plum blossom."
[2] Center 1 yd. (.9 m) of monofilament in a 4 mm. With each thread, pick up an 11º seed bead (figure 10, a–b and aa–bb), cross the red thread through the 11º on the black thread, and sew through the next 4 mm in the ring (b–c).
[3] With the red thread, pick up an 11º (c–d). Cross the black thread through the 11º, and sew through the next 4 mm in the ring (bb–cc). Repeat around the

materials

all beaded beads
- monofilament 6 lb. test
- red and black marker

basic plum blossom ½-in. (1.3 cm) diameter
- 30 4 mm fire-polished beads

plum blossom with seeds ¾-in. (1.9 cm) diameter
- 30 4 mm fire-polished beads, Czech glass disks, or fringe drops
- 60 11º seed beads

embellished plum blossom ¾-in. (1.9 cm) diameter
- 30 4 mm fire-polished beads
- 60 11º seed beads

double-embellished plum blossom ¾-in. (1.9 cm) diameter
- 30 4 mm or 6 mm fire-polished beads
- 60 3 mm or 4 mm fire-polished beads
- 60 11º seed beads

necklace 21 in. (53 cm)
- 6 basic plum blossoms (with optional variations)
- 4 plum blossoms with seeds and disks
- 2 embellished plum blossoms
- double-embellished plum blossom
- 12 6 mm fire-polished beads
- 14 4 mm fire-polished beads
- 28 4 mm Czech glass disks
- 28 3 mm fire-polished beads
- 14 3 x 5 mm rondelles
- clasp
- 4 crimp beads
- 4 crimp covers
- 2 wire guards
- flexible beading wire, .012
- chainnose pliers
- crimping pliers
- wire cutters

pair of earrings
- 2 beaded beads
- 4 4 mm Czech glass disks
- 4 11º seed beads
- 2 2½-in. (6.4 cm) head pins
- pair of earring findings
- chainnose pliers
- roundnose pliers
- wire cutters

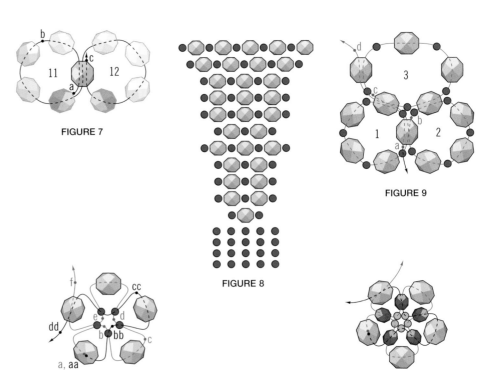

FIGURE 7

FIGURE 8

FIGURE 9

FIGURE 10

FIGURE 11

ring, alternating the threads that cross through the beads (d–e and cc–dd).

[4] When you reach the first 11º, cross the red thread through the 11º and the 4 mm the black thread just exited (e–f).

[5] Repeat around the whole bead, sewing through the beadwork as needed, and end the threads.

Double-embellished plum blossom

Follow the steps to make an "Embellished plum blossom," but pick up a 3 mm fire-polished bead and a seed bead in each embellishment, or use 6 mm fire-polished beads instead of 4 mms, and pick up a 4 mm and a seed bead in each embellishment stitch, then cross through the 3 mm or 4 mm (figure 11).

Necklace

[1] Cut 25 in. (64 cm) of beading wire, and center a double-embellished plum blossom.

[2] On each side, string a 6 mm fire-polished bead, a basic style A (see "Editor's notes") plum blossom, a 6 mm, a plum blossom with seeds and disk beads, a 6 mm, an embellished plum blossom, a 6 mm, a basic style B plum blossom, a 6 mm, a plum blossom with seeds and 3 x 5 mm rondelles, a 6 mm, and a basic style C plum blossom, then string 4½ in. (11.4 cm) of 4 mm fire-polished beads, 4 mm Czech glass disks, 3 mm fire-polished beads, and 3 x 5 mm rondelles in a pleasing arrangement.

[3] On each side, string a crimp bead, a rondelle, a crimp bead, a 3 mm, the first hole of a wire guard, half of the clasp, and the other hole of the wire guard. Go back through the last few beads and crimp beads added, and test the fit. Add or remove beads as desired, crimp the crimp beads (Basics), and close crimp covers over them.

Earrings

[1] Make the beaded bead of your choice.

[2] On a head pin, string an 11º seed bead, a 4 mm Czech glass disk, a beaded bead, a 4 mm, and an 11º.

[3] Make a wrapped loop (Basics).

[4] Open the loop of an earring finding (Basics), attach the wrapped loop, and close the loop.

[5] Make a second earring. ●

EDITOR'S NOTES:

• **You can use Fireline 6 lb. test and #12 beading needles to make your beads. They will turn out a little less stiff, but will be easy to embellish because the beads can take multiple thread passes.**

• **Follow the instructions for "Basic plum blossom," and experiment with different sized and shaped beads to make beaded beads like those that frame Kathryn's focal bead in her necklace. To make the different bead styles mentioned in the necklace instructions, lay out the beads as follows:**

Basic Style A Plum Blossom

• five 3 mm fire-polished beads
• 4 mm fire-polished bead, two fringe drops, 4 mm
• 4 mm, two fringe drops
• two fringe drops, 4 mm
• 4 mm, two fringe drops
• two fringe drops
• 4 mm, 3 mm, 4 mm
• 4 mm, 3 mm
• 4 mm, 3 mm
• 3 mm, 4 mm
• 3 mm

Basic Style B Plum Blossom

• five repetitions of an alternating pattern of a 3 mm fire-polished bead and an 11º seed bead
• 11º, four 3 x 5 mm rondelles, 11º
• 11º, three rondelles
• three rondelles, 11º
• 11º, three rondelles
• two rondelles
• rondelle, 11º, 3 mm, 11º, rondelle
• 11º, 3 mm, 11º, rondelle
• rondelle, 11º, 3 mm, 11º
• 11º, 3 mm, 11º, rondelle
• 11º, 3 mm, 11º

Basic Style C Plum Blossom

• five 11º seed beads
• 3 mm fire-polished bead, two fringe drops, 3 mm
• 3 mm, two 3 mm fringe drops
• two fringe drops, 3 mm
• 3 mm, two fringe drops
• two fringe drops
• 3 mm, 11º, 3 mm
• 3 mm, 11º
• 3 mm, 11º
• 11º, 3 mm
• 11º

The gold standard

Create a gorgeous necklace using flat spiral stitch

designed by **April Bradley**

materials

necklace 17 in. (43 cm)

- 1⅛ x ¹¹⁄₁₆-in. (2.9 x 1.7 cm) crystal pendant
- round beads
  - **3** 10 mm
  - **16** 8 mm
  - **12** 6 mm
  - **132** 3 mm
  - **192** 2 mm
- bicone crystals
  - **86** 6 mm
  - **2** 4 mm
- clasp
- 8 mm jump ring
- **2** crimp beads
- **2** crimp covers (optional)
- Fireline, 8 lb. test
- flexible beading wire, .014
- beading needles, #12
- Bead Stopper or tape (optional)
- **2** pairs of chainnose pliers
- crimping pliers
- wire cutters

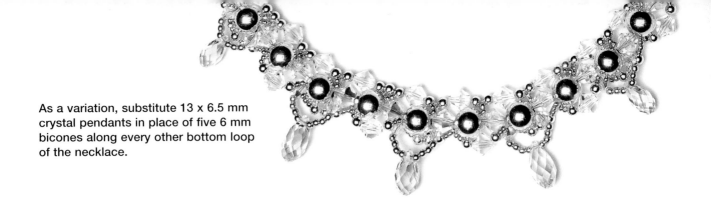

As a variation, substitute 13 x 6.5 mm crystal pendants in place of five 6 mm bicones along every other bottom loop of the necklace.

Adorn your neckline with sparkling crystals and bright gold beads in a necklace that works up so quickly, you'll be able to make it the evening before an evening out.

step by step

Base row

[1] On 24 in. (61 cm) of beading wire, string a crimp bead and half of the clasp 2 in. (5 cm) from one end. Go back through the crimp bead, and crimp it (Basics, p. 13). Trim the short tail.

[2] String four 3 mm round beads, a 4 mm bicone crystal, a repeating pattern of a 6 mm round bead and a 6 mm bicone crystal six times, a repeating pattern of an 8 mm round bead and a 6 mm bicone eight times, a repeating pattern of a 10 mm round bead and a 6 mm bicone three times, a repeating pattern of an 8 mm round and a 6 mm bicone eight times, a repeating pattern of a 6 mm round and a 6 mm bicone six times, a 6 mm round, a 4 mm bicone, and four 3 mm rounds.

[3] String a crimp bead and the other half of the clasp, and go back through the crimp bead. Leaving about 4 mm of space between the last bead strung and the crimp bead, crimp the crimp bead. Or, temporarily secure this end with a Bead Stopper or tape until you finish the necklace.

Spiral loops

[1] On 2 yd. (1.8 m) of Fireline, attach a stop bead (Basics), leaving a 6-in. (15 cm) tail. Sew through the first 6 mm round and 6 mm bicone on the base.

[2] Pick up a 2 mm round bead, a 3 mm round, a 6 mm bicone, a 3 mm round, and a 2 mm round. Sew through the first 6 mm round and bicone again, and continue through the next 6 mm round. Push the loop to the right of the base (figure 1).

[3] Repeat step 2, but sew through the bicone and the round your thread exited at the start of this step, and continue through the next bicone. Push the loop to the left (figure 2).

[4] Repeat steps 2 and 3 for a total of ten loops, pushing the loops to alternate sides and always sewing through the two beads your thread exited at the start of the step and the next bead in the base.

[5] Continue making loops, but instead of picking up one 2 mm round, pick up two. Make a total of 19 loops.

[6] Make one loop using two 2 mm rounds, four 3 mm rounds, and two 2 mm rounds.

[7] Make 19 loops as in step 5, and ten loops as in step 4. End the working thread and tail (Basics).

Finishing

[1] Lay the necklace out on your work surface, making sure the first loop lies to the right of the base and the next loop lies to the left of the base. The center loop of just round beads defines the outer center loop of the necklace.

[2] On 1 yd. (.9 m) of Fireline, attach a stop bead, leaving a 6-in. (15 cm) tail. Sew through the first 3 mm round, 6 mm bicone, and 3 mm round in the first loop of the inner edge.

[3] Sew through the 3 mm round, 6 mm bicone, and 3 mm round in the next loop along the inner edge (figure 3). Repeat until you reach the last inner loop.

[4] Pulling gently, snug up the inner edge into a curve that sits comfortably around your neck.

[5] Pick up three 3 mm rounds, and sew through the 3 mm round and the 4 mm bicone on the base. End the working thread. Remove the stop bead, and repeat with the tail.

[6] Open an 8 mm jump ring (Basics), and attach the pendant to the center outer loop of round beads. Close the jump ring.

[7] If you didn't crimp the second crimp bead in step 3 of "Base row," remove the Bead Stopper or tape, and crimp the crimp bead. Use chainnose pliers to close crimp covers over the crimp beads if desired. ●

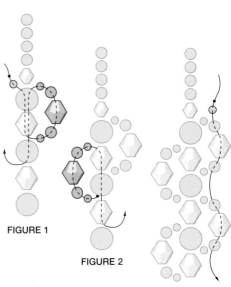

FIGURE 1

FIGURE 2

FIGURE 3

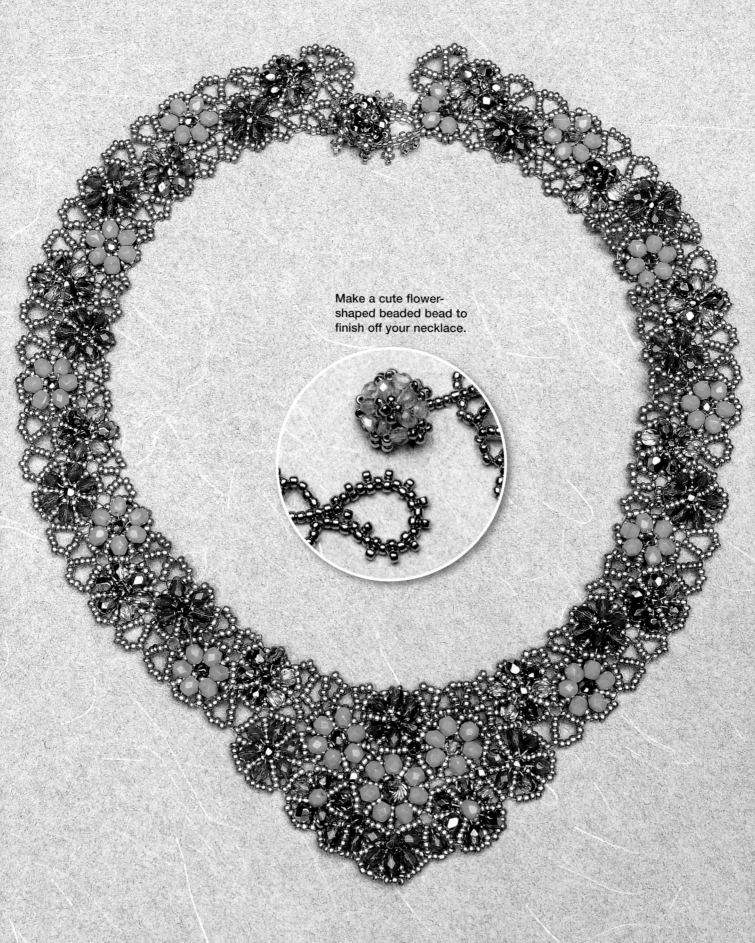

Make a cute flower-shaped beaded bead to finish off your necklace.

Flowers and lace

Embellish a triangle stitch base to make a gently draping floral bib

designed by **Ludmila Raitzin**

An alternating arrangement of triangles creates six-sided flower shapes that are perfect for embellishing with fire-polished beads.

step by step

Necklace base
Row 1
[1] On a comfortable length of Fireline, pick up 12 11º seed beads, and sew through the first eight 11ºs again (figure 1, a–b).
[2] Pick up seven 11ºs, and sew through the last four 11ºs your thread exited in the previous step and the first four 11ºs just added (b–c). This creates a triangle with three 11ºs along the top edge.
[3] Pick up eight 11ºs, and sew through the last four 11ºs your thread exited in the previous step and the first four 11ºs just added (c–d). This creates a triangle with four 11ºs along the bottom edge.
[4] Repeat steps 2 and 3 until the strip is about 16 in. (41 cm) or the desired necklace length, ending and adding thread (Basics, p. 13) as needed. The

strip will curve due to the difference in the number of beads along the top and bottom edges.

Row 2
[1] Sew through the bottom four 11ºs of the last triangle in row 1 (figure 2, a–b).
[2] Pick up eight 11ºs, sew through the four 11ºs in the previous row again, and continue through the first four 11ºs just added (b–c).
[3] Pick up nine 11ºs, and sew through the four 11ºs your thread exited in the

materials
necklace 17 in. (43 cm)
- 5 mm rondelle (to fill center flower – optional)
- 80–90 4 mm fire-polished beads in each of **3** colors: A, B, C
- 55 3 mm fire-polished beads, color D
- 25 g 11º seed beads
- Fireline, 6 lb. test
- beading needles, #12

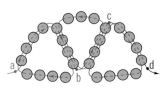

FIGURE 1

FIGURE 2

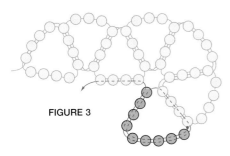

FIGURE 3

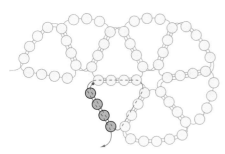

FIGURE 4

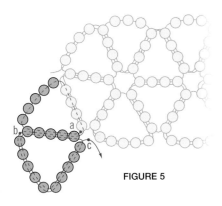

FIGURE 5

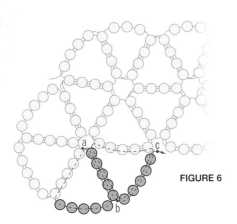

FIGURE 6

previous stitch, the nine 11°s just added, and the next four 11°s in the previous row (figure 3).

[4] Pick up four 11°s, and sew through the last four 11°s added in the previous stitch, the last four 11°s your thread exited in the previous row, and the four new 11°s (figure 4).

[5] Repeat steps 3 and 4 along the length of row 1.

Row 3

[1] Pick up 10 11°s, and sew through the last four 11°s your thread exited in the previous row and the first five 11°s just added (figure 5, a–b).

[2] Pick up 10 11°s, and sew through the five 11°s your thread exited in the previous stitch and the 10 new 11°s (b–c).

[3] Pick up 10 11°s, and sew through the last five 11°s your thread exited in the previous stitch and the first five 11°s just added (figure 6, a–b).

[4] Pick up five 11°s, and sew through the next five 11°s in the previous row, the five side 11°s in the previous stitch, and the five 11°s just added (b–c).

[5] Repeat steps 3 and 4 along the length of row 2. At the very end of the row, you'll need to add one extra triangle to match the starting end. End the thread.

Row 4

[1] Identify the center stitch in row 1. If the center stitch does not have three beads along the top edge, choose one

of the adjacent stitches. This will be the center point of the necklace. Find the stitch in row 3 that is directly below the one you just identified as the center in row 1. Count seven stitches to one side. Add a new thread in the beadwork, and exit the seventh stitch from the center, with the needle pointing toward the center of the necklace.

[2] Work eight stitches as in row 3 (figure 7, a–b). Work one additional stitch with 10 11°s (b–c) to add an extra triangle in the central flower, then finish the flower motif with a stitch, using five 11°s (c–d).

[3] Work six more stitches as in row 3 to complete the row.

Row 5

[1] Sew through the beadwork to exit the fourth stitch from the end of row 4, with the needle pointing toward the center of the necklace.

[2] Work 12 stitches as in row 4 (figure 8).

Embellishment

[1] Begin adding the fire-polished beads in the middle of the top row: Sew through the beadwork to exit a middle 11° of a triangle along the outer edge of the flower shape. Pick up a color A 4 mm fire-polished bead, cross the empty space in the middle of the stitch, and sew through an adjacent "wall" of 11°s and the next two 11°s in the outer edge (figure 9). Repeat around to fill each triangle of the flower shape with a 4 mm.

EDITOR'S NOTE:
If you use Japanese seed beads for the base, you may find that a fair amount of thread remains exposed when you're adding the 4 mm fire-polished beads. To hide the extra thread, pick up a 15° seed bead in the same color as the base after each 4 mm so it sits near the center of the flower.

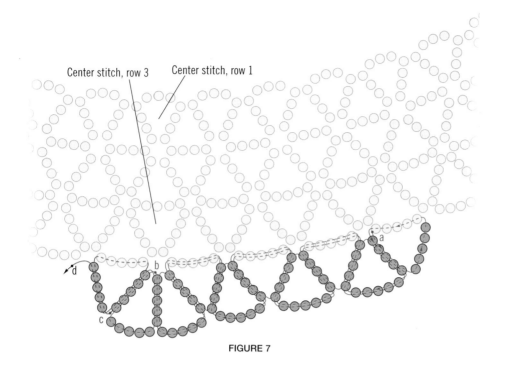

Center stitch, row 3   Center stitch, row 1

FIGURE 7

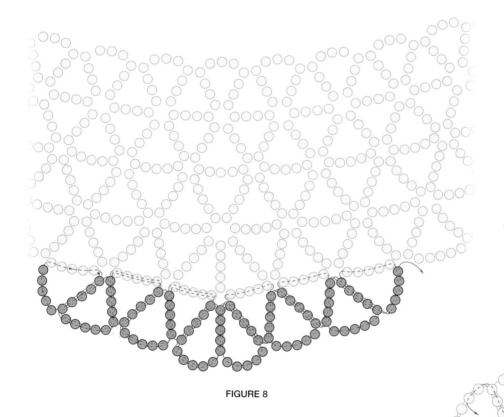

FIGURE 8

FIGURE 9

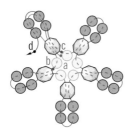

FIGURE 10

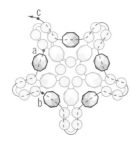

FIGURE 11

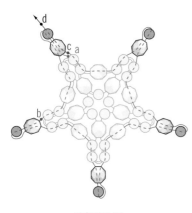

FIGURE 12

FIGURE 13

[2] To fill the center of the flower, sew through the beadwork to exit a bead in the center circle, pick up a 3 mm fire-polished bead, and sew through the opposite "wall" of 11ºs (figure 10).
[3] Repeat steps 1 and 2 to add flowers along the length of the necklace. Alternate them in a zigzagging fashion, using colors A, B, and C as desired. When you fill the center flower, you'll need to add seven 4 mms. If desired, use a 5 mm rondelle in the middle of the center flower. Fill in the area below the center flower as desired. End all remaining threads.

Clasp
Flower bead
[1] On 2 ft. (61 cm) of Fireline, pick up five 11ºs, leaving a 6-in. (15 cm) tail. Tie the beads into a ring with a square knot (Basics).
[2] Pick up one 3 mm and four 11ºs. Skip the four 11ºs, sew back through the 3 mm, and continue through the next 11º in the ring (figure 11, a–b). Repeat around four times (b–c), and sew through the first 3 mm and four 11ºs again (c–d).
[3] Pick up a 3 mm, and sew through the next four 11ºs (figure 12, a–b). Repeat around, but in the last stitch, sew through only two 11ºs (b–c).

[4] Pick up a 3 mm and an 11º, skip the 11º, and sew back through the 3 mm. Sew through the next pair of 11ºs, the next 3 mm, and the following pair of 11ºs (figure 13, a–b). Repeat four times (b–c), then step up through the first 3 mm and 11º (c–d). Sew through the five 11ºs added in the round several times to pull the beads into a button shape, and end the thread.
[5] Add a new 18-in. (46 cm) thread at one end of the necklace base. Pick up eight 11ºs, sew through the center of the flower bead, and pick up one 11º. Skip the last 11º, and sew back through the flower bead, the eight 11ºs, and the bead your thread exited in the base. Retrace the thread path several times, and end the thread.

Loop
Add 18 in. (46 cm) of thread at the other end of the necklace, and pick up enough 11ºs to fit around the flower bead. Sew through two beads in the base to form a ring. Work a round of peyote stitch (Basics), retrace the thread path through the loop at least once, and end the thread. ●

DAISY CHAIN

Get to the
point

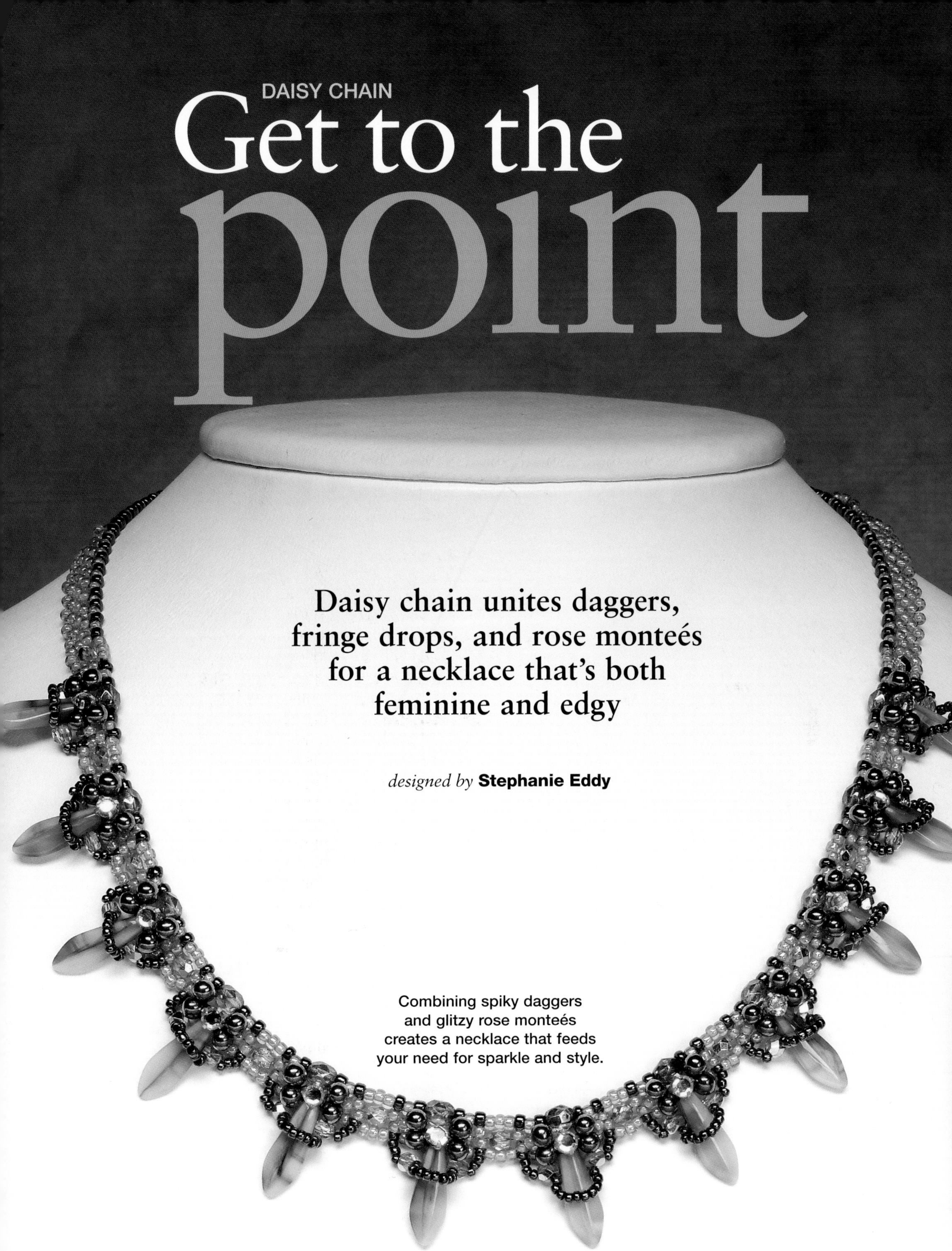

Daisy chain unites daggers,
fringe drops, and rose monteés
for a necklace that's both
feminine and edgy

designed by **Stephanie Eddy**

Combining spiky daggers
and glitzy rose monteés
creates a necklace that feeds
your need for sparkle and style.

Daisy Chain

129

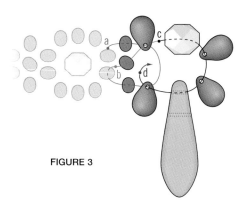

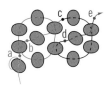

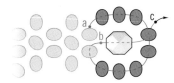

FIGURE 1

FIGURE 2

FIGURE 3

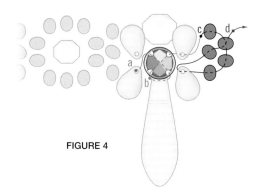

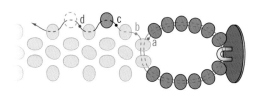

FIGURE 4

FIGURE 5

materials

necklace 18 in. (46 cm)

- **12** 15 mm two-hole daggers
  (U Bead It, ubeaditsacramento.com)
- **12** 3–4 mm rose monteés
- **12** 4 mm fire-polished beads
- **37** 3 mm fire-polished beads
- **48** fringe drops
- **11º** seed beads
  10 g color A
  3 g color B
- **3 g** 15º seed beads
- shank button
- Fireline, 6 lb. test
- beading needles, #12

Take advantage of two-hole components for a richly layered necklace. Double-drilled daggers and cross-hole rose monteés allow you to add embellishments, change direction, and create a necklace that adds another dimension to classic daisy chain.

stepbystep

[1] On a comfortable length of Fireline, attach a stop bead (Basics, p. 13), leaving a 2-yd. (1.8 m) tail. Pick up six color A 11º seed beads, and sew through the first A again to form a ring (figure 1, a–b). Pick up an A, skip two As in the ring, and sew through the next A in the opposite direction (b–c).
[2] Pick up four As, and sew through the next A in the previous ring to form a six-bead ring (c–d). Pick up an A, skip two As in the ring, and sew through the next A in the opposite direction (d–e).

[3] Pick up eight As, and sew through the next A in the previous stitch (figure 2, a–b). Pick up a 3 mm fire-polished bead, skip four As in the ring, and sew through the fifth A in the opposite direction (b–c).
[4] Pick up an A, two fringe drops, and an A, and sew through the next A in the previous stitch (figure 3, a–b). Pick up an A, skip two As, and sew through the first drop in the opposite direction (b–c). Pick up a 4 mm fire-polished bead, two drops, and the top hole of a two-hole dagger, and sew through the next drop in the previous stitch (c–d). As you pull the stitches tight, make sure

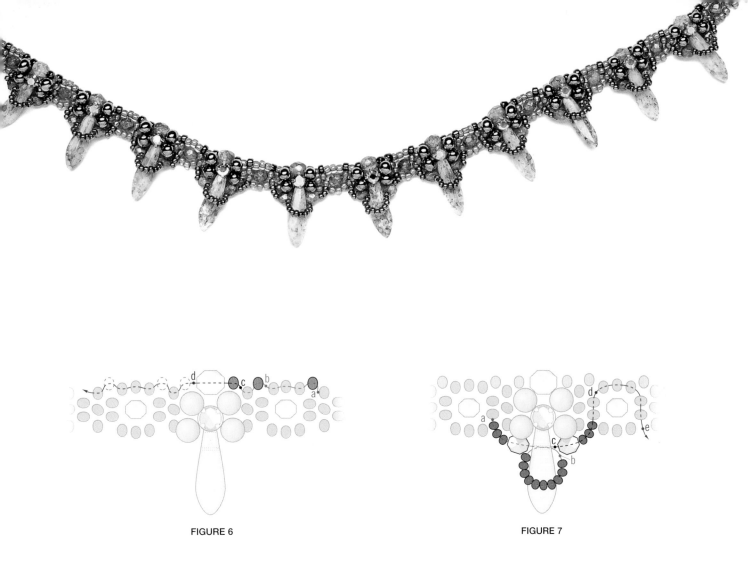

FIGURE 6

FIGURE 7

the drops are positioned on the front of the necklace.

[5] Pick up a rose monteé, slide it up to the beadwork, and sew through the top hole of the dagger to make a diagonal **(figure 4, a–b)**. Sew through the other hole in the rose monteé and through the top drop on the other side of the ring **(b–c)**.

[6] Pick up four As, and sew through the next drop in the previous stitch. Pick up an A, skip a drop and an A, and sew through the next A in the opposite direction **(c–d)**. Make sure the drops are positioned on the front of the necklace.

[7] Repeat steps 3–6 until you've added a total of 12 daggers, ending and adding thread (Basics) as needed. Repeat step 3 to add another stitch with a 3 mm. Resume stitching in regular daisy chain, as in step 2, until the regular daisy chain segment is about 4 in. (10 cm) long.

[8] Remove the stop bead from the tail, and stitch in regular daisy chain until the segment is about 4 in. (10 cm) long.

[9] At one end of the necklace, pick up six As, the button shank, and six As. Sew through both As on the end of the last stitch, and retrace the thread path through the beads **(figure 5, a–b)**. Sew through the top A on the last daisy chain stitch **(b–c)**. Pick up a color B 11º seed bead, and sew through the next top A **(c–d)**. Repeat until you reach the first daisy stitch with a 3 mm.

[10] Pick up a B, and sew through the three As on top of the next stitch **(figure 6, a–b)**. Pick up a B, and sew through the next top A **(b–c)**. Pick up a B, and sew through the 4 mm **(c–d)**. Continue adding Bs, sewing through the top bead or beads of each stitch, until you reach the other end of the necklace.

[11] Pick up enough As to fit around the button, and sew through the two As

at the end of the necklace to make a loop. Retrace the thread path.

[12] Sew through the beadwork to exit the two As between the first 3 mm stitch and the first stitch with drops **(figure 7, point a)**. Pick up three 15º seed beads and a 3 mm, and sew through the bottom hole of the next dagger **(a–b)**. Pick up 10 15ºs, and sew through the bottom hole of the dagger again, making a loop in front **(b–c)**. Pick up a 3 mm and three 15ºs, and sew up through the two As between the next set of drops and the next 3 mm stitch **(c–d)**. Sew through the next five As around the stitch **(d–e)**.

[13] Repeat step 12 to embellish the remaining daggers. End the threads. ○

Filigree fling

An art glass bead
created by lampwork
artist Melissa Vess
inspired this design.

Transform straight peyote segments into curving loops and swirls

designed by **Cynthia Newcomer Daniel**

Capture the colors of a lampworked focal bead in filigree-like beadwork. This versatile design accommodates focal beads of different sizes and shapes.

step by step

Stitching sequence

Follow the same stitching sequence to make each component:

Base rows or rounds: Pick up an alternating pattern of a color D 15º seed bead and a color A 11º seed bead for the specified length. These beads form rows or rounds 1 and 2.

Row/Round 3: Pick up one 15º per stitch.
Row/Round 4: Pick up one color B 11º seed bead per stitch.
Row/Round 5: Pick up one 15º per stitch.
Row/Round 6: Pick up one color C 11º seed bead per stitch.

Focal bead component

[1] On 2 yd. (1.8 m) of thread, attach a stop bead (Basics, p. 13), leaving a 6-in. (15 cm) tail.

[2] Following the stitching sequence described above, pick up an even number of beads to frame the focal bead, leaving enough space for two more inner rounds to be added between this ring of beads and the focal bead. Sew through the first four beads again to form a ring.

[3] Working in tubular peyote (Basics), follow the stitching sequence for rounds 3–6, stepping up at the end of each round through the first bead added in the round, and ending and adding thread (Basics) as needed. Remove the stop bead, and end the tail.

[4] Zip up (Basics) the edges of the ring to form a circular tube, stitching the seam on the outside of the tube **(photo a)** to position the As on the outside, the Cs on the top, and the Bs on the inside of the ring. Exit an A in the outer round.

[5] Continue in circular peyote stitch along the outer edge of the frame:
Round 7: Alternate working a stitch with a 15º and a stitch with a color D 11º seed bead. Step up through the first 15º added in the round.
Round 8: Pick up one C per stitch. Step up through the first C added in the round.
Round 9: Pick up one B per stitch. End the working thread.

[6] Center 18 in. (46 cm) of Fireline on two Cs in the inner round of the ring. Working with each end of the Fireline, cross the Fireline through the 15º between the pair of Cs.

[7] Over both strands of Fireline, string a C, a 4 mm bicone crystal, the focal bead, a 4 mm, and a C **(photo b)**. If the hole in the focal bead is large, string enough seed beads to fill the hole before stringing the focal bead.

[8] Separate the strands of Fireline, and cross the ends through a 15º on the opposite side of the ring. Sew through the Cs and Ds around the inner edge of the ring to stiffen the beadwork. Retrace the thread path through the focal bead, and end the Fireline. Set the focal bead component aside.

Component A
Frame

[1] On 2 yd. (1.8 m) of thread, attach a stop bead, leaving a 12-in. (30 cm) tail.

[2] Following the stitching sequence, pick up 101 beads, beginning and ending with a 15º. Work in flat odd-count peyote (Basics) for rows 3–6.

[3] Zip up the edges to form a tube. Exit the end A in the direction of the tube.

[4] Continue in flat odd-count peyote stitch along the outer edge of the tube:
Row 7: Pick up one D 11º per stitch between the As. Sew through an end 15º.

[5] From the working-thread end of the tube, count back 15 Bs, and sew through the 15th B in the direction of the end of the tube to form a loop **(photo c)**. Sew through a 15º in the end of the tube. Retrace the thread path a few times. Do not end the working thread. Repeat on the other end with the tail. Do not end the tail.

[6] With the working thread, sew through the beadwork toward the end of the tube nearest the loop connection, and exit the fifth D 11º from the end of the tube.

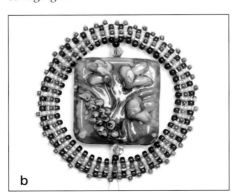

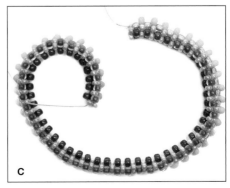

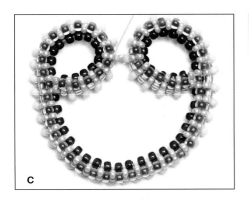

c

d

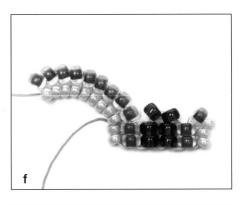

f

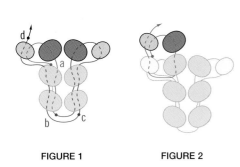

FIGURE 1   FIGURE 2

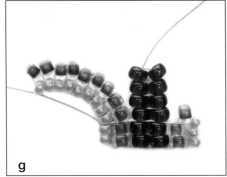

g

h

[7] Line up the loops, and sew through the fifth D 11º from the other end of the tube. Sew the two Ds together (photo d). Retrace the thread path a few times.

[8] Sew through the beadwork to exit the sixth D 11º from an end of the tube, and sew it to the corresponding D 11º as in step 7. Sew through the beadwork to the top of the component. Do not end the working thread.

[9] Repeat steps 1–8 to make another A component.

Filigree inset

[1] On 1 yd. (.9 m) of thread, attach a stop bead, leaving a 12-in. (30 cm) tail. You may need to modify the inset depending on the size of your A component, changing its width and height.

[2] Pick up two 15ºs, two Bs, four Cs, two Bs, and two 15ºs. Following the "Alternative method" for stitching a ladder (Basics), sew through the pairs of beads to make a ladder two beads high and six beads wide (photo e). Remove the stop bead.

[3] Working in flat herringbone stitch (Basics), pick up a 15º and a B in the first stitch, two Cs in the next stitch, and a B and a 15º in the third stitch.

[4] Working in the first two columns, stitch a two-bead column of a 15º and a B until you have a column with 11 15ºs

on the edge, including the beads in the previous rows (photo f).

[5] Sew down through 10 Bs and up through the next two Cs. Work three herringbone stitches using Cs (photo g).

[6] Working in split herringbone stitch, pick up a 15º and a C, and sew down through two Cs in the column you exited (figure 1, a–b).

[7] Sew up through two Cs in the adjacent column, pick up a C and a 15º, and sew down through two Cs in the column you just exited (b–c). Sew up through two Cs in the first column and the 15º added in step 6 (c–d).

[8] Pick up a 15º and a C, and sew through the C and 15º below and the new 15º (figure 2). Repeat three times.

[9] Sew down through six Cs in the split column and up through two Cs in the adjacent column. Repeat step 8 to form a second split column to mirror the first.

[10] Sew down through all the Cs in the right side of the center column and up through the three adjacent Bs. Repeat step 4 to stitch a second curved column.

[11] Center the filigree inside an A component, and attach it to the loops and ring (photo h).

[12] Repeat steps 1–11 to make a second filigree inset to embellish the second A component.

Component B

[1] Repeat steps 1–8 of "Component A: Frame" but with the following changes:
Step 2: Pick up 81 beads, beginning and ending with a 15º.
Steps 6–8: Connect the fourth and fifth D 11ºs.

[2] Make a second B component.

Assembly

[1] Center an A component at one side of the focal bead component, and attach it using the working thread and tails.

[2] With one of the threads, exit an edge C of the focal component that is opposite the connection between the A component loops. Pick up a 4 mm bicone, and sew under the thread bridge of the connection (photo i). Sew back through the 4 mm, retrace the thread path a few times, and end the threads.

[3] Repeat steps 1 and 2 on the other side of the focal bead component with the other A component.

[4] Center a B component at the side of an A component, and attach it as in step 1.

[5] Repeat step 2 on the A component, but exit a D 11º.

[6] Repeat steps 4 and 5 with the other B component.

i

j

k

Toggle bar

[1] On 1 yd. (.9 m) of thread, attach a stop bead, leaving a 12-in. (30 cm) tail.

[2] Following the stitching sequence, pick up 21 beads, beginning and ending with a 15º. Work in flat odd-count peyote for rows 3–6.

[3] Zip up the edges to form a tube. Zigzag through the end 15ºs to make sure they are joined, then exit an end A in the direction of the tube.

[4] Pick up a 15º, and sew through the next A. Repeat to work a row of "stitch-in-the-ditch" between the As. Zigzag through the end 15ºs, and exit an end C in the direction of the tube.

[5] Use 15ºs to work a row of stitch-in-the-ditch between the Cs. This alters the toggle bar into a triangular shape with one edge having three rows of 15ºs. End the working thread and tail.

[6] Repeat steps 1–5 to make a second toggle bar.

[7] On a comfortable length of thread, pick up two D 11ºs, and sew through the first one again, leaving a 12-in. (30 cm) tail. Pick up two D 11ºs, sew down through the next D 11º, and sew up through the adjacent D 11º and the first D 11º just added. Repeat eight times to make a strip 10 beads long and two beads wide.

[8] Using the tail, attach the strip to a toggle bar, sewing through the center 15º on the side with three 15ºs. Sew back through a few Cs in the strip (photo j). Retrace the thread path a few times.

[9] Test your bracelet for fit. If you need to extend its length, add more stitches to the strip. Also measure the distance between the two toggle bars to make sure the strip is long enough to fit between the two B components. Attach the second toggle bar to the strip.

[10] Using the working thread, attach a toggle bar to one end of the bracelet, sewing through the beads in the toggle bar and the strip as needed (photo k). End the working thread. ●

materials
bracelet 7¼ in. (18.4 cm)
- 37 x 20 mm lampworked focal bead (Melissa Vess, melissabeads.etsy.com)
- 6 4 mm bicone crystals
- 4 g 11º seed beads in each of 4 colors: A, B, C, D
- 4 g 15º seed beads, color D
- Fireline, 8 lb. test
- nylon beading thread
- beading needles, #12

EDITOR'S NOTES:
• In steps 4 and 5 of "Toggle bar," we used the term "stitch-in-the-ditch," which indicates you should use a peyote thread path to add beads in the "ditches" where two rows of beads come together in the previous layer of an existing piece of peyote beadwork.
• The shape of your seed beads will affect the size of your components. The seed beads used in the how-to photos were shorter than Cynthia's, making each component smaller, so the size of the filigree insets had to be modified.

PEYOTE STITCH / NETTING

Pleated cuff

Stitch a band with a ruffled channel in the center

designed by **Rebecca Peapples**

Monochromatic
hues create a
sophisticated bracelet.

Combining two techniques and sizes of beads creates a band with a soft, rippling center. Surface embellishments can add elegance or whimsy, depending on your color choices.

stepbystep

[1] On a comfortable length of thread, attach a stop bead (Basics, p. 13), leaving a 6-in. (15 cm) tail. Pick up eight 11º cylinder beads, 13 11º seed beads, and eight cylinders **(figure 1, a–b)**.
[2] Pick up two cylinders, skip the previous two cylinders, and sew back through the next two cylinders **(b–c)**.

Work another two-drop peyote stitch (Basics and **c–d**).
[3] Pick up three 11ºs, skip three 11ºs in the previous row, and sew through the next 11º **(d–e)**. Repeat twice, and sew through the last 11º in the previous row **(e–f)**. Work two stitches of two-drop peyote using cylinders **(f–g)**.
[4] Repeat steps 2 and 3 **(figure 2)** until the band is the desired length, ending

and adding thread (Basics) as needed. The netted section in the center will ruffle and pleat as you stitch. End the working thread and tail. Add a new thread to the bracelet, leaving a 12-in. (30 cm) tail, and exit an edge pair of cylinders at one end of the bracelet.
[5] Pick up a 15º seed bead, a fringe drop, and a 15º, skip the next pair of cylinders on the edge, and sew down through the following pair of cylinders **(figure 3, a–b)**. Pick up a 15º, and sew up through the next pair of cylinders on the edge **(b–c)**. Repeat **(c–d)** along the length of the bracelet. Sew through

136

FIGURE 1

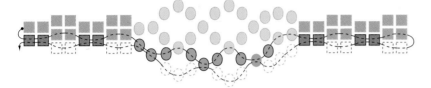

FIGURE 2

Combine
bold,
contrasting
colors for a
playful cuff.

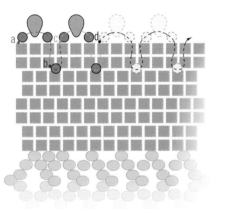

FIGURE 3

FIGURE 4

FIGURE 5

the beadwork to exit an edge pair on the other side of the bracelet, and repeat along the opposite edge. Do not end the thread.

[6] Add a new thread to the beadwork, and exit the beadwork as shown in **figure 4, point a.**

[7] Sew down through the next pair of cylinders, pick up a 15º, and sew up through the following pair of cylinders **(a–b).** Repeat to the end of the band, and then along the opposite edge.

[8] Weave through the beadwork to exit a lower 15º on one end of the bracelet. Pick up six 15ºs, skip the first 15º in the upper row of embellishment, and sew through the next 15º **(figure 5, a–b).** Pick up a 15º, a 3 mm round bead, and a 15º, skip a 15º in the lower row, and sew through the next 15º **(b–c).** Repeat to the end of the row, keeping in mind that the irregular spacing between the rows will dictate whether

or not you skip a 15º as you add the embellishment. Repeat on the other side of the bracelet.

[9] Using one of the remaining threads or tails, weave through the beadwork to exit the front of the bracelet between the first and second stitches on one end. Pick up the loop of one half of a clasp, and sew into the beadwork. Retrace the thread path several times, and end the thread. Using another thread or tail, exit the beadwork on the back of the opposite end of the bracelet, so that the two halves of the clasp will line up and close comfortably. Sew the second half of the clasp to the bracelet as you did the first. Repeat on the other end with the other clasp. End all the threads and tails. ●

materials

bracelet 6½ in. (16.5 cm)
- 52–66 3 mm round beads
- 3 g fringe drops
- 8 g 11º seed beads
- 7 g 11º Japanese cylinder beads
- 3 g 15º seed beads
- 2 magnetic clasps
- nylon beading thread
- beading needles, #12 or #13

DESIGNER'S NOTE:

As you add and end thread, try to make any knots in the netted portion of the cuff rather than the peyote sections. This will make it easier to sew through the beadwork and add embellishments later.

The illusion of a twist is achieved by alternating colors along the neck strap.

Bonus Earrings

PEYOTE STITCH / NETTING

Rivoli twist

Use two versatile stitches to create an elaborate necklace and a classic bracelet

designed by **Carolyn Cave**

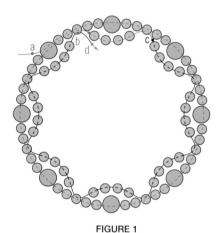

FIGURE 1

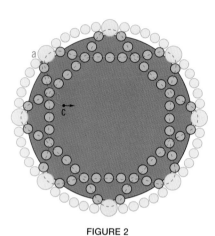

FIGURE 2

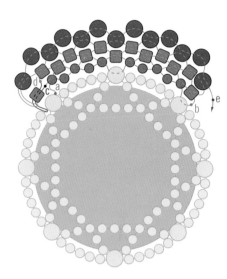

FIGURE 3

Stitch up a winning combination of netting and peyote stitch while capturing six rivolis as a centerpiece for this stunning necklace. The peyote design twists and turns throughout the necklace and can be adapted to make a matching bracelet. Fashion a pair of earrings to round out the set.

step by step

Necklace
Rivoli centerpiece
[1] On 1 yd. (.9 m) of Fireline, pick up a repeating pattern of a color A 11º seed bead and five color A 15º seed beads eight times. Sew through the first A 11º and three A 15ºs to form a ring, leaving a 12-in. (30 cm) tail **(figure 1, a–b)**.
[2] Pick up four A 15ºs, and sew through the center A 15º in the next group of five 15ºs **(b–c)**. Repeat around **(c–d)**. Retrace the thread path through the center ring, and sew through the beadwork to exit an A 11º in the original ring. Do not end the thread.
[3] Using the tail, pick up five A 15ºs, and sew through the next A 11º in the ring. Repeat around, and step up through the first three A 15ºs **(figure 2, a–b)**.

[4] Pick up three A 15ºs, and sew through the center A 15º in the next stitch. Using medium tension, repeat around the ring **(b–c)**. Place a color A rivoli face down into the netting, and retrace the thread path through the center ring, pulling tight. End the tail (Basics, p. 13) but not the working thread.
[5] Repeat steps 1–4 to make a total of six rivoli components, using color A seed beads with color A rivolis and color B seed beads with color B rivolis.

Peyote fans
[1] Using the working thread of a rivoli component, pick up five B 15ºs, and sew through the next 11º in the ring. Repeat **(figure 3, a–b)**.
[2] Pick up a color B cylinder bead, and sew back through the last B 15º picked up. Using B cylinders, work back across

materials
necklace 17 in. (43 cm)
- 3 14 mm rivolis in each of **2** colors: A, B
- 9 6 mm bicone crystals, color A
- 10 6 mm bicone crystals, color B
- 134 2 mm round crystals in each of **2** colors: A, B
- 5 g 11º cylinder beads in each of **2** colors: A, B
- 5 g 11º seed beads in each of **2** colors: A, B
- 5 g 15º seed beads in each of **2** colors: A, B
- clasp
- Fireline, 6 lb. test
- beading needles, #12
- bobbins

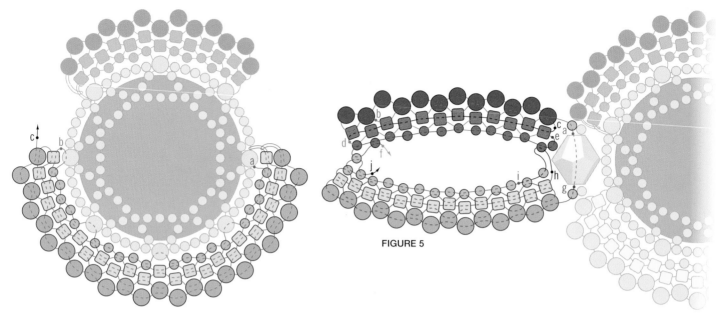

FIGURE 4

FIGURE 5

the row in peyote stitch (Basics and **b–c**). For the last stitch, pick up a B cylinder, and work an odd-count turn (Basics and **c–d**). Work a row of B cylinders, then work a row of B 11ºs with an odd-count turn. Work another row of B 11ºs **(d–e)**.

[3] Sew through the beadwork to exit the next 11º in the original ring. Pick up five color A 15º seed beads, and sew through the next A 11º in the ring. Repeat three times **(figure 4, a–b)**.

[4] Repeat step 2, but use color A cylinders and 11ºs instead of Bs **(b–c)**.

[5] Pick up an A 15º, a color A 6 mm bicone crystal, and an A 15º. Sew through the opposite B 11º. Sew through the edge B 11ºs on the top fan. Pick up a B 15º, a color B 6 mm bicone crystal, and a B 15º, and sew through the edge A 11ºs on the bottom fan **(photo a)**.

[6] Work steps 1–5 with the remaining five rivolis, alternating colors A and B,

but in step 5, sew through an existing 6 mm from the previous component instead of picking up the first one **(photo b)**.

Neck straps

[1] Attach a stop bead (Basics) at the center of 3 yd. (2.7 m) of Fireline. Wind half of the thread on a bobbin. Sew through an end 6 mm of the centerpiece.

[2] Pick up an A 15º and 12 B 11ºs. Pick up a B cylinder, skip a B 11º, and sew back through the next B 11º **(figure 5, a–b)**. Continue in peyote to complete the row using B cylinders **(b–c)**. Work a second row of B cylinders **(c–d)**. Work a row using B 15ºs **(d–e)**. In the first stitch of the next row, pick up two B 15ºs, then complete the row using one B 15º per stitch. Work one stitch using an A 15º as if to begin a new row **(e–f)**. Do not complete the row, but zigzag through the end of the crescent to exit the end B 11º.

[3] Pick up a B 15º and a B 6 mm **(photo c)**. Attach a stop bead, and wind the thread on a bobbin to keep it out of the way.

[4] Remove the bobbin and stop bead from the other half of the thread. Pick up an A 15º, 14 A 11ºs, and an A cylinder. Skip the last A 11º, and sew through the next. Continue in peyote to complete the row using A cylinders. Work another row using A cylinders. Work a row using A 15ºs **(g–h)**. For the last row, sew through the second B 15º of the first stitch in the last complete row of the opposite crescent. Pick up an A 15º, and sew through the next A 15º in the previous row **(h–i)**. Complete the row using A 15ºs. Sew through the edge A 15º added on the opposite crescent **(i–j)**. Zigzag through the end of the crescent to exit the end A 11º.

[5] Pick up an A 15º. Remove the stop bead added after the 6 mm in step 3,

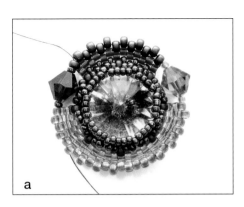

a

b

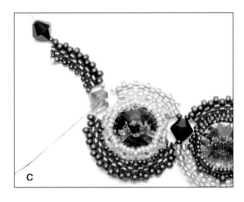

c

and sew through the 6 mm so the threads exit it in opposite directions.

[6] Repeat steps 2–5, alternating colors A and B and ending and adding thread (Basics) as needed, for a total of six pairs of crescents, but don't add the 15º to connect the end of the last pair of crescents. Instead, exit the end 15º on each crescent, and pick up an A 15º with each thread. With both threads together, pick up an A 6 mm.

[7] With one thread, pick up three B 15ºs, half of the clasp, and three B 15ºs. Sew back through the A 6 mm, retrace the thread path, and end the thread. Retrace the thread path using the other thread, and end the thread.

[8] Repeat steps 1–7 on the other side of the necklace, alternating colors.

Crystal embellishment

[1] Center 2 yd. (1.8 m) of Fireline in the clasp loop at one end. With both thread ends, sew through the 6 mm. With one thread, zigzag through the end

beads of an end crescent to exit the first edge 11º, with the needle exiting toward the centerpiece.

[2] Pick up a color A or B 2 mm round crystal to match the 11º your thread is exiting, and, working in peyote, sew through the next up-bead. Continue along the edge, adding one 2 mm per stitch. Sew through the 6 mm and the next two edge beads on the inner edge of the next crescent. Continue in peyote, adding a 2 mm for each stitch, and alternating between colors A and B to match the edge beads.

[3] When you reach the centerpiece, continue in the same manner, but pick up a matching 15º, a 2 mm, and a 15º for each stitch. Switch back to one 2 mm per stitch when you reach the other neck strap. End the thread.

[4] With the other thread, repeat to complete the remaining edges, and end the thread.

Earrings

[1] To make earrings, follow steps 1–5 of "Necklace: Rivoli centerpiece" using 18 in. (46 cm) of thread.

[2] On the working thread, pick up 11 A or B 15º seed beads, and sew through the 11º your thread exited at the start of this step. Reinforce the loop, and end the thread (Basics).

[3] Open the loop of an earring finding (Basics), and attach the loop of 15ºs. Close the loop.

[4] Make a second earring.

Bracelet

To make a bracelet, follow steps 1–7 of "Necklace: Neck straps" for a total of seven pairs of crescents, but pick up 14 11ºs in step 2 so both crescents are the same length. ◐

Combined Techniques

Bead intuitive

Let your intuition be your guide as you embellish a beaded bead

designed by **Connie Lorig**

Follow your intuition to embellish a beaded bead with vines, leaves, and flowers.

a

b

c

A humble wooden bead serves as the core of this embellished focal bead. Wrap it first in peyote stitch, then get creative and cover it with vines, leaves, and flowers. Finally, center it on a beaded kumihimo rope for a one-of-a-kind creation you'll love to wear.

You can customize these instructions to suit any size core bead. The counts listed in the instructions are for a ¾ x 1-in. (19 x 25 mm) bead. If you use the larger bead size listed in the materials list, see the sidebar, p. 145, for counts.

step by step

Beaded bead

[1] If desired, carefully place a strip of double-sided tape around the middle of the oval wood bead. This isn't necessary, but it helps to keep the beadwork in place as you start stitching.

[2] On a comfortable length of thread, pick up an even number of color A 15º seed beads, enough to make a ring around the widest part of the wooden bead (here, 60). Leaving a 6-in. (15 cm) tail, tie the beads into a ring with a square knot (Basics, p. 13). This ring of beads will be the first two rounds of peyote stitch.

[3] Remove the backing from the tape, and carefully position the ring of 15ºs around the middle of the wood bead **(photo a)**.

[4] Work in tubular peyote stitch (Basics), using one 15º per stitch, stepping up at the end of each round, and ending and adding thread (Basics) as needed:

Rounds 3–10: Work 30 regular stitches.

Round 11: Work five stitches, then work a decrease (Basics) by sewing through the next up-bead without adding a bead **(photo b)**. Repeat this pattern around for a total of 25 stitches.

Rounds 12–13: Work 25 regular stitches.

Round 14: Work two stitches, then decrease by sewing through the next up-bead without adding a bead. Work a repeating pattern of four stitches and a decrease four times, then work two more stitches.

Rounds 15–16: Work 20 regular stitches.

Round 17: Work a repeating pattern of a decrease and three stitches five times.

Rounds 18–19: Work 15 regular stitches.

Round 20: Work one stitch, then decrease. Work a repeating pattern of two stitches and a decrease four times, then work one stitch.

Round 21: Work a repeating pattern of a stitch and a decrease five times.

Round 22: Work five stitches.

[5] If your thread is still relatively long, sew through the beadwork to the other edge of the initial ring of 15ºs. If your thread is short, end it, and start a new one, exiting the other edge of the initial ring. Repeat rounds 4–22 to cover the rest of the wood bead as a mirror image of the first half, but keep in mind that you may need to change the order of the stitches and decreases in order to place them in the same columns as those on the first half of the bead. You may need to work more or fewer rounds if your initial ring was not centered precisely.

[6] Embellish the surface of the bead in a free-form manner, covering the bead with vines, leaves, buds, and flowers as desired:

Vines: Pick up five to seven 15ºs in the desired color, place them on the surface of the beaded bead, and sew through an A in the base and the last bead picked up **(photo c)**. Continue in this

materials

beaded bead ⅞ x 1⅛ in. (22 x 29 mm)

- oval wooden bead, ¾ x 1 in. (19 x 25 mm) or ⅞ x 1¼ in. (22 x 32 mm)
- 5 6 mm Swarovski margaritas and/or pressed-glass flower beads
- assorted 2–3 mm accent beads (optional)
- 15º seed beads 10 g color A 2–3 g each of 3–5 accent colors
- nylon beading thread, size B
- beading needles, #12 or #13
- double-sided tape (optional)

necklace 16 in. (41 cm)

- **16–20** 4–8 mm accent beads
- 15º seed beads, 15–20 g color A; or 8–10 g in each of **2** colors: A, B
- **10–12** 6–10 mm copper spacers
- clasp
- **2** 8 mm cones or large-hole spacers
- **2** 10–12 mm bead caps
- scrap wire
- **4** crimp beads
- flexible beading wire, .014 or .015
- YLI Jeans cord, 008 (or equivalent)
- Big Eye needle
- binder clip or weight
- G-S Hypo Cement
- kumihimo disk with **8** thread bobbins
- crimping pliers
- wire cutters

143

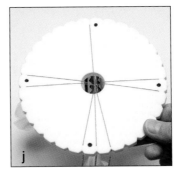

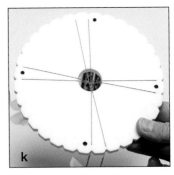

manner to make vines as desired. If you wish to tack down the vines in other places as you add them, sew back through a few beads, sew through a bead in the base (photo d), and sew back through the vine beads.

Leaves: Exiting a vine bead, pick up five to seven 15ºs, sew through a bead in the base, skip the last 15º picked up, and sew back through the previous 15º (photo e). Pick up four or five 15ºs, sew through the first 15º that was picked up to begin the leaf (photo f), and continue through a few vine beads.

Buds: Exiting a vine bead, pick up three to five 15ºs, and sew back through the vine bead (photo g). If desired, sew through a bead or two, tack the bud to the base, and continue.

Flowers: Exiting a vine bead or a base bead, pick up a 6 mm margarita or pressed-glass flower and a 15º. Sew back through the 6 mm and the vine or base bead (photo h).

[7] Continue adding flowers, buds, leaves, and vines, adding 2–3 mm accent beads if desired. Don't forget to use your creativity to design your own embellishments. End all remaining threads.

Kumihimo rope

[1] Cut 2 yd. (1.8 m) of cord, and attach a Big Eye needle to one end. Pick up 16 in. (41 cm) of color A 15º seed beads.

[2] Center the beads on the cord, and wind each end around a bobbin, leaving about 20 in. (51 cm) in the center.

[3] Repeat steps 1 and 2 three times. If desired, use a different color of 15ºs for two of the cords. This will allow you to create a cord with two spiraling colors.

[4] Pick up one of the strands, and slide half the beads toward each end of the cord, leaving the center open. Center the strand over the kumihimo disk, positioning one end in the slot to the right of the top dot and the other end in the slot to the left of the bottom dot.

Repeat with another strand of the same color beads, but position it to the left of the top dot and the right of the bottom dot.

[5] Give the disk a one-quarter turn, and repeat step 4 with the remaining two strands.

[6] Wrap a small piece of scrap wire loosely around the spot where the four cords cross in the middle of the disk. Attach a binder clip to the wire, letting it hang below the disk (photo i).

[7] Bring the top right strand straight down to fit in the slot next to the bottom right strand (photo j). Bring the bottom left strand straight up to fit in the slot to the left of the top strand (photo k). Give the disk a one-quarter turn.

[8] Repeat step 7 seven times to establish the beginning of the braid.

[9] Pick up the top right strand, and slide a bead down to fit under the cord crossing over it (photo l). Pull the top right strand straight down to the slot next to the bottom right strand. Pick up the bottom left strand, slide a

bead up to sit under the cord crossing over it (photo m), and pull the bottom left strand up to the slot to the left of the top strand. Give the disk a one-quarter turn.

[10] Repeat step 9 to make a one-bead-at-a-time kumihimo rope that is 5 in. (13 cm) or the desired length. If you need to take a break, set the braid down when you have three cords at the bottom of the disk. That way, you will always know where you are in the braiding sequence.

[11] Braid two rounds (eight one-quarter turns) without beads, as in steps 7 and 8.

[12] Carefully unwind the eight cords from the bobbins, and remove the rope from the disk. Thread the Big Eye needle onto one cord, and string a bead cap, the beaded bead, and a bead cap. Be sure to pull all the beads still on the cord through the bead and bead caps. Repeat with the remaining cords (photo n).

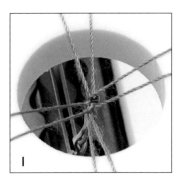

l

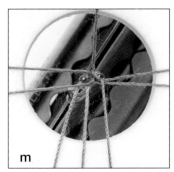

m

n

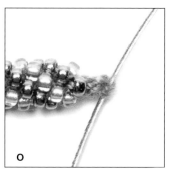

o

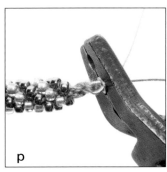

p

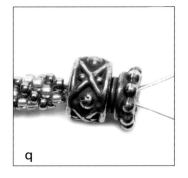

q

[13] Reposition the rope in the disk, wind the strands back onto the bobbins, and line up the strands as in steps 4 and 5.

[14] Repeat steps 7–10 until the second part of the rope is the same length as the first.

[15] Position a piece of scrap wire across the top of the strands, and braid two rounds over the wire.

[16] Unwind the bobbins from the cords, remove any excess beads, and take the beadwork off the disk. Tie opposite pairs of strands (top and bottom and left and right) together with square knots, and lightly cover the knots and part of the unbeaded braid with glue. Let dry, and trim the cords close to the knot.

Finishing

[1] Cut a 6-in. (15 cm) piece of beading wire. At one end of the rope, remove the scrap wire, and string the beading wire through the gap in the cords **(photo o)**. String a crimp bead on the beading wire, and guide the short tail through it. Crimp the crimp bead **(photo p)**.

[2] String a cone or one or more large-hole spacers on the wire so they cover the end of the rope and the crimp bead **(photo q)**. String about 2 in. (5 cm) of accent beads and spacers as desired. String a crimp bead and half of the clasp, and go back through the crimp bead.

[3] Repeat steps 1–2 at the other end of the necklace. Test for fit, and add or remove beads as needed. Crimp the crimp beads, and trim the excess wire. ◐

DESIGNER'S NOTES:
• For a little extra pizzazz, embellish the beaded rope with embroidered leaves, vines, and flowers.
• Instead of centering the bead on a kumihimo rope as in the instructions, finish your necklace however you wish. You can string your bead on a simple chain, make it the focal point of a multi-strand necklace, or create a beaded chain with your favorite stitch, such as bead crochet, herringbone stitch, peyote stitch, or spiral rope.

Using a larger core bead

[1] To use a ⅞ x 1¼-in. (2.2 x 3.2 cm) wood bead, begin with a ring of 64 15ºs, then work in peyote stitch as follows:

Rounds 3–15: Work 32 stitches with one 15º per stitch.

Round 16: Work a repeating pattern of 15 stitches and a decrease twice.

Round 17: Work 30 stitches.

Round 18: Work eight stitches, and decrease. Work 14 stitches, and decrease. Work six stitches.

Round 19: Work 28 stitches.

Round 20: Work three stitches, and decrease. Work a repeating pattern of six stitches and a decrease three times, then work three stitches.

Rounds 21–22: Work 24 stitches per round.

Round 23: Work 10 stitches, and decrease. Work 11 stitches, and decrease. Work one stitch.

Round 24: Work 22 stitches.

Round 25: Work six stitches, and decrease. Work 10 stitches, and decrease. Work four stitches.

Round 26: Work a repeating pattern of four stitches and a decrease four times.

Round 27: Work one stitch, and decrease. Work a repeating pattern of three stitches and a decrease three times, then work two stitches.

Round 28: Work 12 stitches.

Round 29: Work a repeating pattern of two stitches and a decrease four times.

Round 30: Work a repeating pattern of a decrease and one stitch four times.

[2] Work rounds 3–30 on the other side of the bead.

Susan collaborated with
glass-bead maker Leslie Thiel to
create the necklace *Earthly Wonders* for
the 2009 Convergence competition, which was
co-sponsored by *Bead&Button* and the International
Society of Glass Beadmakers (ISGB).

Wander•about

Combine a wide range of art beads, seed beads, and accents for a vibrant showpiece

designed by **Susan Jo Rochlin**

Trying to unite three beads with dramatically different shapes can be a challenge, but this free-form necklace pulls it together. Choosing beads that pick up a variety of hues and tones from the focal pieces allows you to create a unique mix that flows from one segment to the next. Have fun with your focal beads and accents, and create a necklace that's a break from the norm.

step by step

Centerpiece unit

Cut a 7-in. (18 cm) piece of 20-gauge wire. Center the tube-shaped focal bead, and string two 10–12 mm round beads or rondelles on each end. Make a wrapped loop (Basics, p. 13) at each end of the wire **(photo a)**. Set aside.

Embroidered art bead

[1] On a comfortable length of Fireline, tie an overhand knot (Basics). Sew up through the beading foundation, and attach the flower art bead or shanked bead to the foundation by sewing through the bead and the foundation several times.
[2] With your needle, come up through the foundation right next to the flower bead. Working in beaded backstitch (Basics), stitch a round of seed beads next to the bead **(photo b)**. Backstitch a second round of seed beads.
[3] Trim the foundation close to the beadwork, being very careful not to cut any threads.
[4] Trace the outline of the embroidered bead onto the Ultrasuede or felt, and

cut out the shape. Using whip stitch (Basics), attach the backing to the edge of the foundation **(photo c)**.
[5] Sew through the beads to exit the top edge. Pick up six to 10 15º or 11º seed beads, and sew through the last four beads your thread exited and the beads in the loop again. Sew through the beads in the loop a few more times to reinforce the connection, and end the thread (Basics).

Embellished art bead

[1] On a comfortable length of thread, leave a 6-in. (15 cm) tail, and pick up enough seed beads to fit loosely around the outside of the 25 mm art bead from hole to hole. You can pick up individual beads or group them by color.
[2] Work back along the strand in modified peyote stitch (Basics): Pick up a few seed beads, skip an equal number or length of beads on the strand, and sew through the next few seed beads **(photo d)**. Repeat to the end of the strand, then turn, and work back the other way. Continue stitching back and forth, ending and adding thread (Basics) as necessary. To make the free-form

a

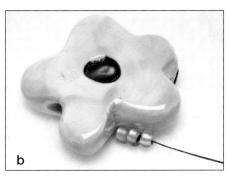

b

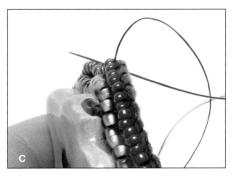

c

d

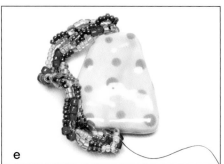
e

f

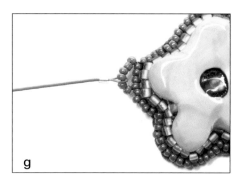
g

materials

necklace 18 in. (46 cm)

- 50–70 mm curved tube-shaped focal bead
- 25 mm art bead
- 20 mm flower art bead or shanked bead
- 4 10–12 mm rondelle or round beads
- 20 8–12 mm round beads
- assorted accent beads, such as pressed-glass shapes (optional)
- 20 g seed beads, in a variety of shapes, sizes, and colors
- clasp
- 7 in. (18 cm) 20-gauge wire
- 4 crimp beads
- 4 crimp covers (optional)
- French bullion wire (optional)
- Fireline, 6 lb. test
- flexible beading wire, .018
- beading needles, #12
- 1-in. (2.5 cm) square of Lacy's Stiff Stuff beading foundation
- 1-in. (2.5 cm) square Ultrasuede or felt
- chainnose pliers
- crimping pliers
- roundnose pliers
- wire cutters

strand curve, pick up an increasing number of beads in each row.

[3] Once the strip is the desired thickness, attach it to the 25 mm by exiting an end bead on the strip and sewing through the 25 mm. If your art bead has a large hole, you may want to pick up 11°s or 15°s to sit inside the hole and stabilize it. Sew through a few beads on the other end of the strip, turn, and sew through a few beads to exit the end. Sew through the 25 mm again. Continue sewing back and forth through the 25 mm to attach the ends of the strip (photo e). End the thread.

Assembly

[1] Add a comfortable length of thread to the free-form strip surrounding the 25 mm, exiting near the bottom edge.

[2] Working in free-form peyote as in step 2 of "Embellished art bead," stitch a segment of beads about 1 in. (2.5 cm) wide and 2 in. (5 cm) long, ending and adding thread as needed.

[3] Exit near the bottom of the strip, and pick up enough seed beads to make a loop through the wrapped loop at one end of the centerpiece unit. Sew back into the strip (photo f).

[4] Continue working in free-form stitching, working up and down the strip, including the section that curves around the 25 mm. Add accent beads as desired. Make sure you pass through the loop of the centerpiece unit several more times, adding enough beadwork to conceal the wire. Once you are satisfied with the fullness of the free-form section, end the thread.

[5] Add a new thread to the embroidered art bead, exiting the seed beads along the bottom edge. Repeat steps 2–4 to attach the embroidered art bead to the other loop of the centerpiece unit.

[6] Measure your joined segments, and subtract that length from the desired length of the necklace. Divide that length by two, and add five inches. Cut two pieces of beading wire to that length. (For example, the joined

segments of this necklace measured 11 in./28 cm, and the desired finished length was 18 in./46 cm: 18 − 11 = 7, 7 ÷ 2 = 3.5, 3.5 + 5 = 8.5, so I cut two 8½-in./21.6 cm pieces of beading wire.)

[7] String a crimp bead, and go through the loop of beads at the top of the embroidered art bead and back through the crimp bead. Crimp the crimp bead (Basics and photo g). String half of the 8–12 mm round beads, a crimp bead, and the loop of half of the clasp, covering the wire with French bullion wire if desired. Go back through the crimp bead, but do not crimp it.

[8] Repeat step 7 on the other end of the necklace, stringing the beading wire through a loop of beads at the top of the strip surrounding the 25 mm art bead.

[9] Test the fit, and add or remove beads from both ends as needed. Crimp the crimp beads, and trim the excess wire. If desired, close crimp covers over the crimps. ◓

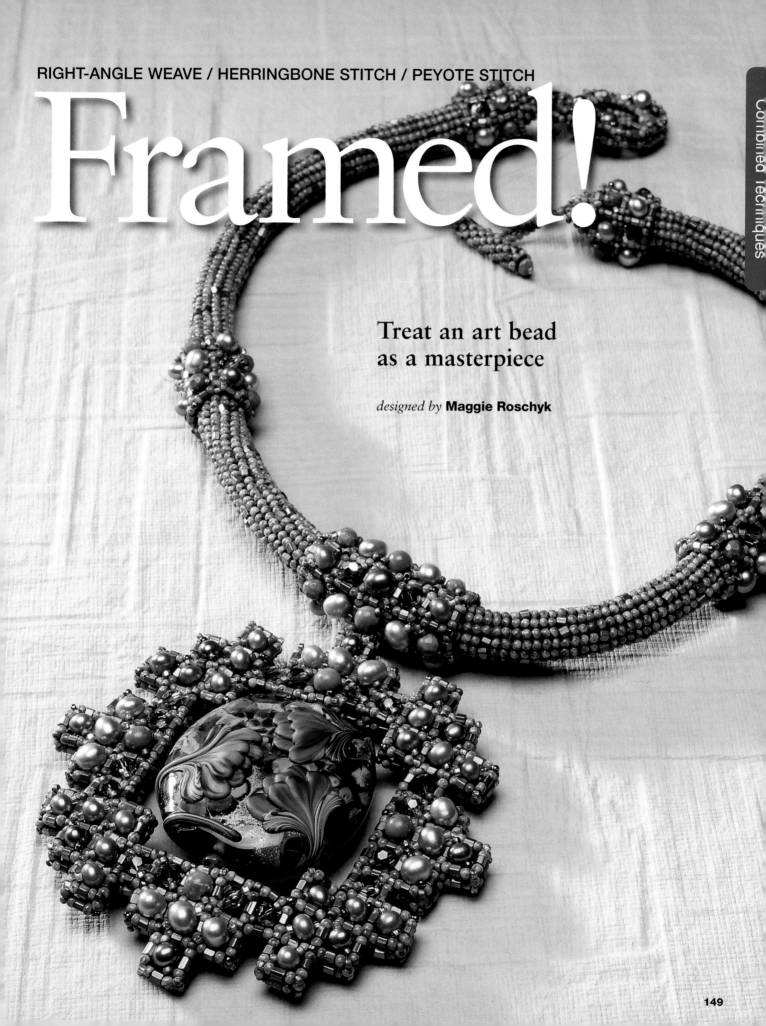

RIGHT-ANGLE WEAVE / HERRINGBONE STITCH / PEYOTE STITCH

Framed!

Treat an art bead as a masterpiece

designed by **Maggie Roschyk**

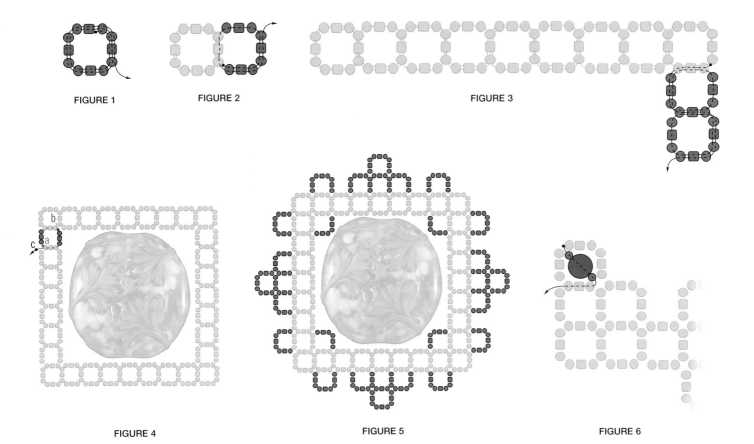

FIGURE 1

FIGURE 2

FIGURE 3

FIGURE 4

FIGURE 5

FIGURE 6

To highlight an art glass bead, make an elaborate beaded frame. Then stitch a sturdy rope from which to suspend your masterpiece.

step by step

Framed focal piece

[1] On a comfortable length of Fireline, pick up a repeating pattern of two 11º seed beads and a 10º hex-cut bead four times, leaving an 18-in. (46 cm) tail. Sew through all the beads again, then sew through four more to exit between two 11ºs **(figure 1)**. This will form a square, and each "wall" will have an 11º, a hex-cut, and an 11º.
[2] Pick up an 11º, a hex-cut, two 11ºs, a hex-cut, two 11ºs, a hex-cut, and an 11º, sew through the three-bead wall your thread exited in the previous stitch, and continue through the next two walls **(figure 2)**.
[3] Working in right-angle weave (Basics, p. 13), repeat step 2 until you have an odd number of stitches that is two stitches wider than the focal bead. Work with tight tension so each stitch pulls into a square shape.

[4] Sew through the next wall, and continue in right-angle weave **(figure 3)** to make another strip that is the same length as the first. Adjust the length as needed if the height and width of your focal bead aren't the same, making sure to end with an odd number of stitches in the strip (including the stitch that is shared with the first strip).
[5] Repeat step 4 twice to create a frame around your focal bead, stopping when the fourth strip is one stitch short of the finished length. To connect the fourth strip to the first strip, pick up an 11º, a hex-cut, and an 11º, and sew through the adjacent wall of the first stitch in the first strip **(figure 4, a–b)**. Pick up an 11º, a hex-cut, and an 11º, and sew through the end wall in the fourth strip **(b–c)**.
[6] Continuing in right-angle weave, add units as desired to complete the shape of the frame. **Figure 5** shows where additional units were stitched to

make the necklace shown on p. 149. Add thread (Basics) as needed, but do not tie any knots so that you don't block the holes. Leave the tails to end later.
[7] Repeat steps 1–6 to make another layer of beadwork identical to the first.
[8] Place one layer on top of the other. To stitch the layers together, pick up an 11º, and sew through the corresponding stitch in the other layer **(photo a)**. Pick up an 11º, and sew through the stitch in the first layer again **(photo b)**. Following a right-angle weave thread path, repeat along the outer and inner edges, connecting all the corresponding stitches in the two layers.
[9] To add the embellishment beads, sew through the beadwork to exit an 11º at the corner of a unit. Pick up a 15º seed bead, a 4–6 mm accent bead, and a 15º. Cross the right-angle weave unit at an angle, and sew through the opposite wall **(figure 6)**. Repeat to add a 15º, an accent bead, and a 15º in each unit. Add the beads randomly, or follow a pattern, as in **figure 7**. As you add the accent beads, vary the direction in which they cross the base, or the base could get skewed.

a

b

c

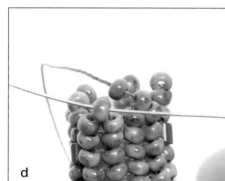

d

materials

necklace 20 in. (51 cm) plus 3½-in. (8.9 cm) pendant

- 35 mm art glass bead (Kristen Frantzen Orr, kristenfrantzenorr.com)
- **210–230** assorted 4–6 mm pearl, gemstone, crystal, and/or glass accent beads
- **4** 3 x 5 mm glass rondelles
- **5–10 g** 10º hex-cut seed beads
- **30–40 g** 11º seed beads
- **5–7 g** 15º seed beads in a mix of **3–5** colors
- Fireline, 6 lb. test
- beading needles, #12
- 20 in. (51 cm) 5 mm-outside-diameter plastic, rubber, silicone, or vinyl tubing

FIGURE 7

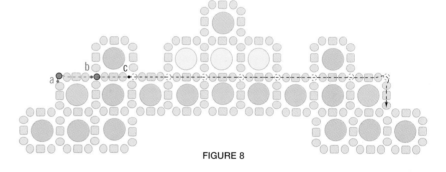

FIGURE 8

[10] Repeat step 9 on the other surface, varying the design as desired. The "Designer's Note," p. 153, shows the flip side of Maggie's frame.

[11] To add the focal bead, sew through the beadwork to exit the center hex-cut where the focal bead will be attached. Pick up a 3 x 5 mm rondelle, the focal bead, and a rondelle, and sew through the opposite hex-cut. Sew back through the rondelle, focal, rondelle, and the first hex-cut **(figure 7)**, and repeat several times, sewing through the corresponding hex-cuts on both layers of the base.

[12] Sew through the beadwork to exit any three-bead wall. Pick up a 15º, and sew through the next three-bead wall **(figure 8, a–b)**. Repeat **(b–c)** along the row, and continue in this manner to add a 15º at every juncture between the right-angle weave units. Repeat on the other surface. End all remaining threads (Basics) except the 18-in. (46 cm) tail.

Herringbone rope

[1] Working on a comfortable length of Fireline and leaving an 8-in. (20 cm) tail, use 11ºs to make a ladder (Basics) that is 12 beads long. Form the ladder into a ring (Basics).

[2] Using 11ºs, work in tubular herringbone stitch (Basics) for three rounds. Work another round, but use hex-cuts for one of the stitches.

[3] Continue as in step 2, working three rounds of herringbone with 11ºs and in the next round substituting hex-cuts for the 11ºs in one stitch. Rotate the position of the hex-cuts, so if you place them in the first stitch in one round, place them in the second stitch the next time. Work in this manner, ending and adding thread as needed, until the rope is about 20 in. (51 cm).

[4] Work one more round, picking up three 11ºs per stitch instead of two **(photo c)**. Step up through the middle 11º in the first stitch.

[5] Work a round of peyote stitch (Basics), sewing through the middle 11ºs in the previous round **(photo d)**. Step up through the first 11º added in this round.

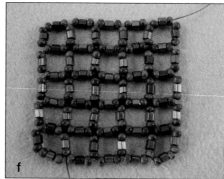

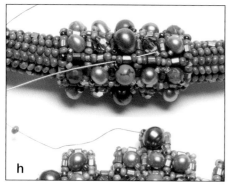

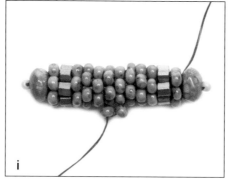

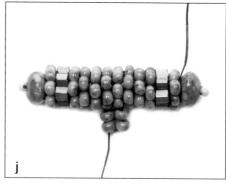

[6] Work one peyote stitch, and sew through the next up-bead to make a decrease (photo e). Repeat twice, and sew through the three beads added in this round to close the end of the tube. Do not end the thread.

[7] Slide the herringbone rope over the rubber tubing. Cut the tubing so it fits within the beadwork, and repeat steps 4–6 to close this end. Set the rope aside.

Rope accents

[1] On a comfortable length of Fireline, work in right-angle weave as in steps 1 and 2 of "Framed focal piece" to make a strip five stitches long. Continue in right-angle weave until you have a strip that is five stitches long and five stitches wide (photo f).

[2] Repeat step 1 to make two strips that are three stitches wide by five stitches long and two strips that are two stitches wide by five stitches long.

[3] Wrap the five-stitch-wide strip around the center of the herringbone rope, and stitch the edges together, as in step 5 of "Framed focal piece" (photo g).

[4] Embellish the beadwork and add 15°s between the stitches as in steps 9 and 12 of "Framed focal piece." Tack the accent strip to the herringbone rope in several places. Do not end the threads.

[5] Repeat steps 3 and 4 to attach the remaining strips to the rope. Attach the three-stitch-wide strips about 2¼ in. (5.7 cm) from each side of the center strip, and attach the two-stitch-wide strips near the ends of the rope.

[6] To attach the focal piece to the center accent strip, sew through the beadwork in the focal piece to exit the three-bead wall at the top of the pendant. Pick up an 11°, and sew through a center three-bead wall in the middle accent strip (photo h). Pick up an 11°, and sew through the three-bead wall of the pendant again. Repeat several times, sewing through the top wall on each layer of the pendant at least twice. End the threads.

Clasp
Toggle bar

[1] On a comfortable length of Fireline, pick up an 11°, a hex-cut, eight 11°s, a hex-cut, and an 11°. Following the established color pattern, work a total of 12 rows in flat even-count peyote stitch (Basics) to make a strip that is 12 beads wide and has six beads on each straight edge. Zip up (Basics) the ends to form a tube.

[2] Sew through the beadwork to exit one end of the tube, and pick up a rondelle and a 15°. Sew back through

the rondelle and the tube, and repeat at the other end.

[3] Sew through the beadwork to exit two adjacent 11°s in the center of the tube. Pick up two 11°s, sew through the two 11°s in the tube, and continue through the first 11° picked up in this stitch (photo i).

[4] Pick up two 11°s, sew through the two 11°s added in the previous stitch, and continue through the first 11° just added (photo j). Repeat until you have a strip that is 10 beads long and two beads wide.

[5] Exiting one of the end 11°s in the strip, sew through an 11° at one end of the rope, and sew back into the strip. Repeat a few times to connect both end beads of the strip to the rope, and end the thread.

Toggle loop

[1] On a comfortable length of Fireline, pick up a repeating pattern of a hex-cut and three 11°s five times, leaving a 6-in. (15 cm) tail. Sew through the first six beads again to form a ring, and exit a three-bead (11°/hex-cut/11°) wall.

[2] Pick up an 11°, a hex-cut, two 11°s, a hex-cut, two 11°s, a hex-cut, and an 11°. Sew through the three-bead wall your thread exited at the start of this step and the next four beads

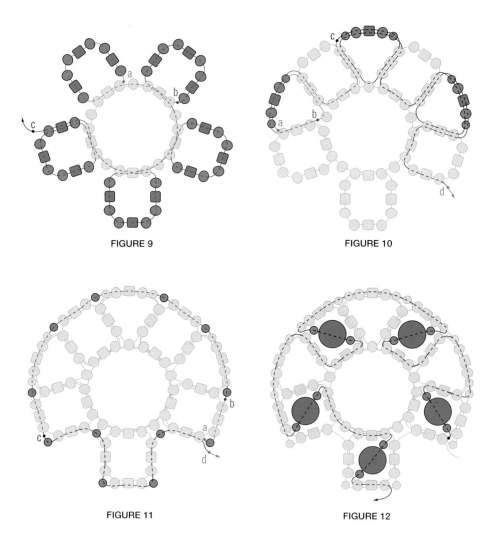

FIGURE 9

FIGURE 10

FIGURE 11

FIGURE 12

DESIGNER'S NOTE:
Let the shape of the art glass bead dictate the shape of the frame. In her necklace, Maggie found she needed to add the inner "corners" of the frame to help stabilize the focal bead.

(figure 9, a–b). Repeat four times, but at the end of the last repeat, sew through the next three-bead wall instead of four beads in the ring (b–c).

[3] Pick up a 15º, an 11º, a hex-cut, an 11º, and a 15º, and sew through the next three-bead wall and the 11º between the two adjacent walls (figure 10, a–b). Sew through the beadwork to exit the next unattached wall (b–c). Repeat twice (c–d) to connect four of the loops.

[4] Pick up a 15º, and sew through the next outer wall (figure 11, a–b). Repeat around to add a second 15º between each pair of outer walls (b–c) and a 15º at each corner of the loop base (c–d).

[5] Repeat steps 1–4 to make another toggle loop component.

[6] Working as in steps 8 and 9 of "Framed focal piece," stitch the two layers together, and embellish both sides with accent beads (figure 12).

[7] Exiting a layer of the toggle loop as in figure 12, pick up an 11º, a hex-cut, and an 11º, and sew through an 11º at the remaining end of the rope. Pick up an 11º, a hex-cut, and an 11º, and sew through the end wall of the toggle loop again. Sew through the beadwork to exit the other layer of the toggle loop, and repeat, sewing through an adjacent 11º at the end of the rope. Retrace the thread path a few times, securing the toggle loop to all three 11ºs at the end of the rope. End the threads. ●

The horseshoe-shaped clasp finishes the necklace perfectly.

Combined Techniques

153

Creative
connections

All three bracelet styles
are created using the
same basic component.

**Versatile
components
lead to several
bracelet options**

designed by **Antonio Calles**

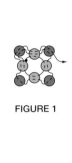
FIGURE 1

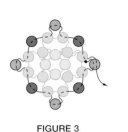
FIGURE 3

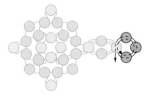
FIGURE 5

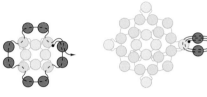
FIGURE 2

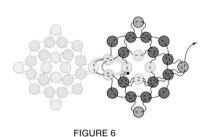
FIGURE 4

FIGURE 6

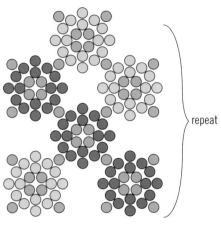
FIGURE 7

repeat

Learn how one simple technique can be the starting point for a wide range of easy to intermediate projects. After working up a quick component, use one of the bracelet ideas provided below, or challenge yourself to create a design of your own.

step by step

The basic component is explained in steps 1–4 of the single-row bracelet.

Single-row bracelet

[1] On a comfortable length of thread, pick up four color A 11º seed beads, leaving a 6-in. (15 cm) tail. Sew through the beads again to form a tight ring.
[2] Pick up a color B 11º seed bead, and sew through the next A in the ring. Repeat three times, and step up through a B **(figure 1)**.
[3] Pick up two Bs, and sew through the next B in the previous round. Repeat three times, and step up through the first B added in this round **(figure 2)**.
[4] Pick up an A, and sew through the next B in the previous round. Pick up a B, and sew through the next B. Repeat three times, and step up through the first A added **(figure 3)**.
[5] To begin the next component, pick up a B, an A, and a B. Sew through the A your thread exited at the start of this step. Retrace the thread path to secure the ring, and exit the new A **(figure 4)**.
[6] Pick up three As, and sew through the A your thread exited at the start of

this step. Retrace the thread path to secure the ring **(figure 5)**.
[7] Repeat steps 2–4 **(figure 6)**, but in steps 3 and 4, sew through the beads added in step 5 when you get to them instead of picking up new ones. Continue adding components until you reach the desired length, ending and adding thread (Basics, p. 13) as needed.
[8] Make a basic component to use as a clasp, and attach it at one end. Retrace the thread path, and end the thread. Make a loop on the other end of the bracelet to accommodate the clasp component.

Three-row bracelet

[1] Refer to figure 7 and work as in "Single-row bracelet," alternating component colors A and B and A and C, connecting the components at the corners.
[2] Make a basic component to use as a clasp, and attach it at one end. Retrace the thread path, and end the thread. Make a loop on the other end of the bracelet to accommodate the clasp component.

materials

all projects 7½ in. (19.1 cm)
- nylon beading thread, size B
- beading needles, #12

single-row bracelet
- 11º seed beads
  1–2 g color A
  4–5 g color B

three-row bracelet
- 11º seed beads
  3–4 g color A
  4–5 g in each of **2** colors: B, C

tube bracelet
- 11º seed beads
  4–5 g color A
  9–10 g color B
- 5–6 g 11º cylinder beads, color C

EDITOR'S NOTE:
You can use 6 mm round gemstone beads in place of the strands of seed beads in the tube bracelet. Just make sure you work with the bracelet clasped, or your bracelet will not bend.

Tube bracelet

[1] Work as in "Single-row bracelet" to make a strip of 18 components, and exit an end A **(figure 8, point a)**.

[2] Pick up 21 Bs, and sew back through the end A **(a–b)**. If desired, add a second loop to extend the length of the bracelet: Sew through the first 11 Bs, pick up 21 Bs, and sew back through the 11th B again **(b–c)**. Retrace the thread path, and end the thread.

[3] With a new thread, make a single component using As and Bs. Exit an A in the center ring of As. Pick up an A, and sew through the opposite A in the ring. Sew back through the new A, and retrace the thread path to secure the new A **(d–e)**.

[4] Pick up an A, and sew through the previous A and the new A **(e–f)**. Pick up three Bs, and sew through the A on the end of the bracelet opposite the loops made in step 2 **(f–g)**. Pick up three As, and sew through the first A picked up in this step **(g–h)**. Retrace the thread path, and end the thread.

[5] Add a new thread in an end component of the bracelet, and exit a side A.

[6] Work as in steps 5–7 of "Single-row bracelet," but omit two corner As to add a component **(figure 9)**. Repeat to add one more component, but omit all three corner As.

[7] Exit an end B on the third component, and sew through the opposite side A on the first component to join the three components into a ring. Sew through the beadwork to exit a side A of the next component.

[8] Repeat steps 6 and 7, ending and adding thread as needed, until you reach the last component on the opposite end.

[9] Exit the A between the two end components added in step 8. Pick up six Bs, and sew through the end A **(photo a)**. Retrace the thread path, and end the thread. Repeat on the other end.

[10] To fill the tube with strands of color C cylinder beads, add a new thread in the beadwork, and exit between the first two Bs added in step 9. Clasp the bracelet as you work, otherwise your strands of Cs will keep the bracelet from curving. Pick up enough Cs to span the inside length of the bracelet, and sew through the tube **(photo b)**. Sew around the thread between the first two Bs on the opposite end of the bracelet. Sew back through the strand of cylinders, and sew through the next B of the six. Repeat, adding six strands of cylinders, or as many strands as desired. End any remaining threads. ◗

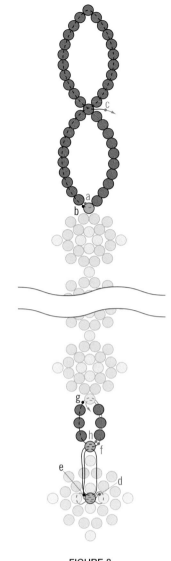

FIGURE 8

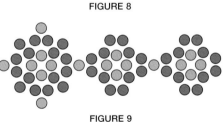

FIGURE 9

a

b

If small beads intimidate you, use 8° seed beads. The components will work up the same, and you'll need fewer components to make a bracelet.

Choose your style. Use pearls and gemstones to create the look of fine jewelry, as in the bejeweled bracelet at right; use drops and seed beads for a hint of sophistication, as in the center bracelet; or go for fresh casual with seed beads, as in the necklace, far right.

MODIFIED LADDER STITCH /
RIGHT-ANGLE WEAVE

Layered
LADDERS

A twisted double ladder forms the foundation of this customizable design

designed by **Lisa Keith**

Start with a double ladder base that twists as you stitch it, then decide how much you want to embellish your base — if at all. Whatever style you choose, this piece can be made to suit your tastes perfectly.

stepbystep

Bejeweled bracelet

Layer one: Twisted double ladder
[1] On a comfortable length of Fireline, pick up four color A 1.5 mm cube beads, and sew through all four beads again to form two stacks of two beads, leaving a 6-in. (15 cm) tail.
[2] Pick up two As, and sew down through the previous pair of As and up through the prior pair of As (figure 1).
[3] Pick up two color B 1.5 mm cube beads, and zigzag through the last two pairs of As (figure 2).
[4] Repeat steps 2 and 3 until the band is the desired length, ending and adding thread (Basics, p. 13) as needed. You'll see the twist form after a few inches.

Layer two: Side embellishments
Layer two follows the thread path between the ladders, but adds beads to hide the thread between the layers.

[1] Exiting an A, pick up two color C 11º seed beads, and sew through the next pair of Bs (figure 3, a–b).
[2] Pick up a color D 10º hex-cut bead, and sew through the next pair of As (b–c).
[3] Repeat steps 1 and 2 along the length of the bracelet.

Layer three: Edge embellishments
Layer three adds embellishment to each corner of the square shape.
[1] Exiting an end C, pick up a 2 mm pearl, and sew through the next pair of Cs (figure 4, a–b). Pick up a 2 mm gold-filled bead, and sew through the pair of Cs your thread exited at the start of this step, the pearl, and the next pair of Cs (b–c). Following a right-angle weave thread path (Basics), repeat along the length of the band, alternating a pearl and a 2 mm gemstone bead on one edge and a gold-filled round and a 2 mm crystal on the other edge (c–d).

[2] Sew through the beadwork to exit the end D on the other side. Pick up a 3–4 mm pearl or drop bead, and sew through the next D (figure 5, a–b). Pick up a 3–4 mm gemstone chip or rondelle and a 13º Charlotte, sew back through the gemstone, and sew through the previous D, the pearl, and the following D (b–c). Following a right-angle weave thread path, continue to add a pearl or drop bead in each stitch along one edge and a gemstone and a Charlotte in each stitch along the other edge (c–d).
[3] Still working on the D surface, continue following a right-angle weave thread path through the Ds, but pick up two Charlottes for each stitch on the edge with the gemstones (photo a), and a C, a Charlotte, and a C for each stitch on the edge with the pearls or drops (photo b), positioning the new beads under the beads in the previous layer. This helps the gemstone and pearl or drop embellishments stand up. Complete both edges.
[4] Exiting the end hex-cut on the edge with the pearls or drops, sew through the pearl or drop, going toward the middle of the bracelet. Pick up a 2 mm gold-filled bead or crystal, and sew through the next pearl or drop (photo c).

a

b

c

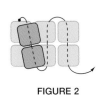
FIGURE 1

FIGURE 2

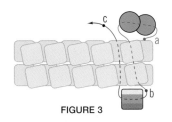
FIGURE 3

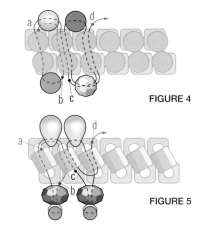
FIGURE 4

FIGURE 5

Repeat along the edge, inserting a 2 mm gold-filled bead or crystal between each pair of pearls or drops.

Clasp

Exiting an end pair of As, pick up ¼ in. (6 mm) of French bullion wire and one half of the clasp, and sew through the end pair of As (photo d). Retrace the thread path, and end the thread. Repeat at the other end of the bracelet with the tail.

Curly necklace

[1] Substitute 11º cylinder beads for the As and 11º seed beads for the Bs to make layer one of "Bejeweled bracelet."
[2] Add a clasp as in "Bejeweled bracelet."

Curly bracelet

[1] Substitute 10º seed beads for the As and 4 mm drops for the Bs to make layer one of "Bejeweled bracelet."
[2] Work as in "Bejeweled bracelet: Layer two," using one color C 11º seed bead instead of two and three color D 15º seed beads instead of a 10º hex-cut.
[3] Add a clasp as in "Bejeweled bracelet." •

EDITOR'S NOTES:

• **For the modified ladder base, if you use beads that are the same size, you will get a blocky, gradual twist. The shape of the beads affects the twist too. Beads that fit together more tightly, like cylinders and cubes, form a somewhat angular twist.**

• **Pairing beads of different sizes creates a loopy spiral. To achieve this look, use the smaller beads as the As and the larger beads as the Bs.**
• **The thread shows in layer one, so if you are not adding embellishment, the thread color should be a design consideration.**

materials

all projects
• Fireline, 4 lb. test
• beading needles, #12 or #13

bejeweled bracelet 8½ in. (21.6 cm)
• 42–48 3–4 mm gemstone chips or faceted rondelles
• 42–48 3–4 mm top-drilled pearls, drop beads, or keshi pearls
• 42–46 2 mm round gemstone beads
• 42–46 2 mm button pearls
• 63–69 2 mm round crystals
• 63–69 2 mm round gold-filled beads
• 5 g 1.5 mm cube beads in each of **2** colors: A, B
• 5 g 10º twisted hex-cut beads, color D
• 5 g 11º seed beads, color C
• 2 g 13º Charlottes
• clasp
• ½ in. (1.3 cm) French bullion wire

curly necklace 16 in. (41 cm)
• 5 g 11º cylinder beads, color A
• 5 g 11º seed beads, color B
• clasp
• ½ in. (1.3 cm) French bullion wire

curly bracelet 7½ in. (19.1 cm)
• 8 g 4 mm fringe drop beads, color B
• 4 g 10º or 11º seed beads, color A
• 2 g 11º seed beads, color C
• 2 g 15º seed beads, color D
• clasp
• ½ in. (1.3 cm) French bullion wire

d

Bicone bijoux

The ladder stitch band allows you to create any ring size, which will come in handy — after you see how quick and easy one is, you'll want to make 10!

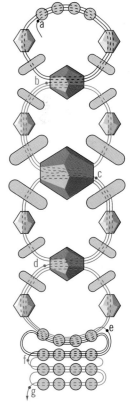

Add a little glam to your digits in a flash

designed by **Nancy Owens**

Use the shapes of this ring's components to nestle crystals between spacers, creating the look of gems in settings.

materials
one ring
- 8 mm bicone crystal
- 2 6 mm bicone crystals
- 8 4 mm bicone crystals
- 50–100 11º metal or glass seed beads
- 4 5 mm daisy spacers
- 8 4 mm daisy spacers
- Fireline, 6 lb. test
- beading needles, #12

stepbystep

[1] On 2 yd. (1.8 m) of Fireline, pick up four 11º seed beads, a 4 mm bicone crystal, a 4 mm spacer, a 6 mm bicone crystal, a 4 mm spacer, and a 4 mm bicone, leaving a 10-in. (25 cm) tail. Tie the beads into a ring with a square knot (Basics, p. 13). Sew through all the beads again, and continue through the beads to exit the 6 mm **(figure, a–b)**.

[2] Pick up a 4 mm spacer, a 4 mm bicone, a 5 mm spacer, an 8 mm bicone crystal, a 5 mm spacer, a 4 mm bicone, and a 4 mm spacer. Sew through the 6 mm and all the beads added in this step, and continue through the beads to exit the 8 mm **(b–c)**.

[3] Pick up a 5 mm spacer, a 4 mm bicone, a 4 mm spacer, a 6 mm, a 4 mm spacer, a 4 mm bicone, and a 5 mm spacer. Sew through the 8 mm and all the beads added in this step, and continue through the beads to exit the 6 mm **(c–d)**.

[4] Pick up a 4 mm spacer, a 4 mm bicone, four 11ºs, a 4 mm bicone, and a 4 mm spacer. Sew through the 6 mm and all the beads added in this step, exiting the 6 mm again. Secure the thread in the beadwork, tying half-hitch knots (Basics) between beads, and exiting the four 11ºs added in this stitch **(d–e)**.

[5] Pick up four 11ºs, and, working in ladder stitch (Basics), sew through the last four 11ºs. Sew through the eight 11ºs again, then sew through the four new 11ºs **(e–f)**. Continue in this manner **(f–g)** until the band is the desired length. To check the fit of the ring, wrap the band around your finger. Add or remove rows as needed.

[6] Join the ladder into a ring (Basics) by sewing through the four 11ºs from

EDITOR'S NOTE: For a more organic look, use 4 mm nugget-style spacers in place of the 4 mm and 5 mm daisy spacers Nancy used.

step 1, on the opposite end of the band. Sew back through the last row. Retrace the thread path of the join several times, then zigzag back through the ladder until you reach the other end. End the working thread and tail (Basics). ●

FIGURE

Set in stOne

Faceted navettes and a matching focal create a sparkling necklace that's both icy and beautiful.

Surround set crystals or stones with columns of beads

designed by **Elizabeth Pullan**

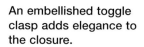

An embellished toggle clasp adds elegance to the closure.

Even- and odd-count herringbone create perfect channels to inset the stone of your choice. With the wide range of navette and marquise-cut stones available, it's easy to create sparkling necklaces reminiscent of fine gemstones or to highlight the subtle glow of vintage glass.

stepbystep

Stones
Set navettes
Set a navette stone face up in the sew-through setting, and hold it firmly in place. Using chainnose pliers, gently press each prong down against the navette (photo a). Repeat with the remaining navettes and settings.

Bezel centerpiece
On 1 yd. (.9 m) of Fireline, center an even number of 11º cylinder beads to fit around the widest part of the 18 x 24 mm stone. Sew through the first cylinder again. Begin a tubular peyote bezel (Basics, p. 13)

by working one round of tubular peyote using cylinder beads and two rounds using 15º seed beads. Work two rounds with Charlottes or true-cuts before placing the stone face down in the beadwork. Using the tail, stitch two rounds with 15ºs and two rounds with Charlottes, and end both threads (Basics).

Clasp
Toggle bar
[1] On 2 yd. (1.8 m) of Fireline, attach a stop bead (Basics), leaving a 6-in. (15 cm) tail. Pick up 14 cylinders. Working in flat even-count peyote (Basics), stitch 12 rows using

cylinders. Remove the stop bead, and zip up (Basics) the edges to make a tube.
[2] Exit a cylinder at one end of the tube. Pick up three 15ºs, and sew down through the next cylinder. Pick up three 15ºs, and sew up through the following cylinder (photo b). Repeat twice for a total of three picots on the edge and three picots around the tube below the edge row.
[3] Exit a cylinder on the edge between two picots. Pick up a 3 mm bicone crystal and three 15ºs. Sew back through the 3 mm and the adjacent cylinder on the edge of the tube (photo c). Sew up through the next cylinder.

materials
necklace 17 in. (43 cm)
- 18 x 24 mm stone, crystal, or cabochon
- 10 15 x 7 mm navette or marquise-cut stones or crystals (Costume Jewelry Supplies, costumejewelrysupplies.com)
- 10 sew-through settings for 15 x 7 mm stones (Costume Jewelry Supplies)
- 4 8 mm crystal rondelles
- 2 4 mm bicone crystals
- 18 2.5 or 3 mm bicone crystals
- 12 g 11º Japanese cylinder beads
- 1 g 11º seed beads
- 3 g 15º Japanese seed beads
- 3 g 15º Charlotte or true-cut seed beads
- Fireline, 6 lb. test
- beading needles, #12 or #13
- chainnose pliers

a

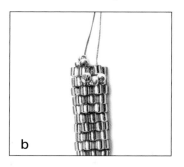

b

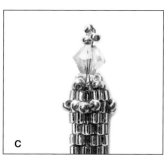

c

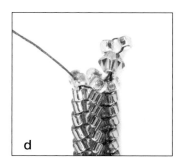

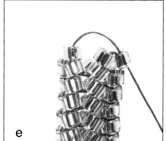

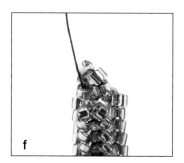

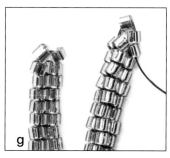

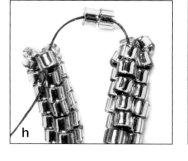

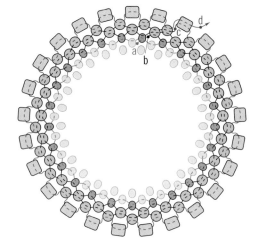

FIGURE

Repeat twice to add two more 3 mms, and exit an edge cylinder.

[4] Pick up an 8 mm crystal rondelle and three 15⁰s. Sew back through the 8 mm and through the next cylinder on the edge. Sew up through the adjacent cylinder, and retrace the thread path through the 8 mm and 15⁰s. Repeat around so the 8 mm is securely centered at the end of the tube.

[5] Sew through the bead-work to exit the opposite end of the tube, and repeat steps 2–4. End the working thread and tail.

Toggle loop

[1] On 1½ yd. (1.4 m) of Fireline, center 50 Charlottes. Sew through the first bead again to form a ring. Work one round of tubular peyote using Charlottes (figure, a–b), two rounds using 15⁰s (b–c), and one round using cylinders (c–d).

[2] Using the tail, stitch two rounds using 15⁰s and two rounds using cylinders. Zip up the edges to form a circular tube.

[3] Exit a cylinder in the center outer round, pick up three Charlottes, and sew through the next cylinder in the round. Repeat around the edge to add a picot trim, but for the last stitch pick up just one 15⁰. Retrace the thread path through the 15⁰, and end both threads.

Ropes

[1] Working on a comfortable length of Fireline and leaving a 10-in. (25 cm) tail, pick up two 11⁰ seed beads, and sew through both 11⁰s so they sit side by side. Continue working in ladder stitch (Basics) until you have a total of six 11⁰s. Sew through the first 11⁰ and the last 11⁰ again to form the ladder into a ring.

[2] Exiting an 11⁰ in the base ring, begin working in tubular herringbone stitch (Basics), picking up two cylinder beads per stitch. Continue working in tubular herringbone until you have a total of 12 rounds of cylinders.

[3] Work one round of herringbone using 11⁰s, and step up. Pick up a 3 mm and two 11⁰s, and sew back through the 3 mm, down through the next 11⁰, and up through the following 11⁰ (photo d). Repeat twice to complete the round, and step up through the first 3 mm and 11⁰ added in the round.

[4] Pick up two cylinders, and sew down through the adjacent 11⁰ and up through an 11⁰ in the next pair. Repeat around, and step up.

[5] Repeat steps 2–4, then continue working in herringbone until you have 12 rows of cylinders in the last section. End and add thread (Basics) as needed.

[6] Pick up two cylinders, and sew down through the next cylinder. Sew up through the following cylinder, pick up a cylinder, and sew down through the first cylinder added in this

step (photo e). Sew up through the adjacent cylinder. Repeat (photo f), working in odd-count herringbone until the three-bead section is 12 rounds long, taking care to pull the thread snug with each stitch.

[7] Sew down through a column of beads and through the beadwork to exit one of the remaining three cylinders from the last round of the six-bead rope. Repeat step 6 to stitch an identical three-bead section.

[8] Examine your rope at the point of the split. One side has a thread bridge on top of the last round before the split. This is the front of the rope. Sew through the beadwork to exit the column of cylinders at the back of the rope at the end of the leg.

[9] Pick up two cylinders, and sew down through the top cylinder in the outer column of beads (photo g). Sew up through the next cylinder, pick up two cylinders, and sew down through the top cylinder in the front column of cylinders on the other leg (photo h). Sew up through the next cylinder, pick up two cylinders, and sew down

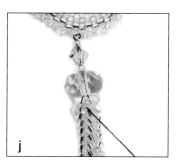

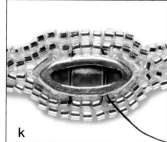

through the remaining cylinder. Sew up through the top two cylinders in the front column (photo i). Work three rounds of herringbone stitch, treating the legs as a six-bead tube.

[10] Repeat steps 6–9 until you have made a total of five splits, ending and adding thread as needed.

[11] Repeat steps 1–10 to make a second rope.

Assembly

[1] Using the tail from one rope, pick up an 8 mm, an 11º, a 4 mm bicone crystal, and an 11º. Sew through the single 15º on the edge of the toggle loop and back through the 11º, 4 mm, 11º, 8 mm, and the next 11º on the rope (photo j). Exit the next 11º, and retrace the thread path. Repeat several times until the join is secure, and end the thread.

[2] Using the tail of the other rope, repeat step 1, sewing into a cylinder near the middle of the toggle bar.

[3] Add a new thread to a rope. Determine which side is the front and which is the back, and push a navette setting into the first opening. Sew through the beadwork

to exit a back column of beads near the sew-through channel on the setting. Sew through the channel on the setting and into the back column on the other side. Retrace the thread path several times, and repeat with the second channel on the setting (photo k). Attach the remaining navettes the same way. Repeat with the other rope and navette settings. End the threads.

[4] Add a new thread to the end of a rope. Begin making a new three-bead section, as in step 6 of "Ropes," but continue stitching until the segment is 2½ in. (6.4 cm) long. Add a second thread to the same rope, and make a second three-bead section about 1 in. (2.5 cm) long.

[5] Arrange your ropes and centerpiece on your work surface as you would like them to sit in the finished necklace. The longer three-bead section should wrap under the centerpiece, while the shorter three-bead section will meet its side. The natural lines of this necklace will keep it from sitting flat on the work surface. Add a thread to the second rope,

EDITOR'S NOTE:
This version of the necklace has two long sections in the center with the centerpiece nestled between them. Both sections are attached to the centerpiece like the long section, but the top segment is a few rows shorter to fit the curve of the necklace.

DESIGNER'S NOTE:
When purchasing supplies, make sure your 15º Charlottes or true-cuts are smaller than the 15º Japanese seed beads.

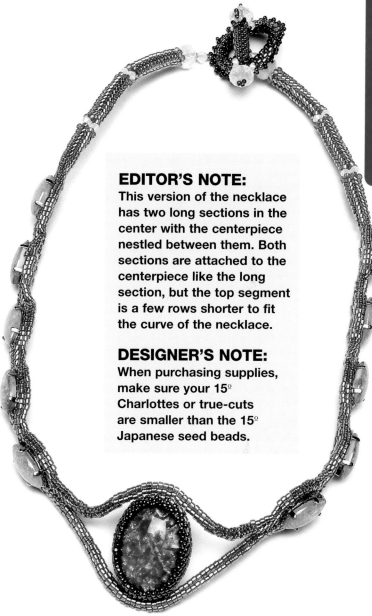

and stitch a 1-in. (2.5 cm) section to mirror the short section of the first rope.

[6] Check that the centerpiece fits within the three-bead sections, and add or remove beads from each section as needed. Stitch the end of the long section to the corresponding point on the other rope, using the same

thread path you would use to start the section. Sew back through the section to exit near the centerpiece, and sew back and forth between the rope and the centerpiece to join them. End the thread.

[7] Stitch the end of each short section to the side of the centerpiece (photo l), and end the threads. ●

Add a splash of sparkle

Looking for an easy way to do something special with herringbone? Intersperse crystals to create a little drama in a classic band.

step by step

Herringbone band

[1] On a comfortable length of Fireline, pick up four color E 11º cylinder beads, leaving a 24-in. (61 cm) tail. Sew through all four Es again, and snug them up to form two stacks of two Es each **(figure 1, a–b)**.

[2] Working in ladder stitch (Basics, p. 13), pick up two Es, and sew through the previous pair of Es and the two Es just added **(b–c)**.

[3] Continue working in ladder stitch to add a stack of two Es, two stacks of color F 11º cylinders, eight stacks of color G 11º cylinders, two stacks of Fs, and four stacks of Es.

[4] To step up, with your thread exiting downward, skip the bottom E, and sew through the top E **(figure 2, a–b)**. To work a herringbone stitch (Basics), pick up two Es, and sew down through the next E and up through the following E **(b–c)**. Work in flat herringbone across the row, following the established color pattern, then work another row.

[5] Work two rows with an increase stitch between the center column to create a channel: Work the first four stitches of the row, add the beads for the next stitch, and sew down through the

 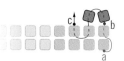

FIGURE 1   **FIGURE 2**

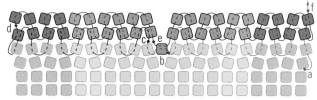

FIGURE 3

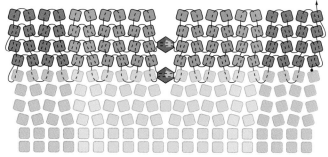

FIGURE 4

Nestle crystal inclusions within a herringbone cuff

designed by **Elizabeth Nance**

next G **(figure 3, a–b)**. To work an increase, pick up a G, and sew up through the next G **(b–c)**. Continue working in herringbone across the row, following the established color pattern, and step up **(c–d)**. Work in herringbone until you reach the increase stitch **(d–e)**, then sew through the increase G, continue working herringbone stitch across the row, and step up **(e–f)**.

[6] Repeat step 5 twice, but substitute a color A 3 mm bicone crystal for each increase G in the channels **(figure 4)**.
[7] Add the beads for the first stitch of the next row, and work an increase with an E **(figure 5, a–b)**. Continue working in herringbone with an A inclusion in the channel **(b–c)**. Work herringbone through the second-to-last column of Es, work an increase with an E, work a

herringbone stitch, and step up **(c–d)**. Work another row of herringbone, following the established pattern and sewing through the increase beads **(d–e)**.
[8] Work two rows of herringbone as in step 7, but substitute a color B 3 mm bicone crystal for each E increase stitch **(e–f)**. Work two more rows using Es again **(f–g)**.

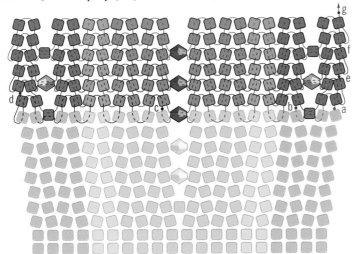

FIGURE 5

materials

bracelet 7 in. (18 cm)

- 3 mm bicone crystals
  47 color A
  8 color B
  12 color C
  6 color D
- 11º cylinder beads
  4–5 g in each of **2** colors: E, G
  2–3 g color F
- Fireline, 6 lb. test
- beading needles, #12

EDITOR'S NOTE:

If you don't want the exposed thread on the edges of the band that comes with the traditional herringbone turn, try one of these invisible turns:

FIGURE A

FIGURE B

• With your thread exiting downward, sew up through the second-to-last bead of the previous row and the last bead of the row just added. Pick up two beads, and sew down through the next bead and up through the following bead (figure a).

• With your thread exiting downward, sew under the thread bridge between the two beads in the previous row and back up through the two edge beads. Pick up two beads, and sew down through the next bead and up through the following bead (figure b).

[9] Work three stitches without an increase, add the beads for the next stitch, and work an increase with a G (figure 6, a–b). Continue working in herringbone with an A inclusion in the channel (b–c). Add the beads for the next stitch, work an increase with a G, work herringbone through the end of the row following the established pattern, and step up (c–d). Work another row of herringbone following the established pattern and sewing through the increase beads and inclusions (d–e).

[10] Work two rows of herringbone as in step 9, but substitute a color C 3 mm bicone crystal instead of each G (e–f). Work two more rows using Gs again (f–g).

[11] Repeat steps 7–10 five times, alternating between Bs and color D 3 mm bicone crystals in step 8. Repeat steps 7 and 8 again.

[12] Work four rows using As for the channel inclusion and two rows using a G to narrow the channel. Work two rows without a channel bead, and work a ladder stitch thread path through the last two rows. Do not end the thread or tail.

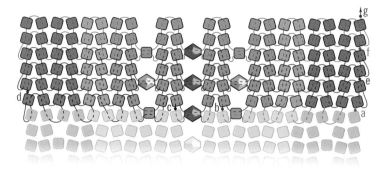

FIGURE 6

Clasp

[1] On 1 yd. (.9 m) of Fireline, attach a stop bead (Basics), leaving a 6-in. (15 cm) tail.

[2] Pick up 12 Es, and work a total of 12 rows of flat even-count peyote stitch (Basics) to make a strip that is 12 beads wide with six beads on each straight edge (figure 7).

[3] Remove the stop bead. Zip up (Basics) the strip to form a tube, and end the working thread and tail (Basics).

[4] Repeat steps 1–3 to make a second toggle bar.

[5] With your working thread exiting an end E of the band, pick up 10 Es, an A, and six Es, and sew through two center Es in a toggle bar (figure 8, a–b). Pick up six Es, and sew through the A (b–c). Pick up 10 Es, and sew down through the fourth G and up through the fifth G in the band (c–d). Repeat to add the second toggle bar. Retrace the thread path a couple of times, and end the thread.

[6] Thread a needle on the tail, and sew through the beadwork to exit an end E on the opposite end of the band. Pick up 10 Es, an A, and 22 Es or enough to form a loop to fit around the toggle bar. Sew back through the A, pick up 10 Es, and sew down through the fourth G and up through the fifth G in the band (figure 9). Repeat to add a second loop. Retrace the thread path a couple of times, and end the tail. ●

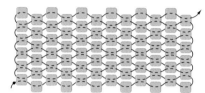

FIGURE 7

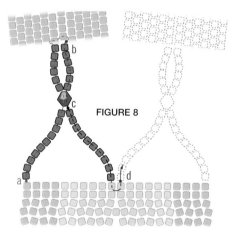

FIGURE 8

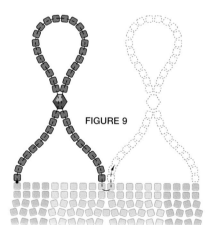

FIGURE 9

Spinner rims

Spin clockwise or counterclockwise — it all depends
on which way you stitch.

Encircle a cabochon with complementary cubes

designed by **Virginia Jensen**

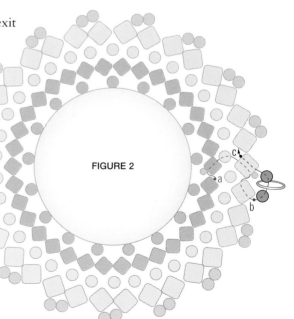

Any cabochon or sew-through button will work with this design, even an irregular shape if the corners are soft and rounded. The beads on the inner edge of the circle are smaller than the beads on the outer edge, creating a natural curve. Use large beads for a pendant or smaller ones for cute earrings.

step by step

Pendant

Herringbone ring

[1] On 2 yd. (1.8 m) of thread, attach a stop bead (Basics, p. 13), leaving a 6-in. (15 cm) tail. Pick up a 1.5 mm cube bead, a color A 11º seed bead, a 2 mm cube bead, and a stop bead. Skip the stop bead, and sew back through the 2 mm (figure 1, a–b).

[2] Pick up a 2 mm, an A, and a 1.5 mm, and sew down through the previous 1.5 mm (b–c). Pick up a color B 11º seed bead, and sew back through the 1.5 mm just added (c–d).

[3] Pick up a 1.5 mm, an A, and a 2 mm, and sew down through the previous 2 mm (d–e). Pick up two color C 11º seed beads, and sew back through the 2 mm just added (e–f).

[4] Repeat steps 2 and 3 until you have enough rows to fit around the circumference of your cabochon, ending with an even number of rows.

[5] With your thread exiting the last 1.5 mm added, sew through the 1.5 mm,

A, and 2 mm in the first row and the 2 mm added in the last row (figure 2, a–b). Pick up two Cs and a 6–8 mm soldered jump ring, and sew through the 2 mm in row 1 (b–c). Sew through a few more rows, and tie a few half-hitch knots (Basics), but do not end the thread. Remove the stop beads from the tail by carefully pulling the thread out of the beads in row 1. If the beadwork comes loose at the join, snug up the beads with the tail. End the tail (Basics).

Bezel

[1] Tape or glue the cabochon or sew the button to the beading foundation. If using E6000 adhesive, allow the glue to dry for 15 minutes. Trim the foundation to about ⅛ in. (3 mm) around the edge of the cabochon or button. If you are using Ultrasuede to cover the foundation, trace the foundation onto the Ultrasuede and trim. Set the Ultrasuede aside.

[2] Sew through the beadwork to exit a 1.5 mm. To stitch the beadwork to the foundation, center the

materials

pendant 1½ x 1¾ in. (3.8 x 4.4 cm) or 1½-in. (3.8 cm) diameter
- ⅞ x 1⅛-in. (22 x 29 mm) cabochon or ⅞-in. (22 mm) sew-through button
- 2–3 g 2 mm cube beads
- 2–3 g 1.5 mm cube beads
- 2–3 g 11º seed beads in each of **3** colors: A, B, C
- 6–8 mm soldered jump ring
- nylon beading thread, size D
- beading needles, #12
- double-sided tape or E6000 adhesive
- felt or Lacy's Stiff Stuff beading foundation
- Ultrasuede (optional)

pair of earrings 1-in. (2.5 cm) diameter
- **2** 12 mm cabochons or flat-back crystals
- 1–2 g 1.5 mm cube beads
- 1–2 g 11º cylinder or hex-cut beads
- 1–2 g 15º seed beads in each of **3** colors: A, B, C
- **2** 4 mm soldered jump rings
- **2** 6 mm jump rings
- pair of earring findings
- nylon beading thread, size D
- beading needles, #12
- double-sided tape or E6000 adhesive
- felt or Lacy's Stiff Stuff beading foundation
- Ultrasuede (optional)
- **2** pairs of chainnose pliers

EDITOR'S NOTE:

If you are sewing a button to the beading foundation, you can tape or glue a piece of Ultrasuede to the back of the beading foundation to hide the button thread, and trim it to the same size as the foundation.

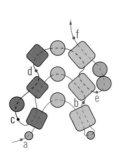

FIGURE 1

FIGURE 2

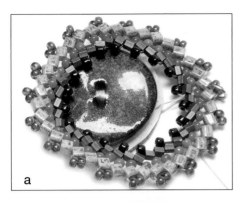

a

b

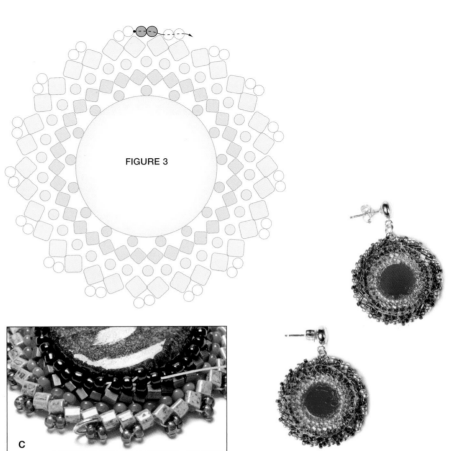

FIGURE 3

beadwork around the cabochon or but-ton, and sew through the foundation and the next cube **(photo a)**. Repeat around the beadwork.

[3] Sew through the beadwork to exit a B. Pick up a B, and sew through the next B **(photo b)**. Repeat around the beadwork, and sew through the first B added.

[4] Pick up a B, skip the next B in the ring, and sew through the following B **(photo c)**. Continue working in tubular peyote stitch (Basics) to complete the round, and step up through the first B added **(photo d)**. If needed, work another round or two. End the thread.

[5] If you are using Ultrasuede to cover the foundation, tape, glue, or whip stitch (Basics) the foundation to the Ultrasuede.

Earrings

[1] Work the steps of "Pendant" with the following substitutions:
• Use 11º cylinders or hex-cut beads in place of the 1.5 mm cube beads
• Use 15º seed beads in place of the 11º seed beads
• Use 1.5 mm cube beads in place of the 2 mm cube beads
• Use a 4 mm soldered jump ring in place of the 6–8 mm soldered jump ring
• At the end of step 4 of "Bezel," do not end the thread.

c

d

[2] Sew through the beadwork to exit a pair of C 15ºs in the outer round. Pick up two B 15ºs, and sew through the next pair of Cs **(figure 3)**. Repeat around the ring. End the thread.

[3] Open a 6 mm jump ring (Basics), attach the 4 mm soldered jump ring and an earring finding, and close the jump ring.

[4] Make a second earring. ◉

DESIGNER'S NOTES:

• To make this project without sewing the beadwork to a foundation, stitch the herringbone ring around the cab, then tape or glue them both to a piece of plastic cut slightly smaller than the beadwork or about ¼ in. (6 mm) larger than the cab.

• Using larger or smaller beads will change the dimensions of the curve. Use small beads for small cabs and large beads for large cabs.

• Make the earrings with or without additional accent beads around the center round.

Garden delight

Stitch with beads in various
shades to give these flowers
a lifelike appearance.

Stitch a floral profusion, and create a necklace, bracelet, earrings, or a set

designed by **Shirley Lim**

Living in Singapore, which is known as the Garden City, Shirley is surrounded by flowers and greenery. She takes inspiration from her surroundings and incorporates nature into her jewelry designs.

step by step

Flowers

[1] On 1 yd. (.9 m) of Fireline or thread, pick up five color H 11º seed beads, and tie them into a ring with a square knot (Basics, p. 13), leaving a 12-in. (30 cm) tail. Sew through the first H again.

[2] Pick up an H, and sew through the next H **(figure 1, a–b)**. Repeat around the ring, and step up **(b–c)**.

[3] Using color A 11º seed beads, work a round in tubular peyote (Basics), and step up **(figure 2, a–b)**.

[4] Pick up two As, and sew through the next A. Repeat around the ring, and step up through the first A added in the round **(b–c)**.

[5] Pick up two color B 11º seed beads, and sew down through the next A and up through the following A **(figure 3, a–b)**. Repeat around the ring, using the pairs of As added in the previous round as a base for tubular herringbone stitch (Basics), and step up **(b–c)**.

[6] Using Bs, work two more rounds in tubular herringbone, and step up.

[7] Work an increase round (Basics): Pick up two color C 11º seed beads, sew down through the next B, pick up a C, and sew up through the following B **(figure 4, a–b)**. Repeat to complete the round, and step up **(b–c)**.

[8] Pick up a C, a color G 11º seed bead, and a C. Sew down through the next C, pick up two Cs, and sew up through the

following C **(c–d)**. Repeat to complete the round, and sew through the beadwork to exit an H in the first round **(d–e)**.

[9] Pick up an H, sew through the center of the flower, and pick up an 8º seed bead, eight color I 11º seed beads, and three Gs. Sew back through the Is, the 8º, the H, and an H in the first round opposite the one your thread exited at the start of this step **(photo)**. Sew back through the first round again to secure the new H. End the thread (Basics).

[10] Repeat steps 1–9, alternating through colors A, B, C, D, E, and F for

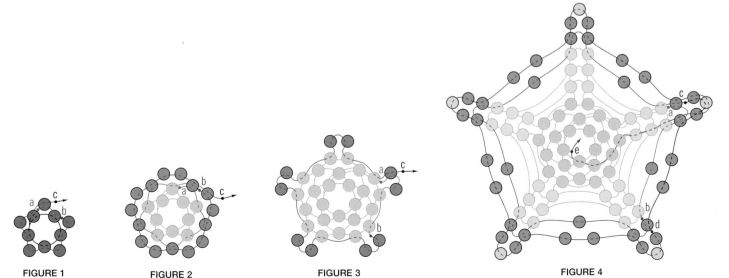

FIGURE 1

FIGURE 2

FIGURE 3

FIGURE 4

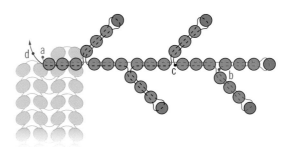

FIGURE 5

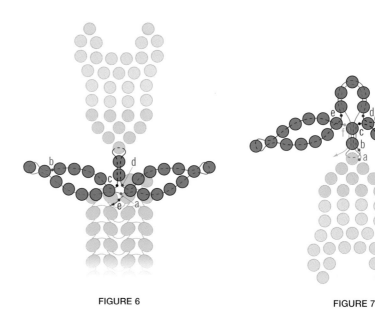

FIGURE 6   FIGURE 7

materials

all projects
- Fireline, 6 lb. test, or nylon beading thread in a color to match the beads
- beading needles, #12

necklace 16 in. (41 cm)
- **14** 8º seed beads
- 11º seed beads
  3–5 g in each of **6** colors: A, B, C, D, E, F
  1 g color G
  5–7 g color H
  1–2 g color I
  12–15 g color J
  10–14 g color K

bracelet 7 in. (18 cm)
- **8** 8º seed beads
- 11º seed beads
  2–3 g in each of **6** colors: A, B, C, D, E, F
  1 g color G
  2–4 g color H
  1 g color I
  6–8 g color J
  5–7 g color K

pair of earrings
- **2** 8º seed beads
- 11º seed beads
  1–2 g in each of **3** colors: A, B, C
  1 g color G
  2 g color H
  1 g color I
- pair of earring findings
- **2** pairs of pliers

the body of the flower, to make a total of 14 flowers for a necklace, eight flowers for a bracelet, or two flowers for earrings.

Necklace base

[1] On a comfortable length of Fireline or thread, pick up six color J 11º seed beads, and tie them into a ring with a square knot, leaving an 8-in. (20 cm) tail. Sew through the first J again.

[2] Using the ring as a base, work in tubular herringbone for about 1½ in. (3.8 cm).

[3] Add fringe: With your thread exiting down a column, pick up 15 color K 11º seed beads and an H. Skip the H, and sew back through the next three Ks (**figure 5, a–b**). To add a branch, pick up three Ks and an H, skip the H, and sew back through the three Ks just added and the next three Ks (**b–c**). Repeat to add three more branches, and exit the first K added (**c–d**). Sew up

through the next J, and work five rounds of herringbone, ending and adding thread (Basics) as needed.

[4] Repeat step 3 three times to add three more fringes.

[5] Add a flower: With your thread exiting a down column, pick up seven Hs, skip the last H added, and sew through the next one (**figure 6, a–b**). Pick up four Hs, skip four Hs, and sew through the first H added (**b–c**). This makes a leaf. Pick up two Hs and the center H in the base of a flower, and sew back through the two Hs just added (**c–d**). Make a second leaf (**d–e**), and sew up through the next J.

[6] Work five rounds of herringbone, and add a fringe as in step 3. Repeat. Work five rounds of herringbone, and add a flower as in step 5.

[7] Repeat step 6.

[8] Work three rounds of herringbone, and add a fringe. Repeat twice. Work

three rounds of herringbone, and add a flower. Repeat this sequence seven times.

[9] Repeat step 6 three times.

[10] Work five rounds of herringbone, and add a fringe. Repeat three times. Work in tubular herringbone for about 1½ in. (3.8 cm).

[11] To adjust the length of your necklace, add or remove rounds of herringbone on both ends of the necklace, taking care to keep the placement of the embellishments symmetrical. You should have one flower left for the clasp.

Clasp

[1] Thread a needle on the tail. Pick up a J, and sew through the next two Js in the end round. Repeat twice, and step up through the first J added. Sew through all three Js just added to bring them together.

[2] Sew through the H in the center of a flower base, the J your thread just exited, and the next J. Continue around to connect the H in the flower base to all three Js at the end of the necklace, and end the thread.

[3] With your working thread, repeat step 1.

[4] Pick up enough Js to form a loop around the flower (about 31 Js). Sew back through the first J added, and continue through the J your thread exited and the next J. Retrace the thread path, connecting the loop to all three Js in the necklace base. End the thread.

Bracelet

Repeat the steps for "Necklace base" with the following changes: Work seven rounds of tubular herringbone at the beginning and the end. Work an alternating pattern of a fringe and three rounds of herringbone three times, then a flower and three rounds of herringbone. To adjust the length, make more or fewer flowers or change the number of rounds of tubular herringbone at the beginning and end.

Earrings

[1] Make a flower as in "Flowers," but do not end the thread. Pick up seven Hs, skip five Hs, and sew back through the first two Hs and the H your thread exited in the base of the flower (figure 7, a–b). Sew back up through two Hs (b–c).

[2] Pick up seven Hs, skip the last H, and sew back through the next H. Pick up four Hs, and sew back through the first H picked up (c–d).

[3] Sew through the five Hs in the loop (d–e).

[4] Repeat step 2 (e–f).

[5] Sew down through two Hs and the H in the base of the flower. End the thread.

[6] Open the loop (Basics) of an earring finding, and attach the five-H loop.

[7] Make a second earring. ○

HERRINGBONE STITCH / CROSSWEAVE TECHNIQUE / SQUARE STITCH

Fine woven rings

Make and wear as many or as few rings as you'd like.

176

Create removable rings you can rearrange on a necklace to your heart's content

designed by **Smadar Grossman**

Customized bead-woven end caps and focal rings create an elegant arrangement in a flexible necklace. Once you learn the basic techniques, you can adjust the bead counts and sizes to suit beaded ropes in a variety of diameters.

step by step

Rope
Twisted tube
[1] On a comfortable length of Fireline, pick up two color A and two color B 8º seed beads, leaving a 24-in. (61 cm) tail. Sew through the four beads again (figure 1, a–b).
[2] Working in ladder stitch (Basics, p. 13), pick up two As, and sew through the two Bs and the two new As again (b–c). Continue adding pairs of 8ºs in alternating colors until you have eight stacks of 8ºs. Join the beads into a ring by sewing up through the first two As, down through the last two Bs, and up through the first two As to exit an A on top of the ring.
[3] Pick up an A and a B, and sew down through the next B in the previous round and up through the following A (figure 2). Repeat around the ring, and sew through the first A added in this round to step up. Work a second round

of tubular herringbone (Basics), following the established color pattern, and step up to start the next round.
[4] To begin working in twisted tubular herringbone (Basics), pick up an A and a B, and sew down through the next B in the previous round (figure 3, a–b). Sew up through the top two As in the next column of beads (b–c). Repeat around, sewing up through three As to step up for the next round.
[5] Continue working in twisted tubular herringbone until the necklace is 15½ in. (39.4 cm) long, ending and adding thread (Basics) as needed. Sew through the last two rows of the rope using a ladder stitch thread path so that the ends match. If the working thread is less than 24 in. (61 cm), end the thread, and add a new thread.

End caps
[1] Exiting an 8º at one end of the necklace, pick up a 4 mm fire-polished bead, an A, and a 4 mm fire-polished.

materials
necklace 17 in. (43 cm)
- **10** 6 mm fire-polished beads
- **68** 4 mm fire-polished beads
- **18** 4 mm bicone crystals
- 12–15 g 8º seed beads, color A
- 11–14 g 8º seed beads, color B
- 3 g 11º seed beads
- 2 g 15º seed beads
- clasp
- **2** 19- or 20-gauge 5–6 mm jump rings
- Fireline, 6–8 lb. test
- beading needles, #12
- **2** pairs of chainnose pliers

FIGURE 1

FIGURE 2

FIGURE 3

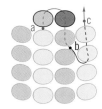

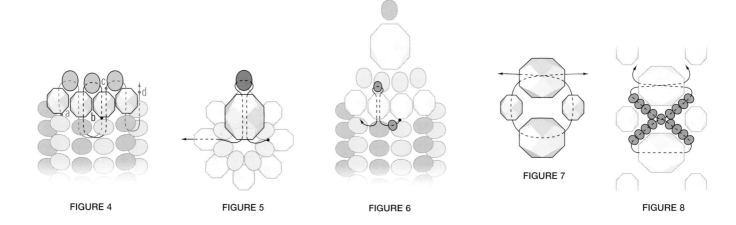

FIGURE 4   FIGURE 5   FIGURE 6   FIGURE 7   FIGURE 8

Sew down through the end 8º in the next column and up through the end 8º in the following column **(figure 4, a–b)**.

[2] Pick up a 4 mm fire-polished and an A, and sew down through the previous 4 mm fire-polished and the 8º below it, and up through the next 8º and 4 mm fire-polished **(b–c)**. Pick up an A and a 4 mm fire-polished, and sew down through the next end 8º, and up through the following 8º **(c–d)**. Repeat around the ring, ending by adding an A between the first and last 4 mm fire-polished beads.

[3] Sew through all the As added in steps 1 and 2 to pull them into a ring. Sew down through a 4 mm fire-polished and up through the next 4 mm fire-polished, sewing under the thread in the ring of As.

[4] Pick up a 6 mm fire-polished bead and a B. Sew back through the 6 mm and down through the 4 mm fire-

polished directly across from the one your thread exited **(figure 5)**.

[5] Sew through the beadwork to exit a 4 mm fire-polished two or three beads away, and sew through the 6 mm and B again. Sew back through the 6 mm and down through the 4 mm fire-polished opposite where your thread exited. Repeat until the 6 mm is secure.

[6] Exit down out of a 4 mm fire-polished. Pick up an 11º seed bead, and sew up through the next 4 mm fire-polished. Pick up an 11º, and sew back through the 4 mm fire-polished **(figure 6)**. Repeat around the ring, and end the thread.

[7] Repeat steps 1–6 on the other end of the necklace.

[8] Open a 5–6 mm jump ring (Basics), and attach it to a B at one end of the necklace and half of the clasp. Close the

jump ring. Repeat on the other end of the necklace.

Rings
Center ring

[1] Attach a needle to each end of 1½ yd. (1.4 m) of Fireline. Center a 4 mm fire-polished, a 6 mm, and a 4 mm fire-polished on the thread, pick up a 6 mm with one needle, and cross the other needle through it **(figure 7)**.

[2] Continue working in crossweave technique (Basics), picking up a 4 mm fire-polished on each needle and crossing the needles through a 6 mm until you have eight 6 mms. To join the ends into a ring, pick up a 4 mm fire-polished on each needle, and cross the needles through the first 6 mm.

[3] With each needle, pick up four 15º seed beads. With one needle, pick up

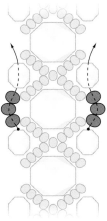

FIGURE 9

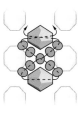

FIGURE 10

FIGURE 11

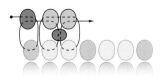

FIGURE 12

a fifth 15º, and cross the other needle through it. Pick up four 15ºs on each needle, and cross the needles through the next 6 mm in the ring **(figure 8)**. Repeat around the ring.

[4] With each needle, sew through the next 4 mm fire-polished on each edge of the ring. Pick up three 11ºs, and sew through the next 4 mm fire-polished on the edge **(figure 9)**. Repeat around the ring on each edge, sew through all the edge beads again, and end the threads.

Crystal rings
[1] Work the crystal rings as in steps 1 and 2 of "Center ring," but substitute 4 mm bicone crystals for the 6 mm fire-polished beads, and work an additional stitch for a total of nine 4 mm bicones in the ring.

[2] With each needle, pick up two 15ºs. With one needle, pick up a 15º, and cross the other needle through it.
With each needle, pick up two 15ºs, and cross the needles through the next bicone **(figure 10)**. Repeat around the ring.
[3] Work as in step 4 of "Center ring." Make two crystal rings.

Seed bead rings
[1] On a comfortable length of thread, pick up enough As to fit around the herringbone tube, making sure that the number of As is divisible by three. Sew through the As again to form a ring, and tie the working thread and tail together with a square knot (Basics).
[2] Pick up an A, and sew through the A directly below the new A and the new A again. Continue working in square stitch (Basics), creating an alternating

pattern of one A and two Bs around the ring **(figure 11)**.
[3] Work round three in square stitch, but after you pick up the first B, pick up an 11º, and sew through the B in the previous round and the new B. Pick up a B, sew through the next B in the previous round, the 11º, and the new B, shifting the 11º to the outside of the ring **(figure 12)**. Repeat around the ring, adding the 11º after the first B of each pair of Bs.
[4] Work a fourth round in square stitch using As. Sew through the round again to snug up the ring, and end the working thread and tail. Make two seed bead rings. ●

DESIGNER'S NOTE:
To fill in the twisted herringbone rope and help it keep a round profile, slide a flexible cord inside the tube before stitching the end caps.

Bougainvillea
bouquet

designed by **Kerrie Slade**

Make as many bougainvillea bracts as you like for a versatile necklace

The small, white flowers of bougainvillea are protected by three paper-like leaves called "bracts," which look like flower petals. This necklace is constructed of two brick stitch ropes that tie together with a bract on the end of each rope. Nine removable bracts slide onto the ropes for multiple options — wear just two, a few, or the whole bunch.

step by step

Bracts

[1] On 4 yd. (3.7 m) of thread, pick up two color A 11º seed beads, leaving a 1-yd. (.9 m) tail. Sew through the As again so they are side by side, and sew through the first A again (**figure 1, a–b**).

[2] Working in brick stitch (Basics, p. 13) and following **figure 1**, increase and decrease as follows:

Row 2: Work an increase row: Work the first stitch with two As and the second stitch with one A, sewing under the same thread bridge as the first stitch (**b–c**).

Rows 3–7: Increase each row by one bead, starting with four As in row 3 and increasing to eight As in row 7 (**c–d**).

Row 8: Work a decrease row with seven As (**d–e**).

Rows 9 and 10: Work a one-bead increase for each row (**e–f**).

Rows 11–14: Alternate between working a decrease row with eight As (**f–g**) and an increase row with nine As (**g–h**), ending up with nine As in row 14 (**h–i**).

Rows 15–21: Decrease each row by one bead, ending with two As in row 21 (**i–j**).

Row 22: Pick up an A, and sew through the other A of row 21 (**j–k**).

[3] To get into position to begin the next bract, sew through the beadwork to exit a bead in row 1 (**figure 2, a–b**).

materials

necklace 20 in. (51 cm)

- **15–20** 8 mm pressed-glass flowers
- 11º seed beads
  50–55 g color A
  25–30 g color B
- clasp
- **2** 7–8 mm jump rings
- nylon beading thread, size D, in **2** colors
- thread conditioner (optional)
- beading needles, #10
- **2** pairs of pliers

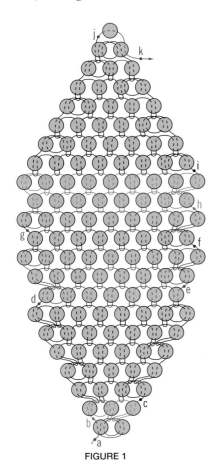

FIGURE 1

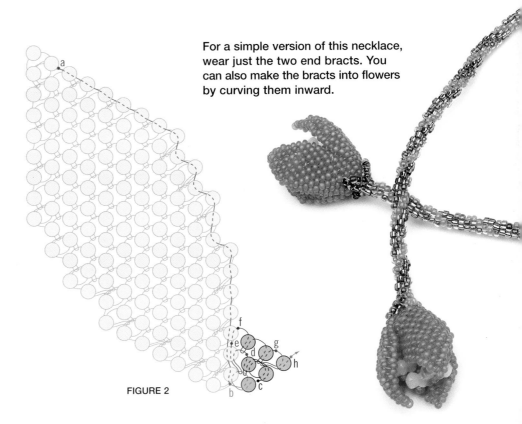

FIGURE 2

For a simple version of this necklace, wear just the two end bracts. You can also make the bracts into flowers by curving them inward.

a

b

c

[4] Work in ladder stitch (Basics) to add an A (b–c).

[5] Work in brick stitch to add two As (c–d). Without adding a bead, work a brick stitch thread path through the next edge A in row 2 of the previous bract (d–e). Exit the edge A of row 3 of the previous bract (e–f).

[6] For row 3, work two stitches with one A per stitch (f–g), and then work an increase stitch with an A (g–h).

[7] For rows 4–7, work an increase for each row, connecting to the previous bract as in steps 5 and 6.

[8] For the remaining rows, repeat rows 8–22 of the first bract, and sew through the beadwork to exit an A in row 1.

[9] To work the third bract, ladder-stitch together the edge As in row 1 of the first two bracts (figure 3, a–b).

[10] Sew through the edge A in row 2 of the first bract (b–c). Work in brick stitch to add an A (c–d), and connect it to the edge A in row 2 of the previous bract (d–e).

[11] For rows 3–7, work an increase for each row, connecting the two previous bracts as in step 10.

[12] For the remaining rows, repeat rows 8–22 of the first bract, and sew through the beadwork to exit an A in row 1. Tie a half-hitch knot (Basics) to secure the thread, but do not trim.

[13] To add a stamen, thread a needle on the tail, and sew up through the center of the bract cluster. Pick up 10–12 As, an 8 mm pressed-glass flower, and an A. Skip the A, and sew back through the remaining beads (photo a). Repeat twice to add two more stamens, anchoring the thread to the base by sewing through a bead in the first row, and omitting the 8 mm flower if desired. Tie a half-hitch knot to secure the thread, but do not trim.

Calyx and hanging loop

[1] On 1 yd. (.9 m) of thread, pick up two color B 11º seed beads, leaving a 20-in. (51 cm) tail. Working in ladder stitch, sew through them again, position them so they are side by side, and sew

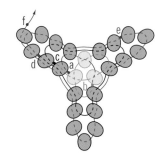

EDITOR'S NOTES:
- To make earrings, attach a pair of earring findings to two bract clusters.
- Select colors close to those found in nature for a realistic-looking bouquet, or if you're feeling adventurous, try making bracts in colors not found in natural bougainvillea.

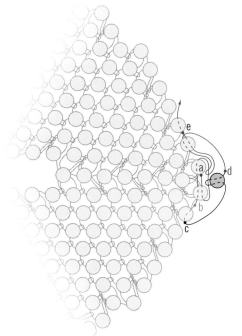

FIGURE 3

FIGURE 4

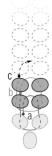

FIGURE 5

d

Use jump rings to attach a clasp
to the end loops of the ropes.

through the first B again. Continuing in ladder stitch, add a third B. Form the ladder into a ring by sewing through the first and third Bs again.

[2] To work in tubular brick stitch (Basics), work the first stitch with two Bs and the second stitch with a B, and connect the third B to the first B following a brick stitch thread path as in step 10 of "Bracts" **(photo b)**.

[3] Work a total of four rounds in tubular brick stitch.

[4] Pick up two Bs, and sew down through the next B and up through the following B **(figure 4, a–b)**. Repeat twice to work a total of three herringbone stitches, and step up through the next B **(b–c)**. Work another round in tubular herringbone (Basics), and step up **(c–d)**.

[5] To form a picot, pick up three Bs, and sew down through the next two Bs and up through the next two Bs **(d–e)**. Repeat twice, and sew through the beadwork to exit a center bead in a picot **(e–f)**. End the working thread (Basics).

[6] Thread a needle on the tail. Pick up two Bs, and sew down through the next B and up through the previous B and the first B added **(figure 5, a–b)**. Repeat **(b–c)** to add a total of 15 rows.

[7] Sew down and up through a pair of Bs in the brick stitch base, one of which is a B your thread exited at the start of step 6, and continue through the last pair of Bs added **(photo c)**. End the thread.

[8] With a thread exiting the bracts, sew through the beadwork to exit an A offset from the center in row 3 of a bract. Sew through a center B in a picot on the calyx, and sew through the other A offset from the center in row 3 **(photo d)**. Retrace the thread path to reinforce the connection. Repeat twice to connect the remaining branches of the calyx to the remaining bracts. End all remaining threads.

Assembly

[1] Make 10 more bract clusters as in "Bracts." For eight of the bract clusters, complete the steps for "Calyx and hanging loop." Set aside the remaining two bract clusters.

[2] On a comfortable length of thread, leave a 20-in. (51 cm) tail, and repeat steps 1 and 2 of "Calyx and hanging loop." Work in tubular brick stitch, ending and adding thread (Basics) as needed, until your rope reaches 12 in. (30 cm).

[3] Using your working thread, make three branches for the calyx as in steps 4 and 5 of "Calyx and hanging loop," and end the thread.

[4] Attach a bract cluster set aside in step 1.

[5] Thread a needle on the tail, and make a loop as in steps 6 and 7 of "Calyx and hanging loop," and end the tail.

[6] Repeat steps 2–5 for a second rope.

[7] Using the loops of the remaining bract clusters, string five bract clusters onto one rope and four bract clusters on the other rope.

[8] Open a jump ring (Basics), and attach an end loop of one rope and one half of the clasp. Close the jump ring. Repeat for the remaining rope and clasp half.

[9] To wear, use an overhand knot (Basics) to tie the ropes above the bract clusters. ◗

Create a wide cuff of
twisted ropes with
crystal connections.

Do the twist

Twine together strands of twisted tubular herringbone for a dramatic cuff

designed by **Jimmie Boatright**

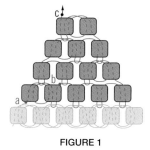

FIGURE 1

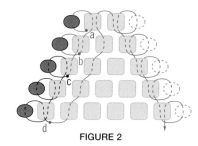

FIGURE 2

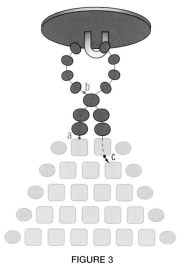

FIGURE 3

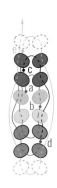

FIGURE 4

This multistrand bracelet offers plenty of opportunities to have fun with color and texture. Three colors play across the twisted ropes while round crystals and a button closure add playful accents.

step by step

Triangular ends

[1] On 1 yd. (.9 m) of thread or Fireline, pick up two 3 mm cube beads, leaving a 6-in. (15 cm) tail. Sew through the 3 mms again so they sit side by side. Continue working in ladder stitch (Basics, p. 13) until the strip is six 3 mms long. Weave through the 3 mms to stabilize the ladder, exiting the first 3 mm.
[2] Pick up two 3 mms, sew through them both again, and sew under the thread bridge between the second and third 3 mm in the first row, then up through the second 3 mm just added **(figure 1, a–b)**. Work in brick stitch (Basics), decreasing one 3 mm in each row, until the final row has two 3 mms **(b–c)**.
[3] Exit the bottom of a 3 mm in the top row **(figure 2,**

point a)**. Pick up an 8º seed bead, and sew down through the 3 mm again, and continue through the next edge 3 mm **(a–b)**. Pick up an 8º, and sew down through the 3 mm your thread just exited and the next edge 3 mm **(b–c)**. Repeat to add an 8º to the edge of each row **(c–d)**, then sew through the beadwork to exit the other top 3 mm, and repeat along the other edge.
[4] Sew through the bead-work to exit a top 3 mm **(figure 3, point a)**. Pick up three 8ºs, four 11º seed beads, the shank of the button, and four 11ºs **(a–b)**. Sew back through the last 8º added, pick up two 8ºs, and sew through the other top 3 mm **(b–c)**. Retrace the thread path, and end the threads (Basics).
[5] Repeat steps 1–3 to create and embellish another

triangular end. Sew through the beadwork to exit a top 3 mm, and pick up enough 8ºs to make a loop around the button. Sew through the other top 3 mm, retrace the thread path, and end the working thread and tail.

Ropes

[1] On a comfortable length of thread, leave a 10-in. (25 cm) tail, and work in ladder stitch to create a ladder of two color A 11º seed beads and two color B 11º seed beads. Join the ends of the ladder to form a ring (Basics), and exit up out of the first A.
[2] Pick up two As, and sew down through the next A in the previous round **(figure 4, a–b)**. Sew up through the next B, pick up two Bs, and sew down through the next B, and up through the two As in the next column **(b–c)**.

materials
bracelet 7 in. (18 cm)
- **11** 8 mm round crystals
- 5 g 3 mm cube beads
- 3 g 8º seed beads
- 8 g 11º seed beads in each of **3** colors: A, B, C
- shank button
- nylon beading thread, size D, or Fireline, 6 lb. test
- beading needles, #12

185

a

b

c

d

[3] Pick up two As, and sew down through the next A in the previous round and up through the top two Bs in the next column **(c–d)**. Pick up two Bs, sew down through the next B in the previous round, and step up through the top three As in the next column **(d–e)**. Continue working in twisted tubular herringbone (Basics), following the established pattern, until the rope is 5 in. (13 cm) long, ending and adding thread (Basics) as needed. Do not end the working thread or tail.

[4] Repeat steps 1–3 to make a second rope with As and Bs.

[5] Work in twisted tubular herringbone as in steps 1–3 to create two ropes using Bs and color C 11º seed beads, one rope using just As, and one rope using just Cs, for a total of six ropes.

Assembly

[1] Using the tail of an A-and-B rope, attach it to the bottom of an edge 3 mm in a triangular end: Sew through the 3 mm, and continue through the 3 mm above it. Sew through the beadwork to exit the bottom of the edge 3 mm, and sew back into the rope **(photo a)**. Exit the next 11º in the round, and sew back into the triangular end. Continue sewing between the rope and the triangular end until the join is secure, and end the thread.

[2] Join the remaining ropes to the same triangular end as in step 1, working across the bottom of the end to join an A-and-C rope, the B rope, the C rope, an A-and-C rope, and the remaining A-and-B rope.

[3] Wrap an A-and-B rope over and under the adjacent A-and-C rope, and join the ropes to the other triangular end as in step 1 **(photo b)**, but do not end the threads. Repeat with the B and C ropes and the other A-and-B and A-and-C ropes.

[4] Using a thread from an A-and-B or A-and-C rope, sew through the rope to exit the middle of the bracelet. Pick up an 8 mm round crystal, and sew through an 11º in the next rope, positioning the 8 mm between the ropes. Sew back through the 8 mm and the 11º your thread exited on the first rope. Retrace the thread path, and exit an 11º on the other side of the inner rope **(photo c)**.

[5] Use a ladder stitch thread path to join the rope to the next rope, a B or C rope **(photo d)**. Exit the other side of the rope. Add an 8 mm between the B and C ropes as you did in step 4, and attach the next two ropes. Add another 8 mm between the other A-and-B and A-and-C ropes, and end the thread. These 8 mms form a line across the middle of the bracelet.

[6] Add an 8 mm between the A-and-B and A-and-C ropes about one-third of the way between a triangular end and the middle. Repeat to add a second 8 mm aligned with the first and two 8 mms at the other end.

[7] Find the point halfway between each row of 8 mms where the ropes cross each other. Using one of the remaining tails, sew through the beadwork to exit a rope at this point, and stitch the ropes together. Repeat to join the other ropes where they cross each other.

[8] Exiting between the ropes where they are joined together, pick up an 8 mm, and sew into the next pair of ropes where they are joined. Sew back and forth through the 8 mm between the ropes. Repeat to add an 8 mm between the center ropes and the pair of ropes on the other side. Repeat at the other end of the bracelet to add two more 8 mms, and end all the threads. ●

SQUARE STITCH / PEYOTE STITCH / BRICK STITCH

A taste of honey

Be busy as a bee when you combine three stitches to create this sweet bracelet

designed by **Barbara Klann**

Gemstone chips glisten like drops of honey on the edges of this band.

Bees play a pivotal role in pollination, carrying pollen from one plant to the next. In recent years, these wonderful workers have begun to disappear due to colony collapse disorder. Barbara made this bracelet as a tribute to bees.

step by step

Condition thread (Basics, p. 13) if desired.

Bracelet base

[1] Attach a stop bead (Basics) on a comfortable length of thread or Fireline, leaving a 12-in. (30 cm) tail. Pick up four 4 x 4 mm cube beads for the first row. To begin the next row, pick up a cube, and work a square stitch (Basics) by sewing through the cube your thread just exited in the previous

materials

bracelet 8 in. (20 cm)

- 21 g 4 x 4 mm cube beads
- 16-in. (41 cm) strand 3–4 mm citrine chips
- 15º seed beads
  4–6 g color A (black)
  1–2 g color B (gold or yellow)
  1–2 g color C (white)
- 3-strand slide clasp
- nylon beading thread in a color to match beads, or Fireline, 6 lb. test
- thread conditioner (optional)
- beading needles, #12

row and the new cube again. Work three more square stitches to complete the row. Continue working in square stitch to the desired bracelet length, ending and adding thread (Basics) as needed.
[2] Remove the stop bead, and thread a needle on the tail. With your thread exiting an end cube, pick up four color B 15º seed beads, a loop of the clasp, and four Bs, and sew back through the cube your thread exited **(figure 1, a–b)**. Pick up four Bs, the middle loop of the clasp, and four Bs, and sew through the next two cubes **(b–c)**. Pick up four Bs, the middle loop of the clasp, and four Bs, and sew through the next cube **(c–d)**. Pick up four Bs, the remaining loop of the clasp, and four Bs, and sew back through the cube your thread exited **(d–e)**. End the thread.
[3] Repeat step 2 with the working thread on the other end, but do not end the thread.
[4] Sew through the bead-work to exit an end cube. Pick up three to five citrine chips, skip two cubes, and sew down through the next cube and up through the previous cube **(figure 2)**. Repeat across the length of the bracelet and along the opposite edge. End the thread.

Bee
Body
[1] On 1½ yd. (1.4 m) of thread or Fireline, pick up six color A 15º seed beads, and tie them into a ring with a square knot (Basics), leaving a little slack and an 8-in. (20 cm) tail. Sew through the next A. Pick up an A, and sew through the next A **(figure 3, a–b)**. Repeat around the ring, and step up through the first A **(b–c)**. Work five more rounds of tubular peyote (Basics), and step up.
[2] Work an increase round (Basics) in tubular peyote, picking up two Bs per stitch, and step up through the first

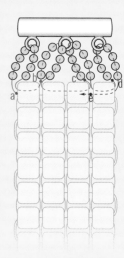

FIGURE 1

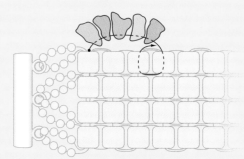

FIGURE 2

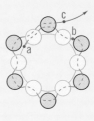

FIGURE 3

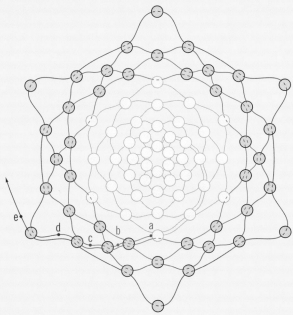

FIGURE 4

a

b

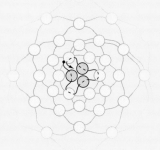

c

FIGURE 5

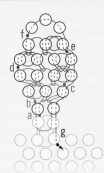

FIGURE 6

B added **(figure 4, a–b)**. Work a round of tubular peyote with Bs, adding a B between each pair of Bs and between the stitches in the previous round, and step up **(b–c)**.

[3] Work a round with As, and step up **(c–d)**.

[4] Work a decrease round with As (Basics), picking up an A and sewing through two As for each stitch, and step up **(d–e)**.

[5] Work two rounds with Bs, three rounds with As, three rounds with Bs, and three rounds with As.

[6] Work a decrease round with As as in step 4, and work another regular round. Sew through the three As added in the previous round to pull them together.

[7] To make the stinger, work a ladder stitch (Basics) with an A, and ladder stitch another A to the previous A.

[8] Thread a needle on the tail, and work a round with three stitches **(figure 5)**. Sew through the three As just added, and pull them together.

[9] To add eyes, sew through the beadwork to exit an A near the first increase round, pick up a color C 15º seed

bead, and sew through the next A. Sew through the next two As, pick up a C, and sew through the next A **(photo a)**. End the thread.

Wings

[1] With the working thread, sew through the beadwork to exit an A near the center of the body. Pick up two Cs, and sew through the next A **(photo b)**. Sew up through the first A your thread exited and the first C added.

[2] Pick up two Cs, and sew down through the next C and up through the previous C **(figure 6, a–b)**.

[3] Working in brick stitch (Basics) following **figure 6**, increase and decrease as follows:

Row 3: Work an increase row: Work the first stitch with two Cs and the second stitch with a C, sewing under the same thread bridge as the first stitch **(b–c)**.

Row 4: Increase by one bead to work a row that has four Cs **(c–d)**.

Row 5: Work a row with four Cs **(d–e)**.

Row 6: Work a decrease row with three Cs **(e–f)**.

[4] With your thread exiting an edge C, pick up three Cs, and sew through the other edge C and the remaining edge Cs **(f–g)**.

[5] Repeat steps 1–4 to make a second wing. Sew through the beadwork to exit an A near the center of the body on the underside.

[6] Repeat "Bee: Body" and steps 1–5 of "Bee: Wings" to make as many bees as desired.

Assembly

[1] With your thread exiting the underside of a bee's body, pick up two As, and sew through two center cubes in the bracelet base. Pick up two As, and sew through an A on the underside of the body **(photo c)**.

[2] Sew through the beadwork to exit a B on the underside of the body. Repeat step 1, using As to attach the bee to the bracelet base, and end the thread.

[3] Repeat steps 1 and 2, evenly spacing your bees across the bracelet. ○

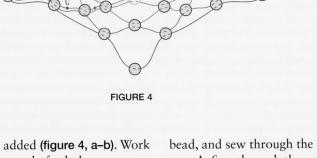

Combined Techniques

189

ST. PETERSBURG CHAIN /
PEYOTE STITCH / FRINGE

Floral inspiration

A blooming mimosa tree inspired
this flower-like clasp that draws
attention to a dainty version of
St. Petersburg chain

designed by **Callie Mitchell**

materials
bracelet 7 in. (18 cm)
- Swarovski 11 x 5.5 mm pendant
- **23** 4 mm Swarovski bicone crystals
- 3 g 11º Japanese seed beads, color C
- 15º Japanese seed beads
  5 g color A
  3 g color B
- nylon beading thread
- beading needles, #13
- bobbin (optional)

Making this supple
bracelet is a great way
to get the hang of
St. Petersburg chain.

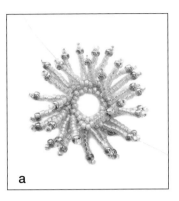

a

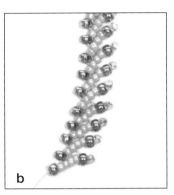

b

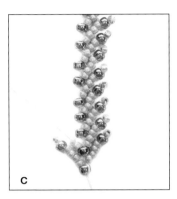

c

d

e

f

A pendant attached to one end of a St. Petersburg band slides through a fringe-embellished ring of seed beads to become the flower's center and bracelet's clasp.

step by step

Flower clasp loop

[1] On 4 ft. (1.2 m) of thread, pick up 20 color A 15º seed beads, leaving an 8-in. (20 cm) tail. Sew through all the beads again to form a ring, and sew through the first bead again.
[2] Working in circular peyote stitch (Basics, p. 13), pick up an A, skip an A, and sew through the next A. Repeat around, and step up through the first A picked up in this round.
[3] Pick up two As, and sew through the next up-bead. Repeat around, and step up through the first A in the pair of As picked up in this round.
[4] To make a fringe, pick up five color B 15º seed beads, an A, a color C 11º seed bead, and a B. Skip the end B, and sew back through the first seven beads. Sew through the next A in the pair of As.
[5] Repeat step 4 around the ring, sewing through the next A in either a pair of As or an A from the third round **(photo a)**. End and add thread (Basics) as needed.

[6] Sew through the beadwork in the ring, and exit an up-bead in the first round. Work a second round of fringe: Pick up four Bs, an A, a C, and a B. Skip the end B, and sew back through the first six beads. Sew through the next A in the first or second round. Repeat around the ring. End the working thread and tail. Set the clasp loop aside.

Bracelet band

[1] Using 4 yd. (3.7 m) of thread, and working in St. Petersburg chain (see "Double St. Petersburg chain," p. 192, and **photo b**), stitch the first side of the band to the desired length. Stitch 47 units for a 7-in. (18 cm) bracelet. If you lengthen the band, stitch an odd number of units.
[2] Work the second side of the band ("Double St. Petersburg chain" and **photo c**). When you complete the second side, if you do not have 30 in. (76 cm) of thread remaining, end the thread, and add a new 30-in. (76 cm) thread to attach the clasp and embellishment.

Clasp and embellishment

[1] Position the clasp loop fringe side down.
[2] Using the working thread from the doubled band, sew through an A in the outer round of the clasp and two As in the other side of the end V **(photo d)**. Retrace the thread path a few times.
[3] Flip the band so the clasp fringe is facing upward, and exit a center C at the end of the band.
[4] Pick up an A, a 4 mm bicone crystal, and an A, skip a center C, and sew through the next center C **(photo e)**. Repeat for the length of the band. Do not end the thread.
[5] Using the working thread from the embellishment, sew through the beadwork to exit an end A at the base of the V.
[6] Pick up a C, two As, the pendant, and two As. Sew back through the C, and continue through the As in the other side of the V **(photo f)**. Retrace the thread path a few times. End the thread. Push the pendant up through the fringe loop to fasten the clasp. ●

EDITOR'S NOTE:
You can substitute
4 mm round crystals
for the 4 mm bicone
crystals, as in the
version of the bracelet
on p. 190. You can
also use a larger
pendant for the clasp,
but if you do, make
the loop larger as well
to fit the pendant.
Just remember to pick
up an even number
of beads and keep
the ring snug around
the pendant.

This clever clasp is an
excellent example of a
well-thought-out design.

Double St. Petersburg chain

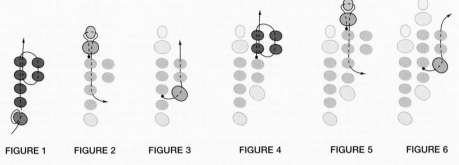

FIGURE 1   FIGURE 2   FIGURE 3   FIGURE 4   FIGURE 5   FIGURE 6

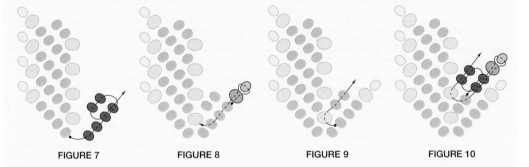

FIGURE 7   FIGURE 8   FIGURE 9   FIGURE 10

[1] Attach a stop bead (Basics) in the center of the thread. Wind the tail around a card or bobbin so it stays out of the way as you work the first half of the chain.
[2] Pick up six color A seed beads. Sew through the third and fourth As again so the fifth and sixth beads form an adjacent column (figure 1).
[3] Pick up a color C and B seed bead, and sew back through the C and the last three As in the column (figure 2).
[4] Pick up a C, and sew through the two As in the newest column (figure 3).
[5] Pick up four As, and sew through the first two As just picked up, sliding the four beads tight to the existing chain (figure 4).
[6] Pick up a C and a B, and sew back through the C and the last three As in the column (figure 5).

[7] Pick up a C, and sew through the two As in the new column (figure 6).
[8] Repeat steps 5–7 to the desired length.
[9] Remove the stop bead from the starting end of the chain. Pick up six As, and sew through the third and fourth As again, as in step 2 (figure 7).
[10] Pick up a C and a B, and sew back through the C and the next three As in column (figure 8).
[11] Sew through the adjacent C from the first side of the chain and the two As in the newest column of the second side (figure 9). Pull tight.
[12] Pick up four As, and sew through the first two As again. Pick up a C and a B, and sew back through the C and the last three As in the column. Sew through the next C in the first chain and through the two As in the newest column (figure 10). Repeat this step to the end of the chain.

KUMIHIMO / SPIRAL ROPE

Come together

Weave a spiral rope through a braided cord to set off an art glass bead

designed by **Lisa Phillips**

EDITOR'S NOTE:
You can use 20-gauge wire instead of 14-gauge to hang the focal bead, as shown here. Make a hook at the end, string the focal bead and a few spacers, and make a wrapped loop (Basics, p. 13). After joining the spiral rope and braid, add a new thread (Basics) at the middle of the spiral rope, and sew the wrapped loop to the beadwork. Cover the join with fringe. Art glass bead by Cathy Lybarger, aardvarkartglass.net.

If you love kumihimo and are looking for a new way to incorporate it into your beadwork, look no further. This clever combination of braiding and stitching fits the bill.

materials

necklace 18 in. (46 cm)

- lampworked focal bead
- 48 4–6 mm Czech glass beads, color C
- **12–15** 4–6 mm Czech glass beads in each of **2** colors: D and E
- 5 g 8º seed beads, color A
- 3 g 8º seed beads, color B
- 5 g 11º seed beads
- 3 g 15º seed beads
- clasp
- 2 cones or bead caps
- 3 in. (7.6 cm) 14-gauge wire
- Fireline, 6 or 8 lb. test
- 3 yd. (2.7 m) fiber cord in each of **2** styles
- beading needles, #12
- anvil or bench block
- G-S Hypo Cement
- hammer
- marudai or kumihimo disk with **8** bobbins and counterweight
- metal file
- scrap wire or cord
- roundnose pliers
- wire cutters

step by step

Kumihimo ladder rope

Lisa learned this rope from Jacqui Carey's book *Beads and Braids*. It creates a flat rope that has openings in it, like the gaps between the rungs of a ladder.

[1] Cut two 1½-yd. (1.4 m) pieces of each type of cord, for a total of four cords. Wind each end of each cord around a bobbin, leaving 10–12 in. (25–30 cm) between the bobbins.

[2] Position the two style A cords on the marudai or kumihimo disk so they are perpendicular and cross in the middle (**photo a**). Move one notch to the right, and position the two style B cords so they are perpendicular and cross in the middle (**photo b**). Tie or twist a piece of scrap cord or wire around the middle of all four cords where they cross. Attach your counterweight to the cord or wire.

[3] Position the marudai or disk so the cords are arranged as in **figure 1**. The cord positions are indicated by a letter, and you will always work with the cords in pairs: A and B, C and D, E and F, and G and H for the sides; and C and H and B and E for the rungs. If you are working on a marudai, grasp the first

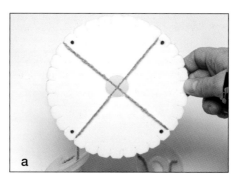

a

b

c

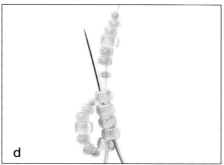

d

e

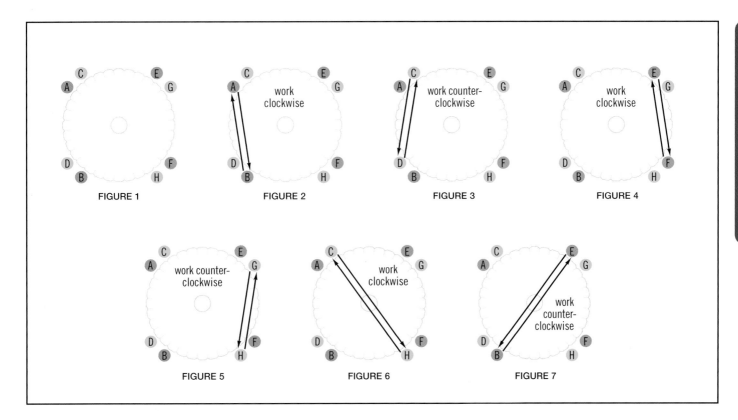

FIGURE 1   FIGURE 2   FIGURE 3   FIGURE 4

FIGURE 5   FIGURE 6   FIGURE 7

cord mentioned with your right hand and the other cord with your left hand, and move them simultaneously in the direction indicated for that movement. If you're working with a disk, pick up the first cord of the pair, move it in the direction indicated to the new position, then pick up the second cord, and move it in the direction indicated to the new position. Begin the ladder rope as follows:

Movement 1: Working clockwise, move cord A to the cord B position, and move cord B to the cord A position **(figure 2)**.

Movement 2: Working counterclockwise, move cord D to the cord C position, and move cord C to the cord D position **(figure 3)**.

Movement 3: Working clockwise, move cord E to the cord F position, and move cord F to the cord E position **(figure 4)**.

Movement 4: Working counterclockwise, move cord H to the cord G position, and move cord G to the cord H position **(figure 5)**.

[4] Repeat movements 1–4 three times. This creates two parallel braids that form the sides of an opening.

[5] Make a ladder rung as follows:

Movement 5: Working clockwise, move cord C to the cord H position, and move cord H to the cord C position **(figure 6)**.

Movement 6: Working counterclockwise,

move cord B to the cord E position, and move cord E to the cord B position **(figure 7)**.

[6] Repeat movements 5 and 6 twice.

[7] Continue as in steps 3–6 until the braid is 18 in. (46 cm). Remove the braid from the marudai or disk, and tie the ends together with a tight square knot (Basics, p. 13). Cut the cords close to the knot, apply glue to the knot, and set the braid aside.

Spiral rope

[1] On 2 yd. (1.8 m) of Fireline, leave an 8-in. (20 cm) tail, and pick up four color A 8º seed beads, a 15º seed bead, two 11º seed beads, a color B 8º seed bead, two 11ºs, and a 15º. Sew through the 8ºs again **(photo c)**. The As are the core beads and the rest of the beads form a loop. Flip the loop to the left.

[2] Pick up an A, a 15º, two 11ºs, a B, two 11ºs, and a 15º, and sew through the top three As from the previous stitch and the A just added **(photo d)**. Pull tight to create a new loop, and flip it to the left so it sits on top of the previous loop. This bead sequence will be referred to as pattern 1.

[3] Repeat step 2 13 times to make a pattern 1 segment with 15 loops.

[4] Continue in spiral rope for three stitches, but pick up the following beads,

which will be referred to as pattern 2:

First stitch: an A, a 15º, an 11º, a color C 4–6 mm Czech glass bead, an 11º, and a 15º.

Second stitch: an A, a 15º, an 11º, a color D 4–6 mm Czech glass bead, an 11º, and a 15º.

Third stitch: an A, a 15º, an 11º, a C, an 11º, and a 15º.

[5] Work pattern 1 for four stitches.

[6] Continue in spiral rope for three stitches as in pattern 2, but substitute a color E 4–6 mm Czech glass bead for each D. This bead sequence will be referred to as pattern 3.

[7] Work four pattern 1 stitches.

[8] Work a repeating sequence of three pattern 2 stitches, four pattern 1 stitches, three pattern 3 stitches, and four pattern 1 stitches until you have 12 sets of both pattern 2 and pattern 3. End the rope with a total of 15 pattern 1 stitches. Do not end the thread.

Assembly

[1] Cut a 3-in. (7.6 cm) piece of 14-gauge wire. Place one end on the anvil or bench block, and hammer the end ⅛ in. (3 mm) to flatten it **(photo e)**. Use a metal file to smooth the edges.

[2] String the focal bead on the wire, then place the other end of the wire on

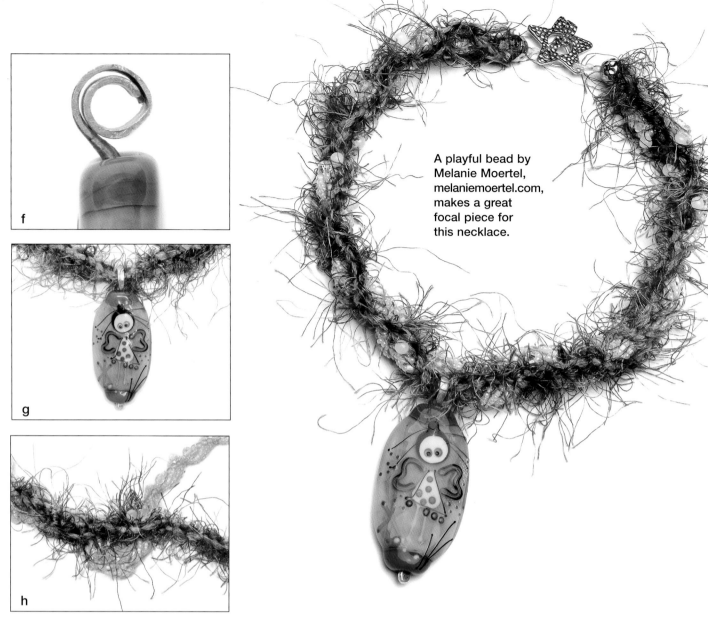

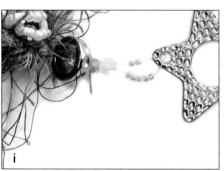

A playful bead by
Melanie Moertel,
melaniemoertel.com,
makes a great
focal piece for
this necklace.

the anvil or bench block, and hammer
it flat, being careful not to hit the focal
bead. Smooth the end with the file.
[3] Use the widest part of your
roundnose pliers to turn the end of the
wire into a large loop **(photo f)**.
[4] Center the pendant on the braid
(photo g).
[5] Weave the spiral rope through the
openings in the braid **(photo h)** until they
are completely intertwined. Sew each end
of the spiral rope to the ends of the braid.

[6] On one end, pick up a cone, an 8º,
a 4–6 mm Czech glass bead, seven 15ºs,
and half of the clasp. Sew back through
the 4–6 mm, the 8º, and the cone, and
sew into the end of the braid **(photo i)**.
Retrace the thread path to secure the
clasp connection, and end the thread
(Basics). Repeat at the other end. ●

Get beadpunk'd

BEAD EMBROIDERY /
JEWELRY ASSEMBLY

Incorporate a touch of steampunk into a necklace with eclectic appeal

designed by **Diane Hyde**

If you've been intrigued by steampunk design but think it can look a little rough around the edges, give this project a try. Designer Diane Hyde has combined her favorite beading techniques with the steampunk aesthetic, creating an elegantly eclectic look she calls "beadpunk."

Bits of pink, orange, and green brighten up the usual steampunk color palette.

stepbystep

Preparation
[1] On a work surface, experiment with designs by placing the components you want to use in a few pleasing arrangements that are balanced in color and visual weight. Sketch or take digital photos of the arrangements you like. You may need to refer back to them when you're ready to assemble your piece.
[2] Select the components that you are going to bead embroider. In this necklace, the round watch plate and the typewriter key are surrounded by bead embroidery. Glue each component to beading foundation using E6000 adhesive. Leave at least ½ in. (1.3 cm) of foundation around each component. Allow the glue to dry completely.

Bead-embroidered components
Watch plate focal piece
[1] Tie an overhand knot (Basics, p. 13) at the end of a comfortable length of thread, and sew up through the beading foundation right next to the watch plate. Working in beaded back-stitch (Basics), pick up two color A 8° seed beads, align

An old family photograph hints that this necklace holds personal meaning for the designer.

them next to the watch plate, and sew down through the foundation. Come up through the foundation between the A 8ºs, and sew through the second A 8º added. Continue around the watch plate in two-bead beaded backstitch until it is surrounded. End and add thread (Basics) as needed.

[2] Using 11º seed beads, work another round of beaded backstitch next to the round of 8ºs, but at the top of the watch plate, sew on an accent bead, pearl, or crystal.

[3] Sew up between the 8ºs and the watch plate. Using color B 15º seed beads, work a round of beaded backstitch between the 8ºs and the watch plate. Do not pull the thread tight — you want the 15ºs to rest on top of the crevice between the 8ºs and the watch plate (**photo a**).

[4] Determine where you want to attach a Lucite flower, and sew up through the foundation and the corresponding hole in the watch plate. Pick up a 19 mm metal flower stamping, an 18 mm Lucite flower, and a 4 mm pearl, and sew back through the flowers, the

watch plate, and the foundation. Retrace the thread path at least twice for security.

[5] Use E6000 to glue one or more 6–9 mm cabochons to the watch plate (**photo b**). Allow to dry.

[6] Using the remaining holes in the watch plate, attach beads, charms, and ephemera as desired. Sew beads and small Lucite flowers on as in step 4. If you want to add watch gears, fill holes in the watch plate with glue, and insert the gear stems (**photo c**).

[7] Trim the foundation just outside the round of 11ºs, being careful not to cut the stitches. Tint the edges of the foundation with a permanent marker that closely matches your Ultrasuede.

[8] Determine where you want this component to connect with others. Tie an overhand knot at the end of a comfortable length of thread, and sew through the foundation near a connection point. Sew a 5 mm soldered jump ring to the connection point, positioning it so half of it extends beyond the edge of the component. Repeat to attach additional jump rings

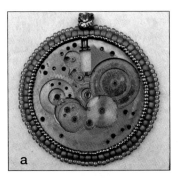

a

b

c

d

e

f

g

h

i

j

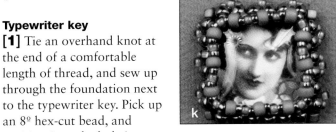

k

l

m

at the other connection points (photo d).

[9] Trace the shape onto a piece of Ultrasuede. Cut the Ultrasuede along the line, and attach it to the foundation using whip stitch (Basics). End the thread (photo e).

Typewriter key

[1] Tie an overhand knot at the end of a comfortable length of thread, and sew up through the foundation next to the typewriter key. Pick up an 8° hex-cut bead, and position it so the hole is perpendicular to the key. Sew down through the foundation, and sew back up a half-bead's width away from the first 8°. Continue to add 8° hex-cuts around the typewriter key, positioning them like the spokes of a wheel (photo f).

[2] Using color C 15° seed beads, work a round of two-bead beaded backstitch (photo g).

[3] Sew up through the foundation between the typewriter key and a hex-cut bead, and sew through the hex-cut. Pick up a 3 mm bicone crystal and a B 15°, skip the B 15°, and sew back through the 3 mm, the hex-cut, and the foundation. Repeat all around, adding a 3 mm and a 15° at the end of each hex-cut (photo h). End the thread.

[4] Finish the component as in steps 7–9 of "Watch plate focal piece."

Photo component

[1] Cut out an image from a photo, photocopy, or other printed image. Cut it slightly larger than the watch crystal you will cover it with.

[2] Apply a light coating of spray mount to the back of the image, press it onto a small piece of cardstock, and allow it to dry. Spray the image with spray sealant, if desired, and let dry.

[3] Place the watch crystal over the photo, and decide how you want to crop the image. Hold the watch crystal in place, trace around it, and then carefully trim the image on the line.

[4] Trace the watch crystal onto the PeelNStick adhesive, and cut along the line. Remove one piece of backing, and attach it to the back of the image. Remove the second piece of backing, and adhere the image to a piece of beading foundation.

[5] If desired, place a few watch parts or other ephemera onto the image (photo i). Using a toothpick, apply a thin line of E6000 around the rim of the watch crystal. Position the watch crystal over the image, and press it in place. Allow to dry completely.

[6] Using color B 8° seed beads, work as in step 1 of "Typewriter key" to surround the watch crystal (photo j). Sew through the B 8°s to exit a B 8°, facing outward (figure, point a).

[7] Pick up a color D 15° seed bead, an 11°, and a D 15°, and sew through the next 8° (a–b). Repeat around to surround the image with three-bead picots (b–c).

[8] If you are using a square watch crystal, add a 1.4 mm cube bead at each corner: Sew down through the foundation, and sew up at

a corner. Pick up a 1.4 mm cube bead, position the cube so it fits squarely in the corner, and sew down through the foundation. Repeat at each corner.

[9] Step up through a D 15° and an 11° in the inner round of picots. Pick up a B 15°, a B 8°, and a B 15°, and sew through the middle 11° in the next inner-round picot. Repeat around (photo k).

[10] Finish the component as in steps 7–9 of "Watch plate focal piece."

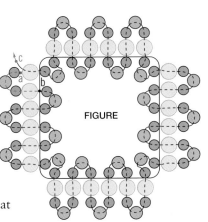

FIGURE

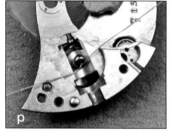

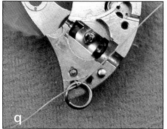

Partial-watch-plate connector

[1] Cut a small circle of Ultrasuede about ¼ in. (6 mm) in diameter.
[2] With a comfortable length of Fireline, sew through the Ultrasuede several times to lock the end in place.
[3] Determine where you want to attach a Lucite leaf and flower, and sew through the hole of the partial watch plate in that spot, from back to front (photo l).
[4] Pick up a 16 x 17 mm Lucite leaf, and sew through an adjacent opening in the watch plate and the Ultrasuede (photo m). Sewing through adjacent holes helps to stabilize the leaf.
[5] Sew back through the Ultrasuede and watch plate, and pick up a 14 mm Lucite flower and a 3 mm accent bead. Skip the 3 mm, and sew back through the flower, the watch plate, and the Ultrasuede (photo n). Retrace

the thread path several times to secure both the flower and the leaf, and end the Fireline.
[6] To add a 7 mm half-ball sew-on or other accent bead to the partial watch plate, attach an 11º stop bead (Basics) to a comfortable length of Fireline, leaving a 6-in. (15 cm) tail. Sew through a hole in the watch plate, and pick up the accent bead and a B 15º. Sew back through the accent bead and the watch plate (photo o), and tie the working thread and tail together with a square knot (Basics and photo p). Retrace the thread path a few times, tying a square knot each time. Squeeze a dot of G-S Hypo Cement onto the knots, letting the glue pool up a bit, and let dry. Trim the Fireline close to the knots.
[7] Determine where you want this component to connect to others. On a comfortable length of Fireline, pick up a 5 mm

soldered jump ring, and sew through a hole in the watch plate from back to front, leaving a 6-in. (15 cm) tail. Pick up an 8º or an 11º (or an accent bead and a 15º), and sew back through the hole in the watch plate. Tie the working thread and tail together with a square knot, capturing the soldered jump ring (photo q). Retrace the thread path several times, tying one or more knots each time. Squeeze a dot of G-S Hypo Cement onto the knots, allowing it to pool up on the jump ring. Let dry, and trim the Fireline close to the knots.
[8] Repeat step 7 to attach additional jump rings at the other connection points.
[9] If you wish to add more beads on the front surface, attach them as in step 7, but

For her homage to the Mexican holiday Día de los Muertos (Day of the Dead), Diane added a filigree crown to a large skull bead, and chose a lampworked heart as an accent. Blue vintage sew-throughs echo the color of the heart.

attach an 11º stop bead on the back instead of a jump ring.

Watch face pendant

[1] Glue a watch face or other object to the center of a 19 mm filigree stamping with openings around the perimeter. These openings will allow you to attach other components to them with jump rings.
[2] Cut a 2-in. (5 cm) piece of 22-gauge wire, and make a plain loop (Basics) at one end. String an 8º, a 42 x 16 mm Lucite leaf, and an 8º, and make another plain loop.
[3] Open an oval jump ring (Basics), and attach one of the loops made in step 2 and an opening at the bottom of the watch face filigree component. Close the jump ring. Repeat to attach the other loop made

s

t

u

v

in step 2 to the watch face component (photo r).

Linking components

[1] Cut a 2-in. (5 cm) piece of 22-gauge wire, make a plain loop, and string an accent bead. If desired, string an 11º before and after the accent bead. Make plain loop.

[2] Repeat step 1 as needed to make the number of bead links needed for your design.

[3] Determine which connections will be made with chain, and cut pieces of chain to the appropriate lengths.

Assembly

[1] Position all your components in the desired order. If you are using a house key top, drill holes in it as needed using a ¹⁄₁₆-in. (2 mm) drill bit.

[2] Using 4 mm two-loop crystal connectors, attach the watch face pendant to the watch plate focal piece (photo s).

[3] Using jump rings, chain, and the loops of the bead links, connect the partial watch plate component to the photo component (photo t). Connect a metal stamping

to the typewriter key, then connect the typewriter key to the partial house key (photo u). Connect the house key and the photo component to the watch plate focal piece.

[4] Cut a piece of chain to the desired length for one end of the necklace. Open a jump ring, attach the end link of chain and an end component, and close the jump ring.

[5] Open a jump ring, attach the end chain link and half of the clasp, and close the jump ring.

[6] Cut 10 in. (25 cm) of .014 beading wire, and string a crimp bead and the jump ring of the other end necklace component. Go back through the crimp bead, and crimp it (Basics). String beads as desired to

make the second end of the necklace the same length as the first.

[7] String a crimp bead and the other half of the clasp, go back through the crimp bead, and crimp it. Trim the excess wire.

[8] Use chainnose pliers to close a crimp cover around each crimp if desired.

materials

necklace 27 in. (69 cm)

Note: Materials listed are for Diane's necklace, p. 198. You may wish to substitute similar materials for your version.

- Lucite components
  42 x 16 mm leaf
  18 mm flower
  16 x 17 mm leaf
  14 mm flower
  9 mm flower
  2 7 mm flowers
- 6–9 mm cabochon
- 45–55 assorted 3–8 mm faux pearl, crystal, or glass accent beads and/or sew-ons
- 7 mm half-ball crystal sew-on
- 2 4 mm two-loop crystal connectors
- 24 3 mm bicone crystals
- 4 1.4 mm micro cube beads
- 1 g 8º hex-cut beads
- 3 g 8º seed beads in each of 2 colors: A, B
- 3 g 11º seed beads
- 1–2 g 15º seed beads in each of 3 colors: B, C, D
- 2½-in. (6.4 cm) diameter round watch plate
- 1½ x ⅞-in. (3.8 x 2.2 cm) partial watch plate
- ⅝-in. (1.6 cm) watch face
- 18–24 mm watch crystal
- 5 9–12 mm watch gears
- typewriter key with flat back
- house key top (optional)
- 3 or more metal stampings and charms, including a 19 mm flower and a 19 mm filigree stamping

- ⅜-in. (1 cm) mesh dome (optional)
- printed image or photo
- clasp
- 1 ft. (30 cm) 22-gauge wire
- 12–15 in. (30–38 cm) chain in 1–3 styles
- 16–20 5 mm soldered jump rings
- 25–36 3 x 4–4 x 5 mm oval jump rings
- 2 crimp beads
- 2 crimp covers (optional)
- nylon beading thread, size D
- Fireline, 6 lb. test
- flexible beading wire, .014
- beading needles, #10 and #12
- cardstock
- drill with ¹⁄₁₆-in. (2 mm) drill bit (optional)
- E6000 adhesive
- G-S Hypo Cement
- Lacy's Stiff Stuff beading foundation
- PeelNStick double-sided adhesive (thermoweb.com)
- permanent marker to match Ultrasuede
- spray mount
- spray sealant like Krylon Preserve It! (optional)
- toothpick
- Ultrasuede
- chainnose pliers
- crimping pliers
- roundnose pliers
- wire cutters

[9] If desired, use E6000 to glue a ⅜-in. (1 cm) round mesh dome or filigree piece over the exposed Ultrasuede on the back of the partial watch plate component (photo v). ●

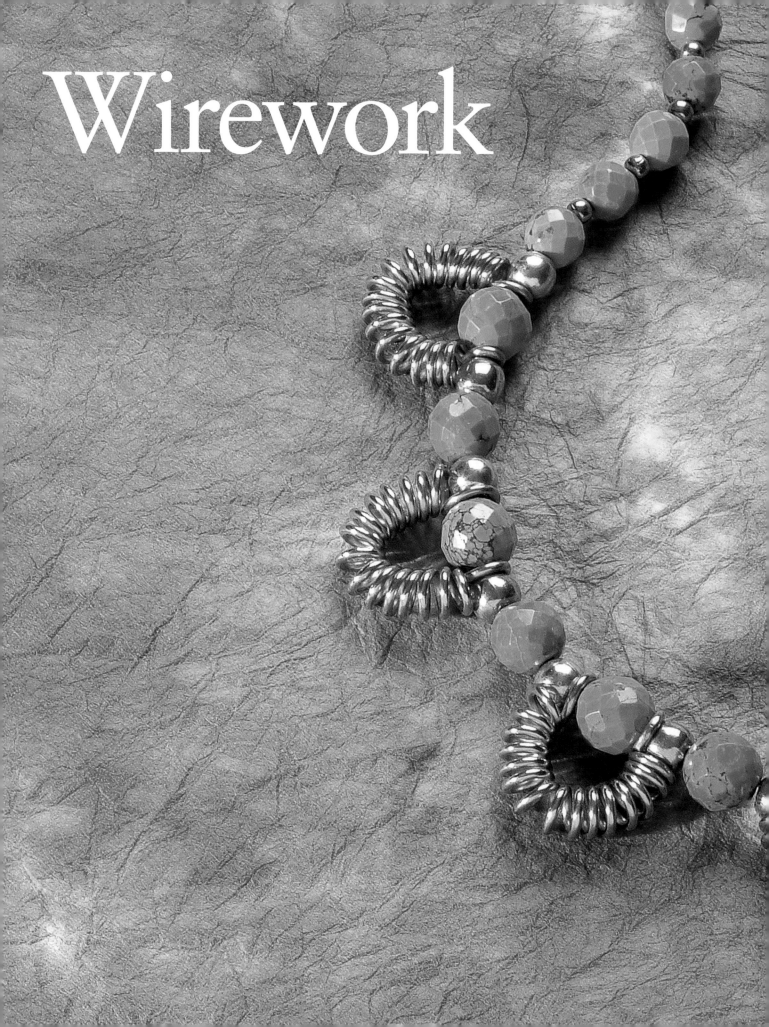

Wirework

CHAIN MAIL

Dahlia ring

Link jump rings
in graduated
sizes to create a
dimensional ring

designed by **Amanda Shero Granstrom**

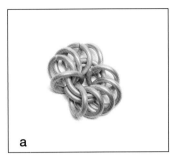

a

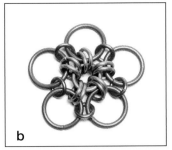

b

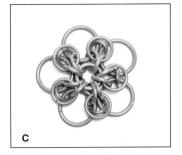

c

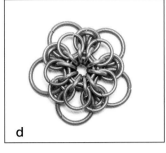

d

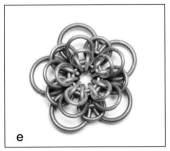

e

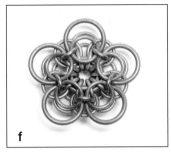

f

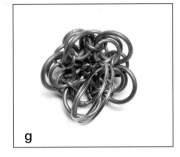

g

DESIGNER'S NOTE:
To make sure you use the right amount of wire, string the flower onto the spool before making the ball. Make the ball, then measure 7–8 in. (18–20 cm) of wire, and cut it from the spool.

Use anodized aluminum jump rings to create distinctive, lightweight jewelry, and have fun experimenting with cheerful colors!

stepbystep

Flower

[1] Close 10 color B 5 mm jump rings, and open two color B 6 mm jump rings (Basics, p. 13). On an open 6 mm jump ring, attach the 10 closed 5 mms, and close it. Slide another open 6 mm through the 10 closed 5 mms, and close it **(photo a)**.

[2] Open five color A 10 mm jump rings. Slide an open 10 mm jump ring through two adjacent 5 mms, and close it. Repeat to attach the remaining 10 mms to the other 5 mms.

[3] Open five color A 4 mm jump rings. Slide an open 4 mm jump ring through two adjacent 10 mms, and close it. Repeat to attach the remaining 4 mms to the other 10 mms **(photo b)**.

[4] Decide which side of the flower is the front and which is the back, and build the next three layers on the front:
Layer 1: Open five color A 6 mm jump rings. Slide an open 6 mm jump ring through a color B 5 mm in one pair and a color B 5 mm in an adjacent pair, and close it. Repeat to attach the remaining 6 mms **(photo c)**.
Layer 2: Open five color A 6 mm jump rings. Slide an open 6 mm jump ring through a pair of color B 5 mms connected in the base layer in step 2, and close it. Repeat to attach the remaining 6 mms **(photo d)**.
Layer 3: Open five color B 5 mms. Slide an open 5 mm jump ring through a pair of color B 5 mms connected in the base layer in step 2, and close it. Repeat to attach the remaining color B 5 mms **(photo e)**.

[5] Open five color A 6 mm jump rings. On the back of the flower, slide an open 6 mm jump ring through two adjacent 4 mms, and close it. Repeat to attach the remaining 6 mms **(photo f)**.

Ring

[1] Cut a 7–10-in. (18–25 cm) piece of 18-gauge wire. Make a free-form wire ball at one end by using chainnose and roundnose pliers to loosely wrap the wire into a small sphere big enough to prevent the wire from slipping through the hole in the center of the chain mail flower.

[2] String the flower onto the wire, with the wire ball on the front of the flower. Bend the wire on the back at a right angle. Wrap the wire twice around the mandrel for your desired size, keeping the wire ball tight against the flower.

[3] Wrap the tail of the wire around the wire at the back of the flower, and trim **(photo g)**. File the end of the wire if desired. ◗

materials

ring 1¼-in. (3.2 cm) diameter

- 7–10 in. (18–25 cm) 18-gauge wire
- **5** 10 mm (⅜-in.) inside-diameter (ID) 16-gauge jump rings, color A
- 6 mm (¼-in.) ID 18-gauge jump rings
  15 color A
  2 color B
- **15** 5 mm (³⁄₁₆-in.) ID 18-gauge jump rings, color B
- **5** 4 mm (⁵⁄₃₂-in.) ID 18-gauge jump rings, color A
- metal file (optional)
- ring mandrel
- 2 pairs of chainnose pliers
- roundnose pliers
- wire cutters

CHAIN MAIL
Bicycle chain
bracelet

Adding glass rings to easy chain mail creates a lively, colorful bracelet

designed by **Luan Carnevale**

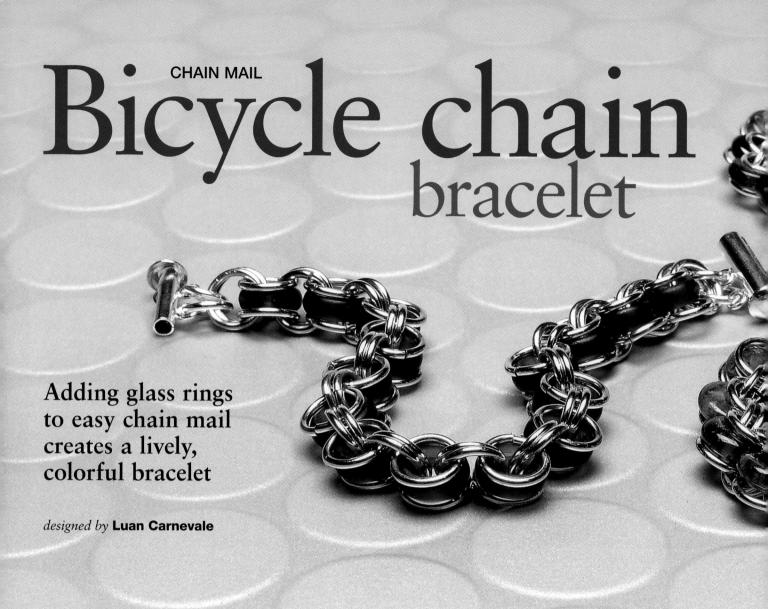

Silver jump rings and shiny glass Cheerios make a cheerful combination. For casual elegance, try gemstones or matte glass in a single color.

Jewelry projects don't get much easier than this. Link glass or gemstone rings and large jump rings into an easy chain for a beautifully layered chain mail bracelet.

step by step

[1] Open a jump ring (Basics, p. 13), attach two glass rings, and close the jump ring **(photo a)**. Open a second jump ring, slide it through the same two glass rings to sit parallel to the first jump ring, and close the jump ring **(photo b)**.
[2] Open a jump ring, attach a new glass ring to the previous glass ring, and close

the jump ring. Repeat with a second jump ring **(photo c)**.
[3] Open a jump ring. Position the four jump rings attached to the second-to-last glass ring near each other, and attach the new jump ring to the four jump rings above the glass ring. Close the jump ring **(photo d)**. Flip the chain over and repeat on the other side, so the glass ring is sandwiched between two jump rings **(photo e)**.

[4] Repeat step 2 **(photo f)** and step 3 **(photo g)**, and continue building the chain until the bracelet is 1 in. (2.5 cm) short of the desired length.
[5] Attach a pair of jump rings to the glass rings at each end of the bracelet, and then repeat step 3 at each end **(photo h)**.
[6] Open a jump ring, and attach the clasp and the two jump rings at one end of the bracelet. Close the jump ring **(photo i)**. Attach a jump ring to the two rings at the other end of the bracelet. ◉

EDITOR'S NOTES:

• Glass rings offer regularly sized holes, but 10 mm gemstone donuts also work well for this project. Make sure the holes in the gemstones are large enough to loosely fit four jump rings. You may need to increase your jump ring size to 6.4 mm or 7 mm to fit around two donuts and four jump rings.

• Is silver too precious for your pocketbook? Get started with an easy-to-maneuver base metal like aluminum, or add some color with anodized aluminum jump rings, like these brown ones from Blue Buddha Boutique (bluebuddhaboutique.com).

• If you have leftover glass rings, make a matching necklace. Follow steps 1–4 of the bracelet, and then link pairs of rings to each end until the necklace is the desired length.

a

b

c

d

e

f

g

h

i

materials
bracelet 7 in. (18 cm)

• **16** 9 mm glass rings, Cheerios, or donuts with 4 mm hole
• **68** 6 mm inside-diameter 18-gauge jump rings
• clasp
• 2 pairs of chainnose pliers

Lampwork *links*

Use a clever construction technique to pull together diverse elements

designed by **Kathy Petersen** *and* **Susan Matych-Hager**

Susan Matych-Hager's mistletoe beads make for a great holiday bracelet, while the carved amber-colored agate beads are appropriate for everyday wear.

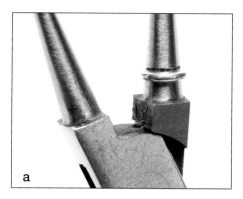

a

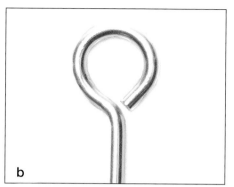

b

c

d

e

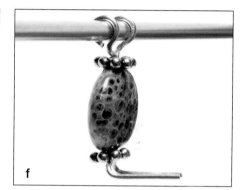

f

g

Use a variation of Byzantine chain to show off a collection of small focal beads. Art glass beads are perfect for this design, though other large-hole focal beads work well, too.

step by step

Bead components

[1] Place a 6 mm jump ring on one jaw of your roundnose pliers, and mark where it sits with a marker (**photo a**). This mark indicates where you should place the wire in the following steps in order to make the loops the same size as the jump rings.
[2] Cut a 3–4-in. (7.6–10 cm) piece of wire, place one end of the wire at the mark made in step 1, and make a plain loop (Basics, p. 13, and **photo b**).
[3] Grasp the loop with your chainnose pliers, and make a right-angle bend (**photo c**).
[4] Grasp the wire right after the bend, and make another right-angle bend going away from the loop (**photo d**).
[5] Repeat steps 2–4 with another wire, but make the first bend in the opposite direction so that when the long ends of the wire come together in the middle, the loops are parallel and sit about ⅜ in. (1 cm) apart.

[6] Over both wires, string one or more spacers, a focal bead, and one or more spacers. Bend the wire ends in opposite directions (**photo e**). At this point, you may find it helpful to slide a knitting needle or dowel through the loops. This will stabilize them as you complete the bead component.
[7] Grasp one wire right next to the bend made in step 6, and bend it in the opposite direction of the loops on the other end. Repeat with the other wire. Trim the wires to about ⅝ in. (1.6 cm) (**photo f**). Using roundnose pliers, make a loop with one of the wires. Repeat with the other wire (**photo g**). The loops should face the same way as the loops on the other side of the focal bead.
[8] Repeat steps 2–7 with the remaining focal beads.

Chain mail sections

[1] Open four and close six 6 mm jump rings (Basics). On an open jump ring, attach four closed jump rings, and close it. Slide another open jump ring through

materials

bracelet 7 in. (18 cm)
- **3–5** art glass beads or other large-hole focal beads (you need to be able to fit two thicknesses of wire through the beads)
- **2** art glass spacer beads (optional)
- **6–10** metal spacers
- **2**-strand clasp
- **120** 6 mm outside-diameter jump rings, 18-gauge
- 18–30 in. (46–76 cm) 18–20-gauge wire, half-hard
- knitting needle or dowel (optional)
- bentnose pliers
- chainnose pliers
- roundnose pliers
- wire cutters

209

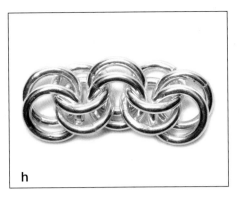

h

i

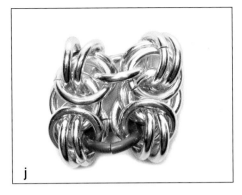

j

EDITOR'S NOTE:
The glass beads add a lot of weight to this project and may cause the work to slip out of your pliers. To prevent this, raise your work surface to shoulder level and rest the piece on it as you assemble the components.

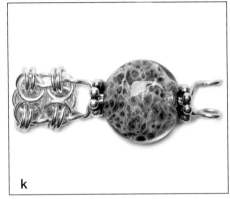

k

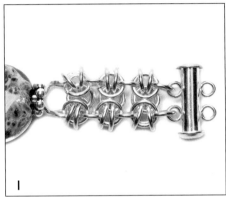

l

the four closed jump rings, and close it. This creates a 2 + 2 + 2 chain.

[2] Slide an open jump ring through an end pair of jump rings, attach the remaining two closed rings, and close the open jump ring. Slide the remaining open jump ring through the four jump rings the previous open ring went through, and close it. This

creates a chain of 10 rings, attached in pairs (photo h).

[3] Repeat steps 1 and 2.

[4] Flip the end pair of rings on one chain back toward the rest of the chain. Repeat with an end pair of rings on the other chain. Open a jump ring, and slide it through the side of each set of flipped rings. Close the ring (photo i).

[5] Repeat step 4 at the other end of the chains (photo j).

[6] Repeat steps 1–5 until you have one more chain mail section than you have bead components.

Assembly

[1] Open a loop of a bead component, and slide it through a pair of flipped rings on a chain mail section, on the side opposite the jump ring that connected the two chains. Close the loop.

[2] To connect the other loop of the component to the remaining pair of flipped rings of the chain mail section, open one of the flipped rings, guide it through the loop, and close the ring. Repeat with the other ring (photo k). This is the most challenging part of this project, and you may need a little extra patience

and persistence to get these rings properly positioned.

[3] Repeat steps 1 and 2 to connect the remaining chain mail sections and bead components.

[4] Test for fit, and add or remove a 10-ring section of chain mail from each end if needed. To add a section, repeat steps 1 and 2 of "Chain mail sections," then connect it to one end of the bracelet as in steps 4 and 5.

[5] To attach the clasp, open a jump ring, slide it through two end flipped rings and a loop on half of the clasp, and close the ring. Repeat with the other loop of the clasp (photo l).

[6] Repeat step 5 at the other end of the bracelet. ●

Mottled green borosilicate lentils by Unicorne Beads (unicornebeads.com) are a lovely option for a casual accessory.

Linkitup

Enjoy everyday elegance with gemstones and chain mail

designed by **Wendy Hunt**

materials

bracelet 8½ in. (21.6 cm)

- **3** 18–20 mm lentil beads (jasper)
- **4** 8 mm beads (jasper)
- lobster claw clasp
- **15 in. (38 cm)** 21-gauge sterling silver wire, half-hard
- **9** 6 mm inside-diameter (ID) 18-gauge sterling silver jump rings
- **84** 5 mm ID 19-gauge sterling silver jump rings
- **18** 3 mm ID 19-gauge sterling silver jump rings
- **180–216** 2 mm ID 19-gauge sterling silver jump rings
- chainnose pliers
- roundnose pliers
- wire cutters

Create chain mail flowers with a clever series of jump ring links, and enclose gemstone lentil beads within them for an intriguing bracelet with a blush of color.

step by step

Bead components

[1] Cut a 3-in. (7.6 cm) piece of 21-gauge wire. Make a wrapped loop (Basics, p. 13) on one end. String an 18–20 mm lentil bead, and make a wrapped loop **(photo a)**. Repeat to make a total of three lentil-bead components.

[2] Cut a 1½-in. (3.8 cm) piece of 21-gauge wire, and make a wrapped loop on one end. String an 8 mm bead, and make a wrapped loop. Repeat to make a total of four 8 mm bead components.

Flower components

[1] Open 24 2 mm jump rings, and close 14 5 mm jump rings (Basics).

[2] On an open 2 mm, attach four closed 5 mms, and close it. Slide another open 2 mm through the four closed 5 mms, and close it. This creates a 2 + 2 + 2 chain **(photo b)**.

[3] Slide an open 2 mm through an end pair of 5 mms, attach two more 5 mms, and close it. Slide another open 2 mm through the four closed 5 mms, and close it **(photo c)**.

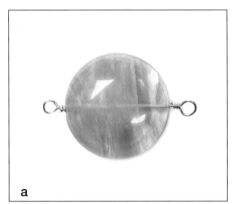

a

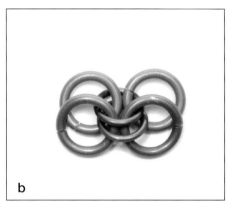

b

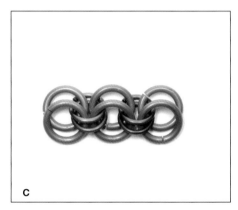

c

d

e

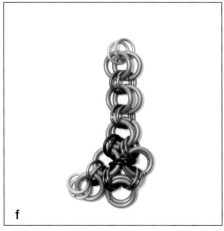

f

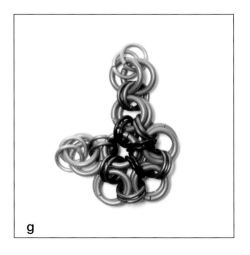

g

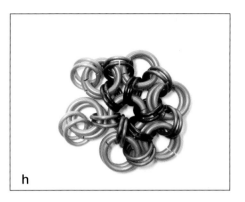

h

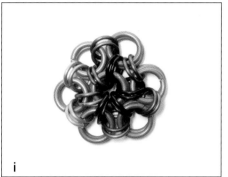

i

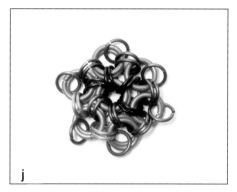

j

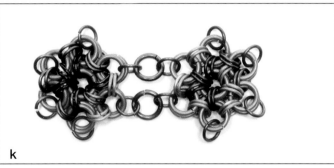

k

l

[4] Repeat step 3 to make a chain that has seven pairs of 5 mms connected with six pairs of 2 mms.

[5] Slide an open 2 mm through an end pair of 5 mms, and close it. Slide another open 2 mm through the end pair of 5 mms, and close it. Repeat on the other end (photo d).

[6] Slide an open 2 mm through the second and fourth pairs of 5 mms, and close it. Repeat with a second 2 mm (photo e).

[7] Slide an open 2 mm through the second and fifth pairs of 5 mms, and close it. Repeat with a second 2 mm (photo f).

[8] Slide an open 2 mm through the second and sixth pairs of 5 mms, and close it. Repeat with a second 2 mm (photo g).

[9] Slide an open 2 mm through the second and seventh pairs of 5 mms, and close it. Repeat with a second 2 mm (photo h).

[10] Attach the end 2 mms of the first and seventh pairs to the adjacent pairs of 5 mms to complete the flower (photo i).

[11] Open a 2 mm, and attach it to an outer pair of 5 mms, and close it. Repeat around the flower (photo j). If desired, attach a second 2 mm to each pair of 5 mms.

[12] Repeat steps 1–11 to make a total of six flower components.

Assembly

[1] Open a 3 mm jump ring, and slide it through a 2 mm or pair of 2 mms attached in step 11 of "Flower components" for each of two flower components. Close the 3 mm. Repeat (photo k).

[2] Place a lentil between the two flower components, and attach the remaining 2 mms with 3 mms as in step 1 (photo l).

[3] Repeat steps 1 and 2 with the remaining flower components and lentils.

[4] Open a 6 mm jump ring, slide it through a wrapped loop of an 8 mm and a lentil, and close the 6 mm (photo m). Repeat to connect the remaining 8 mms and lentils, alternating between them.

[5] Open a 6 mm, slide it through an end wrapped loop of an 8 mm, and close it. Repeat on the other end.

[6] Open a 6 mm, slide it through an end 6 mm and the lobster claw clasp, and close it. Use the 6 mm on the other end as the other half of the clasp. ●

m

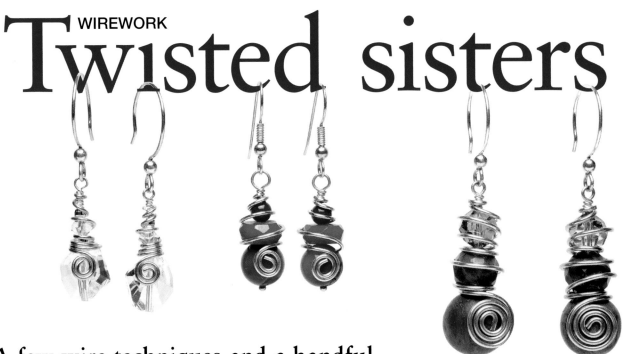

Twisted sisters

A few wire techniques and a handful of materials produce a pair of earrings in minutes

Use smaller beads and 22-gauge wire to make a dainty version of these earrings, like the two pair at left.

designed by **Kimberly Berlin**

a

b

c

d

Wrap wire around a few spare beads for a sophisticated twist on the traditional drop earring. Mix wood, gemstones, and crystals for a natural feel, or go glam with all crystals.

materials

pair of earrings

- wooden, gemstone, glass, crystal, or pearl beads
  2 14 mm
  2 10 mm
  2 8 mm
- 2 4 mm flat spacers
- 12 in. (30 cm) 18-gauge wire
- 2 3-in. (7.6 cm) 24-gauge head pins
- pair of earring findings
- chainnose pliers
- flatnose pliers
- roundnose pliers
- wire cutters

step by step

[1] On a 3-in. (7.6 cm) head pin, string a 4 mm spacer, a 14 mm bead, a 10 mm bead, and an 8 mm bead. Make a wrapped loop (Basics, p. 13, and **photo a**).

[2] Cut a 6-in. (15 cm) piece of 18-gauge wire. On one end, make a small loop with the tip of your roundnose pliers. Hold the loop with your flatnose pliers, and wrap the wire around the loop three times to create a flat spiral (**photo b**).

[3] Hold the spiral against the 14 mm bead, and wrap the wire once around the spot where the 14 mm and the 10 mm beads meet (**photo c**).

[4] Continue wrapping the wire around the 10 mm, the spot where the 10 mm meets the 8 mm, and the 8 mm.

[5] Wrap the wire twice around the wraps of the wrapped loop, and trim the excess wire (**photo d**).

[6] Open the loop (Basics) of an earring finding, and attach the wrapped loop.

[7] Make the second earring as a mirror image of the first. ●

Going green

Pair copper
elements with a
green gemstone
ring and a few
glass beads for
an easy-to-make
three-strand bracelet

by **Julia Gerlach**

materials

bracelet 7¼ in. (18.4 cm)

- 35 mm gemstone ring
  (Eclectica,
  262-641-0910,
  eclecticabeads.com)
- **4** 8 x 10 mm copper and
  sterling triangle beads
  (Eclectica)
- **4** 6 x 8 mm Czech glass
  rondelles
- 3-loop clasp, antiqued
  copper
- 17 in. (43 cm) antiqued
  copper wire, 20-gauge
- 6–8 in. (15–20 cm)
  decorative antiqued
  copper chain
- **15–20** Blue Moon
  antiqued copper oval
  jump rings in **2** sizes:
  9 x 12 mm and 6 x 9 mm
  (createforless.com)
- bentnose pliers
- chainnose pliers
- roundnose pliers
- wire cutters

This lightweight bracelet could be easily
adapted as a necklace as well — simply make
the chains and bead-link sections several
inches longer.

stepbystep

[1] Cut a 3-in. (7.6 cm) piece
of wire, and make the first
half of a wrapped loop
(Basics, p. 13). Attach the
loop to the center loop of
one half of the clasp, and
complete the wraps. String a
6 x 8 mm glass rondelle, and
make a wrapped loop.
[2] Repeat step 1, but attach
the first loop to the finished
loop of the previous bead
link, and string an 8 x 10 mm
copper bead instead of a

glass rondelle. Repeat twice
more alternating between a
glass rondelle and a copper
bead, and attaching each new
link to the previous one.
[3] Open a 9 x 12 mm jump
ring (Basics), and attach the
remaining loop of the end
copper bead link and the
35 mm gemstone ring. Close
the jump ring.
[4] Repeat steps 1–3 to
complete the other half of
the center strand.
[5] Measure each bead-link
section. Cut several short

pieces of chain, and connect
them to jump rings to make
four chains that are the
same length as the bead-link
sections. Make sure one end
of each chain has a 6 x 9 mm
jump ring and the other end
has a 9 x 12 mm jump ring.
[6] Open the 6 x 9 mm jump
ring at the end of one chain,
and connect it to an end loop
of one half of the clasp. Close
the jump ring. Open the
9 x 12 mm jump ring at the
other end of the chain, and
attach it to the gemstone
ring. Close the jump ring.
[7] Repeat step 6 with the
remaining three chains and
clasp loops, attaching each
to the gemstone ring. ●

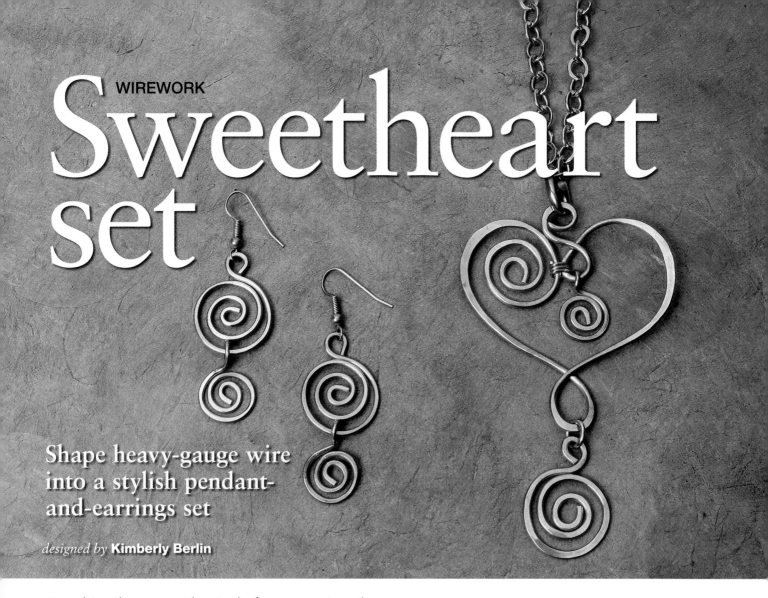

Sweetheart set

Shape heavy-gauge wire into a stylish pendant- and-earrings set

designed by **Kimberly Berlin**

Combine hearts and spirals for pretty jewelry you'll love to wear.

stepbystep

Pendant

[1] Cut a 10-in. (25 cm) piece of 14-gauge wire, and use a file, wire rounder, or bur cup to smooth the ends. Mark the center of the wire with a permanent marker.
[2] Position the widest part of the roundnose pliers on the center mark, and curve the ends around the top jaw of the pliers to make a loop **(photo a)**.
[3] Using your fingers, curve the wire ends to begin forming the heart shape **(photo b)**.
[4] Place the tip of the roundnose pliers at one end, and make a small loop.

Holding the loop flat in chainnose or flatnose pliers, make an open spiral **(photo c)**.
[5] Curve the unspiraled wire end up and around to shape the top of the other side of the heart **(photo d)**. Using roundnose pliers, make a loop next to the spiral **(photo e)**.
[6] Working in the opposite direction, make another loop. Trim the excess wire **(photo f)**. Use a ball-peen hammer to hammer the entire heart,

except in the areas where the wire crosses itself. If the wire spreads as you hammer it, reshape it with your fingers.
[7] Cut a 4-in. (10 cm) piece of 18-gauge wire, and wrap it three times around the spot where the spiral meets the loop made in step 5 **(photo g)**. Trim the ends so they both terminate on the same side of the heart. Squeeze the wrapped wire flat with flatnose pliers to lock it in place and harden it.

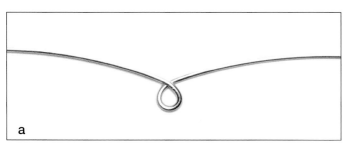

a

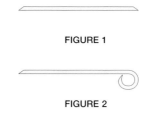

FIGURE 1

FIGURE 2

FIGURE 3

FIGURE 4

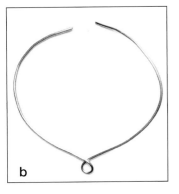

b

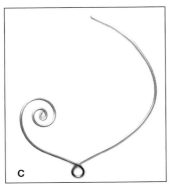

c

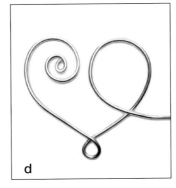

d

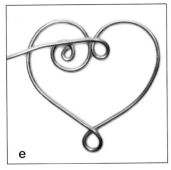

e

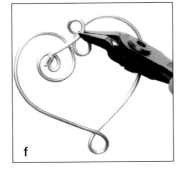

f

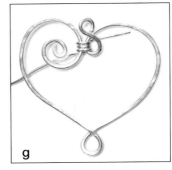

g

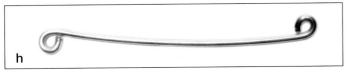

h

i

j

[8] For the inner dangle, cut a 2½-in. (6.4 cm) piece of 16-gauge wire, and file the ends. Make a simple loop at each end, turning them in opposite directions **(photo h)**. Shape the wire into a spiral **(photo i)**. Hammer the spiral.
[9] Using flatnose pliers, turn the top loop so it is perpendicular to the spiral. Open the loop (Basics, p. 13), attach it to the loop made in step 5, and close it.
[10] For the bottom dangle, cut a 4-in. (10 cm) piece of 14-gauge wire, and make and hammer a spiral as in step 8. Open the 4 mm jump ring (Basics), attach the top loop of the spiral you just made and the bottom loop of the heart, and close the jump ring.
[11] For the bail, cut a 2½-in. (6.4 cm) piece of 10-gauge half-round wire, angling the ends **(figure 1)**. With roundnose pliers, make

a simple loop **(figure 2)**. Do not close the loop completely.
[12] Attach the loop to the top loop of the pendant, and close it with roundnose pliers.
[13] Using double-barreled bail-making pliers, make a loop with the remaining wire **(figure 3)**. Trim the excess wire at an angle, file the end, and close the loop **(figure 4 and photo j)**.
[14] Use a polishing cloth to polish the pendant.

Earrings

[1] Cut two 2½-in. (6.4 cm) and two 4-in. (10 cm) pieces of 16-gauge wire. Working as in step 8 of "Pendant," make and hammer a spiral with each piece. Turn the top loop of the two small spirals so they are perpendicular to the spirals.
[2] Open the loop of a small spiral, attach it to the bottom of a large

spiral, and close the loop. Repeat with the remaining two spirals.
[3] Use a polishing cloth to polish the spirals.
[4] Open the loop of an earring finding, attach it to the top loop of a large spiral, and close the loop. Repeat with the remaining earring finding and large spiral. ◐

materials

both projects
- ball-peen hammer
- bench block or anvil
- heavy-duty flush wire cutters
- bur cup, wire rounder, or metal file
- permanent marker
- polishing cloth
- chainnose pliers
- flatnose pliers
- roundnose pliers

pendant 3½ x 1¾ in. (8.9 x 4.4 cm)
- 2½ in. (6.4 cm) 10-gauge half-round wire, dead-soft
- 14 in. (36 cm) 14-gauge wire, dead-soft
- 2½ in. (6.4 cm) 16-gauge wire, dead-soft
- 4 in. (10 cm) 18-gauge wire, dead-soft
- 4 mm jump ring, 16-gauge
- double-barrel bail-making pliers

earrings
- 13 in. (33 cm) 16-gauge wire, dead-soft
- pair of earring findings

DESIGNER'S NOTE:
The large bail on this pendant is designed to be used with large-link chain. To complete a necklace, simply string the pendant on a chain, and use jump rings to attach a clasp.

Paisley
perfection

Add gemstones to wire frames for earrings reminiscent of Persian motifs

designed by **Sonia Kumar**

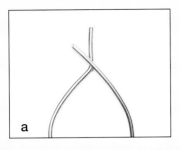 a

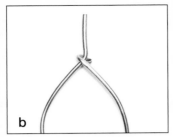 b

 c

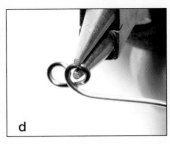 d

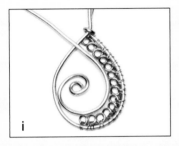 e

 f

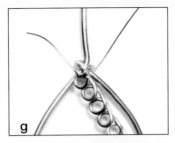 g

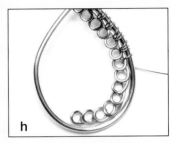 h

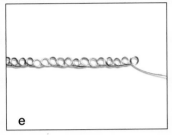 i

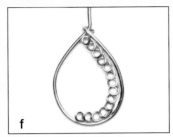 j

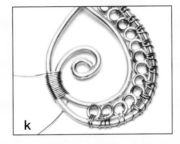 k

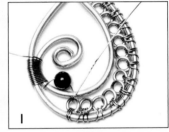 l

 m

Make loops and spirals to adorn a simple wire shape. Add gemstones in the color combination of your choice.

step by step

[1] Cut 5 in. (13 cm) of 16-gauge wire, and bend it from the center to form a teardrop shape, overlapping the ends. Bend one end so it points straight up **(photo a)**. Wrap the other end around the vertical end, and trim **(photo b)**.
[2] Cut 9 in. (23 cm) of 20-gauge wire, and make a simple loop at one end using roundnose pliers **(photo c)**. Reposition the roundnose pliers next to the previous loop, and wrap the long wire around the pliers to make another loop **(photo d)**. Repeat to make a continuous series of loops **(photo e)** that is long enough to fit about halfway around the inside of the teardrop frame. Decrease

the size of the last few loops in the series. Trim the end, and place the series of loops in the teardrop frame **(photo f)**.
[3] Cut about 12 in. (30 cm) of 28-gauge wire, and wrap it a few times around the first loop and the teardrop frame **(photo g)**. Continue along the edge of the teardrop, connecting the loops to the frame **(photo h)**. Trim the ends, and press them close to your work.
[4] Cut 5 in. (13 cm) of 16-gauge wire, and make a simple loop at one end. Hold the loop flat with chainnose pliers, and make an open spiral that will fit within the teardrop frame **(photo i)**. Trim the end **(photo j)**.
[5] Cut 24 in. (61 cm) of 28-gauge wire, and begin wrapping it around the

teardrop frame and the spiral **(photo k)**.
[6] Wrap the wire once around the spiral wire only. String a 4 mm gemstone bead onto the 28-gauge wire, and wrap the wire around the spiral and the nearest loop **(photo l)**. Continue connecting the spiral to the loops, adding 4 mms at regular intervals, until you've added seven 4 mms and reached the top of the frame. Trim the wire, and press the end close to your work.
[7] Using roundnose pliers, make a simple loop with the remaining wire end at the top of the frame **(photo m)**.
[8] Open the loop (Basics, p. 13) of an earring finding, attach it to the loop made in step 7, and close the loop.
[9] Repeat steps 1–8 to make a second earring as the mirror image of the first. ●

materials
pair of earrings
- **14** 4 mm round gemstone beads
- **20 in.** (51 cm) 16-gauge wire, dead-soft
- **18 in.** (46 cm) 20-gauge wire, dead-soft
- **2 yd.** (1.8 m) 28-gauge wire, dead-soft
- pair of earring findings
- chainnose pliers
- roundnose pliers
- wire cutters

Wirework

Copper wire accentuates
turquoise beads.

WIREWORK
Curly cue

Coiled components
add texture to a
strung necklace

designed by
Kimberly Berlin

Bonus Earrings

materials

both projects
- 5 mm mandrel
- metal file or wire rounder
- pencil
- ruler
- chainnose pliers
- wire cutters

necklace 19 in. (48 cm)
- **13** 10 mm gemstone beads or pearls
- **24** 8 mm beads to match the 10 mms
- **14** 6 mm large-hole copper beads, gemstones, or pearls
- **22** 3 mm beads to match the 6 mms
- clasp
- 7 ft. (2.1 m) 16-gauge round copper or silver wire, half-hard
- 4 crimp beads
- 4 crimp covers
- flexible beading wire, .019
- crimping pliers

pair of earrings
- **2** 10 mm gemstone beads or pearls
- **2** 6 mm large-hole copper beads, gemstones, or pearls
- **2** 3 mm beads to match the 6 mms
- 24 in. (61 cm) 16-gauge round copper or silver wire, half-hard
- 8 in. (20 cm) 20-gauge round copper or silver wire, half-hard
- pair of earring findings
- roundnose pliers

Bring out the best in your favorite chunky beads when you pair them with coiled wire. Using beads in graduated sizes adds to the flow of this necklace. The coiled components make elegant earrings, too.

step by step

Necklace

[1] Cut a 12-in. (30 cm) piece of 16-gauge wire, and file the ends or use a wire rounder to smooth them. Coil the wire around the 5 mm mandrel, keeping the coils straight and snugging them tight against each other, but not too tight around the mandrel. Using chainnose pliers, flatten the ends against the mandrel. Slide the coil off the mandrel.

[2] Using chainnose pliers, gently bend an end coil perpendicular to the remaining coils. Repeat on the other end, making sure the end coils are parallel **(photo a)**.

[3] Gently stretch the coils apart so the coil unit measures 1¾ in. (4.4 cm) from end to end **(photo b)**. If needed, use chainnose pliers to neaten the coils.

[4] Wrap the coil unit around the pencil to form a U shape **(photo c)**.

[5] Repeat steps 1–4 to make a total of seven coil units.

[6] Cut a 24-in. (61 cm) piece of beading wire. Center a coil unit with a 10 mm gemstone bead or pearl

sandwiched between the ends **(photo d)**.

[7] On each end, string a 6 mm large-hole copper bead or gemstone or pearl, a 10 mm, a 6 mm, and a coil unit with a 10 mm sandwiched between the ends. Repeat twice, and string a 6 mm.

[8] On each end, string an alternating pattern of an 8 mm gemstone bead or pearl and a 3 mm large-hole copper bead or gemstone or pearl to the desired length.

[9] Test the fit, and add or remove beads as needed.

[10] On each end, string two crimp beads and half of the clasp. Go back through the crimp beads, crimp the crimp beads (Basics, p. 13), and trim the tails. Close a crimp cover over each crimp.

Earrings

[1] Cut a 12-in. (30 cm) piece of 16-gauge wire, and make a coil unit as in steps 1–4 of "Necklace."

[2] Cut a 4-in. (10 cm) piece of 20-gauge wire. Center a coil unit with a 10 mm gemstone bead or pearl sandwiched between the ends.

[3] Bend both ends of the 20-gauge wire up, and cross the wire ends over the top of the 10 mm. Bend one end straight up, wrap the other end around it twice, and trim the tail **(photo e)**.

[4] String a 6 mm large-hole copper bead or gemstone or pearl and a 3 mm large-hole copper bead or gemstone or pearl. Make a wrapped loop (Basics).

[5] Open the loop of an earring finding (Basics), attach the wrapped loop, and close the loop.

[6] Make a second earring. ●

DESIGNER'S NOTE:

If the end coils are not parallel, use pliers to tighten the coil until the ends are aligned. Take care not to change the shape of the coiled piece.

a

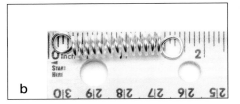

b

c

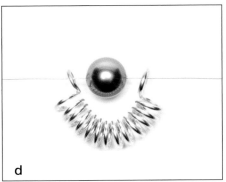

d

e

Following
the curve

Keeping the right-from-the-package curve in jewelry wire makes it easier to shape this ring.

Make a comfortable ring with just a bit of wire and two pretty beads

designed by **Lilian Chen**

a

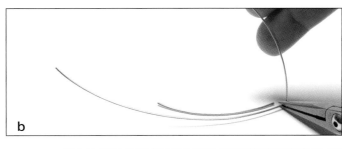

b

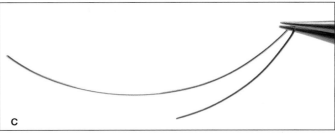

c

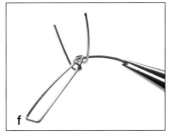

d

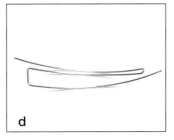

e

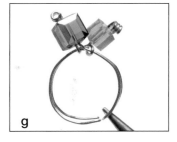

f

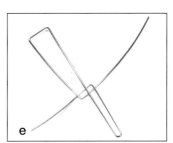

g

materials

ring

- cube crystals
  8 mm
  6 mm
- 6 in. (15 cm) 20-gauge
  square or round wire
- 3-in. (7.6 cm) piece of
  scrap wire
- ring mandrel
- chainnose pliers
- flatnose pliers
- roundnose pliers
- wire cutters

Take a piece of wire, make a few strategically placed bends, attach a pair of crystals, and you have a high-fashion ring.

step by step

[1] Wrap a piece of scrap wire around your finger or a ring mandrel to determine your ring size. Cut the scrap wire to this measurement **(photo a)**.
[2] Straighten the piece of scrap wire with your fingers, leaving it slightly curved, to create a ring template.
[3] Cut a 6-in. (15 cm) piece of 20-gauge wire. Do not straighten it.
[4] With the ring wire lying flat on your work surface, center the template wire next to the ring wire.

[5] Holding your chainnose or flatnose pliers parallel to the work surface with the lower jaw touching the work surface, grasp the ring wire, and make a right-angle bend at the end point of the template wire by slowly pulling the ring wire upward **(photo b)**.
[6] Hold the wire with roundnose pliers at the point of the bend, and slowly pull and twist the end of the wire into a U-shaped curve, maintaining a parallel curve with the longer section of the ring wire **(photo c)**.

[7] Make a right-angle bend at the point of the other end of the template wire, then make another bend about ¼ in. (6 mm) away, so the wire end goes toward the bend made in steps 5 and 6 **(photo d)**.
[8] Make a right-angle bend across the center of the band with each end **(photo e)**.
[9] Wrap the end of one wire around the two parallel wires with the end pointing away from the curve of the band. Repeat with the other wire **(photo f)**.

[10] Curve the wire around the ring mandrel at the appropriate size. String a crystal on one wire end, and make a coil with roundnose pliers to hold it in place. Repeat with the other wire end **(photo g)**.
[11] Adjust the band as needed to fit your finger. ●

All the hoop-la

Hang gemstones from a chain of large jump rings

designed by **Kimberly Berlin**

Feel like a rock star
when you display your
favorite gemstones.

a

b

c

d

Linked jump rings create a flat chain, allowing gemstones to fan out for maximum display. Use large jump rings for a bold statement or smaller jump rings for a more delicate version.

step by step

Note: Some of the step-by-step photos show colored jump rings to make it easier to see the order of attachment.

Gemstone necklace, p. 224
Links
[1] Cut a 2½-in. (6.4 cm) piece of 16-gauge wire. File the ends or use a wire rounder to smooth the ends.
[2] Use roundnose pliers to turn a simple loop at one end of the wire. Make a simple loop on the other end of the wire as a mirror image of the first simple loop.
[3] Using roundnose pliers, bend the wire in half with the backs of the simple loops touching to form a link **(photo a)**. Hammer the link. If the wire spreads, push the link back into shape.
[4] Repeat steps 1–3 11 times to make a total of 12 links.

Clasp
[1] Cut a 5-in. (13 cm) piece of 16-gauge wire, and file or round the ends.
[2] Use roundnose pliers to turn a simple loop at one end of the wire. Bend the wire into a hook so the simple loop touches the straight edge of the working wire **(photo b)**. On the opposite end of the wire, make a wrapped loop (Basics, p. 13).
[3] Hammer the hook and loop of the clasp **(photo c)**.
[4] Cut a 4-in. (10 cm) piece of 16-gauge wire, and file or round the ends. Make a plain loop (Basics) on one end, and make a wrapped loop on the other end. Twist the loops so they are perpendicular to each other, and hammer the loops **(photo d)**.

---

materials
both necklaces
- bench block or anvil
- chasing hammer
- metal file or wire rounder
- ruler
- chainnose pliers
- flatnose pliers
- roundnose pliers
- flush wire cutters

gemstone necklace 17 in. (43 cm)
- 5 15–20 mm gemstone beads
- 4 8–12 mm gemstone beads
- 5 4–6 mm gemstone beads
- 18 4 mm spacers
- 39 in. (.99 m) 16-gauge round sterling silver wire
- 9 2½-in. (6.4 cm) 22-gauge head pins
- 26 12 mm inside-diameter (ID) jump rings, 16-gauge
- 21 6 mm ID jump rings, 16-gauge
- 18 5 mm ID jump rings, 16-gauge

crystal necklace 17 in. (43 cm)
- 3 8 mm round crystals
- 4 6 mm round crystals
- 14 3 mm faceted silver beads
- 7 4 mm spacers
- 65 in. (1.7 m) 16-gauge round sterling silver wire
- 7 2-in. (5 cm) 22-gauge head pins
- 38 10 mm inside-diameter (ID) jump rings, 16-gauge
- 53 4 mm ID jump rings, 16-gauge

Wirework

e

f

g

h

i

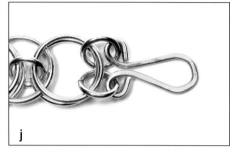

j

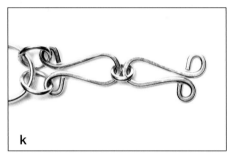

k

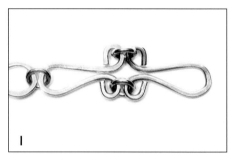

l

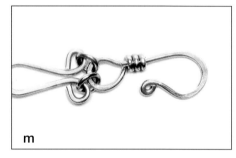

m

Jump ring chain

[1] Close 26 12 mm jump rings, and open eight 6 mm jump rings (Basics).

[2] On a 6 mm jump ring, attach two 12 mm jump rings, and lay one to the left and one to the right of the 6 mm jump ring (photo e).

[3] Lay a 12 mm jump ring over the 6 mm jump ring (photo f).

[4] Attach two 12 mm jump rings as in step 2, and close the 6 mm jump ring (photo g).

[5] Flip the top right 12 mm jump ring to the left. With an open 6 mm jump ring, attach the bottom right 12 mm jump ring and a new 12 mm jump ring. Lay a 12 mm jump ring over the 6 mm jump ring as in step 3 (photo h).

[6] With the open 6 mm jump ring, attach the top right 12 mm jump ring that was flipped in step 5 and a new 12 mm jump ring. Close the 6 mm jump ring (photo i).

[7] Repeat steps 5 and 6 six times to attach all 26 12 mm jump rings.

Necklace assembly

[1] Open a 6 mm jump ring, attach two end 12 mm jump rings and a loop of a link, and close the 6 mm jump ring. Repeat for the other loop of the link (photo j).

[2] Open a 5 mm jump ring, attach the center of the link and the center of a new link, and close the 5 mm jump ring (photo k).

[3] Open a 5 mm jump ring, attach a loop of the link and a loop of a new link, and close the 5 mm jump ring. Repeat for the remaining loops on the links (photo l).

[4] Repeat steps 2 and 3 twice, but in the last repeat of step 3, attach half of the clasp instead of a new link (photo m).

[5] Repeat steps 1–4 for the other half of the necklace.

Gemstone dangles

[1] On a head pin, string a 4 mm spacer, a 15–20 mm gemstone bead, a 4–6 mm gemstone bead, and a 4 mm spacer. Make a wrapped loop to form a large gemstone dangle. Repeat four

times to make a total of five large gemstone dangles, and set them aside.

[2] On a head pin, string a 4 mm spacer, an 8–12 mm gemstone bead, and a 4 mm spacer, and make a wrapped loop. Repeat three times to make a total of four small gemstone dangles, and set them aside.

[3] Determine the order in which you want to attach the gemstone dangles. Open a 6 mm jump ring, attach a gemstone dangle and a pair of 12 mm jump rings, and close the 6 mm jump ring (photo n).

[4] Repeat step 3 for the remaining gemstone dangles.

n

Spiral components add a new twist to the necklace.

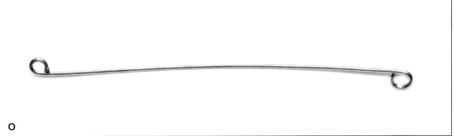

o

Crystal necklace, above right

[1] Follow the steps in "Gemstone necklace: Links" to make 16 links using 2-in. (5 cm) pieces of 16-gauge wire.

[2] Make a clasp as in "Gemstone necklace: Clasp."

[3] Make a jump ring chain as in "Gemstone necklace: Jump ring chain," but use 10 mm jump rings in place of the 12 mm jump rings and 4 mm jump rings in place of the 6 mm jump rings, and continue until you have connected all 38 10 mm jump rings.

[4] Connect the links and clasp as in "Gemstone necklace: Necklace assembly," but connect eight links on each side of the necklace.

[5] To make a spiral dangle, cut a 4-in. (10 cm) piece of 16-gauge wire, and make a small simple loop at one end. Repeat on the opposite end, making the loop face in the opposite direction (photo o). Use roundnose pliers and your fingers to form a spiral with one loop until the spiral touches the other loop. Hammer the spiral.

[6] Repeat step 5 five times to make a total of six spirals.

[7] On a head pin, string a 3 mm faceted silver bead, an 8 mm round crystal, a 4 mm spacer, and a 3 mm. Make a wrapped loop. Repeat twice to make three 8 mm crystal dangles, and four times with 6 mm round crystals instead of 8 mms.

[8] Determine the order in which you want to attach the spirals and crystal dangles. Open a 4 mm jump ring, attach a spiral or crystal dangle and a pair of 10 mm jump rings, and close the 4 mm jump ring.

[9] Repeat step 8 for the remaining spirals and crystal dangles. o

Keshi cuff

Create an organic bracelet with freshwater pearls and crystals

designed by **Candice Sexton**

Weave a wire frame that lends support to center-drilled keshi pearls, which appear to float with clusters of crystals.

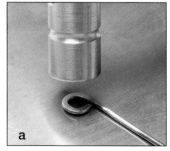

a

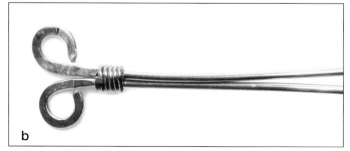

b

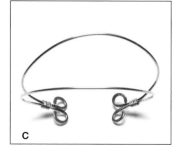

c

Create the frame for this cuff with heavy-gauge wire, then add crystals, pearls, and seed beads for color and texture.

Use pastel-hued crystals and pearls with silver wire for a feminine look or pressed glass with colorful craft wire for a funky edge.

step by step

If the holes in your pearls are too small to accommodate two passes of 28-gauge wire, use a bead reamer to enlarge them, twisting gently to avoid breaking the pearls. To avoid breathing in pearl dust, ream the pearls under water.

Use chainnose pliers to neaten all wire wraps.

Frame

[1] Measure your wrist, add 1½ in. (3.8 cm) to the measurement, and cut two pieces of 14-gauge wire to that length. Use roundnose pliers to turn a simple loop at each end of each wire. If desired, hammer each loop to flatten the wire **(photo a)**.
[2] Cut a 2-in. (5 cm) piece of 20-gauge wire. Hold the 14-gauge wires together so the loops face away from each other, and tightly wrap the 20-gauge wire around them five or six times at one end **(photo b)**.
[3] Bend the 14-gauge wires into a cuff shape to fit comfortably around your wrist. Cut a 2-in. (5 cm) piece of 20-gauge wire, and wrap it two to three times around the remaining ends of the 14-gauge wire. Spread the pieces of 14-gauge wire apart to form a canoe shape,

and finish wrapping the 20-gauge wire to keep the shape **(photo c)**.

Support structure

[1] Cut a 32-in. (81 cm) piece of 20-gauge wire, and tightly wrap one end two or three times around one end of the frame. Working in a loose zigzagging pattern, wrap the wire around the frame, keeping the wraps about ¼–½ in. (6–13 mm) apart. Wrap the wire tightly around the remaining end of the frame **(photo d)**.
[2] Cut a 24-in. (61 cm) piece of 24-gauge wire, and tightly wrap one end two or three times around the 20-gauge wire at one end of the zigzag. Weave the 24-gauge wire lengthwise through the 20-gauge wire, crisscrossing back and forth through the support structure **(photo e)**, and wrap the tail tightly around the 20-gauge wire.

Embellishment

[1] Cut a 12-in. (30 cm) piece of 28-gauge wire. Tightly wrap one end two or three times around a wire in the support structure, and bring the wire up through the front of the frame.
[2] String a 6–8 mm center-drilled keshi pearl and an 11º

seed bead. Skip the 11º, and go back through the pearl and support structure **(photo f)**.
[3] Wrap the 28-gauge wire around the wire in the support structure, feed it back up through the front next to the pearl, and wrap it around the base of the pearl two to three times to tighten the pearl in place **(photo g)**. Feed the wire down through the support structure and back up to exit the front.
[4] Repeat steps 2 and 3 using a combination of pearls, 6 mm bicone crystals, and 4 mm round crystals, sometimes stacking a crystal on top of a pearl, and using 11ºs and 15º seed beads as desired.
[5] To end a wire, wrap it tightly around a wire in the support structure. To add a new wire, repeat step 1, and continue adding pearls and crystals as before until the whole cuff is embellished. ●

DESIGNER'S NOTE: Take care to avoid kinking the wire. If the wire does kink, try to gently straighten it by unfolding it at the point of the kink rather than pulling and breaking the wire.

materials
bracelet 8 in. (20 cm)
- 65–80 6–8 mm center-drilled keshi pearls (Ta Pearlstone, tapearlstone.com)
- 12–15 6 mm bicone crystals
- 15–20 4 mm round crystals
- 1–3 g 11º seed beads
- 1–3 g 15º seed beads
- 14–18 in. (36–46 cm) 14-gauge wire, half-hard
- 1 yd. (.9 m) 20-gauge wire
- 24 in. (61 cm) 24-gauge wire
- 4–5 yd. (3.7–4.6 m) 28-gauge wire
- bead reamer (optional)
- bench block or anvil (optional)
- hammer (optional)
- chainnose pliers
- roundnose pliers
- wire cutters

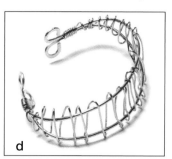

d

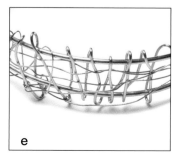

e

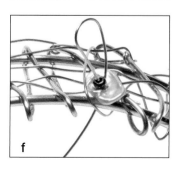

f

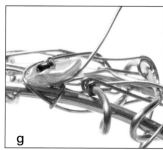

g

Beaded clusters

Twist an assortment of beads into an organic necklace

designed by **Jean Ann Reeves**

Mix colors and finishes for a refreshing blend
of your favorite leftover beads.

materials
necklace 20 in. (51 cm)

- **140–180** 4–10 mm assorted glass beads, crystals, and pearls
- 5–7 g 6º seed beads
- 5–7 g 8º seed beads
- 5–7 g 11º seed beads
- toggle clasp
- 6½ yd. (5.9 m) 24-gauge wire
- 4 crimp beads
- 4 crimp covers (optional)
- flexible beading wire, .018–.020
- chainnose pliers
- crimping pliers
- roundnose pliers
- wire cutters

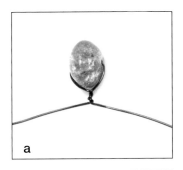

a

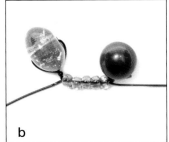

b

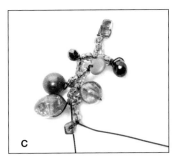

c

d

e

f

g

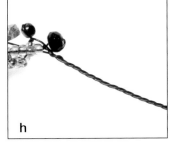

h

Create a bead soup with beads in pleasing shapes, sizes, and colors for a necklace that displays beauty and variety. Choose craft wire in a color that coordinates with the beads, or use a precious-metal wire that will stand out.

stepbystep

Focal cluster

[1] Cut a 5-ft. (1.5 m) piece of 24-gauge wire, and fold it in half. String a 4–10 mm bead to the fold, and twist the wire together three times **(photo a)**.
[2] On one side, string three to seven 6º, 8º, and/or 11º seed beads and a 4–10 mm bead. Twist the wire around the base of the 4–10 mm bead **(photo b)**.
[3] Repeat step 2 seven times for a total of eight units.
[4] Fold the beaded portion of wire in half, and twist the beaded wire together to form a cluster. Bend the larger beads to one surface to create the front of the necklace. This allows the seed beads to serve as the background support structure **(photo c)**.
[5] Weave the unbeaded wire through the bead cluster to exit the opposite end, and repeat steps 2–4.
[6] Twist the unbeaded wire ends around beads in both clusters to hold the clusters together **(photo d)**.
[7] On one wire, repeat steps 2–4. Weave the working wire around the beads in the new cluster and the previous cluster to connect the clusters **(photo e)**. Repeat to the end of the wire, and weave the tail into the beadwork.
[8] Repeat step 7 on the remaining wire.
[9] Cut a 5-ft. (1.5 m) piece of 24-gauge wire, and weave one end into the beadwork to anchor the wire. Continue adding bead clusters as before.
[10] Repeat step 9 on the other side of the beadwork. If needed, continue cutting new wire and adding bead clusters on alternating sides of the original cluster until the bead clusters measure about 6 in. (15 cm) or your desired length.

Bridging clusters

[1] Cut an 18-in. (46 cm) piece of 24-gauge wire, and fold it in half. String it through an end loop of the focal cluster, and twist the wire together **(photo f)**.
[2] On each half of the wire, make five to seven units as in steps 2 and 3 of "Focal cluster." Twist the beaded units together **(photo g)**. Bend the large beads to the front of the necklace.
[3] Repeat steps 1 and 2 on the remaining end of the focal cluster.
[4] Cut a 20-in. (51 cm) piece of 24-gauge wire to reinforce the structure of the necklace. Leaving a 2-in. (5 cm) tail, weave the wire through the bead clusters from one end of the necklace to the other. Add beads to conceal the wire as desired.
[5] On one end, twist the tails of the beaded clusters and the reinforcing wire together **(photo h)**. With all three wires twisted together, make a plain or wrapped loop (Basics, p. 13). Repeat on the other end.

Assembly

[1] Cut an 8-in. (20 cm) piece of beading wire. String a crimp bead, six 11º seed beads, and the loop of a bridging cluster. Go back through the crimp bead, and crimp it (Basics).
[2] Determine the final length of your necklace, and subtract the length of the clasp and focal and bridging clusters. Divide the remainder in two, and string assorted 4–10 mms and seed beads to that length.
[3] String a crimp bead and half of the clasp. Go back through the crimp bead and the next few beads. Crimp the crimp bead, and trim the wire. If desired, close a crimp cover over each crimp with chainnose pliers.
[4] Repeat steps 1–3 on the remaining end. ●

DESIGNER'S NOTE: String your beads in a random order for an organic look.

Miscellaneous Techniques

STRINGING
Outside
the box

Experiment with bead
combinations to create
a variety of necklaces.

**Challenge yourself to
create a chic necklace with different
shapes of beads and a new color palette**

designed by **Jennifer Curran**

Using the copper-edged red Czech glass cube beads as a guide, Jennifer paired red with copper for a warm combination.

a

b

c

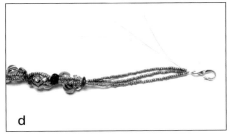

d

EDITOR'S NOTE:
Step up to the creative challenge and play around with a color you don't normally use in your bead-work. This necklace is the result of *Bead&Button* Associate Editor Tea Benduhn's experimentation with her little-used color: pink.

When a friend handed Jennifer a collection of beads, it gave her the creative push she needed to step outside of her color box and work with a hue she doesn't usually use — red.

stepbystep

[1] Cut three 20-in. (51 cm) pieces of illusion cord, and center a 10–20 mm Czech glass cube, gemstone, or metal bead on all three cords. On each end, string a 9–15 mm glass or metal bead, a 10–20 mm, and a 6 mm glass or metal bead (photo a).
[2] On one end of one cord, string three 12 x 8 mm teardrop beads. On each of the remaining two cords, string 12 11º seed beads (photo b).
[3] On all three cords, string a 4 mm spacer (photo c).

[4] Repeat steps 2 and 3 four times, alternating between a 6 mm and a spacer in step 3.
[5] On each cord, string about 2½ in. (6.4 cm) of 11ºs.
[6] On all three cords, string a crimp bead and half of a clasp. Go back through the crimp bead, but do not crimp it (photo d).
[7] Repeat steps 2–6 on the other end of the necklace.
[8] Test the fit, and add or remove 11ºs as needed. Crimp both crimp beads (Basics, p. 13), and trim the cords. Close a crimp cover over each crimp bead with chainnose pliers. ●

materials
necklace 15½ in. (39.4 cm)
- 30 12 x 8 mm teardrop beads
- 3 10–20 mm Czech glass cube, gemstone, or metal beads
- 2 9–15 mm glass or metal beads
- 6 6 mm glass or metal beads
- 4–6 g 11º seed beads
- 6 4 mm spacers
- clasp
- 2 crimp beads
- 2 crimp covers
- illusion cord, 8 lb. test
- chainnose pliers
- crimping pliers

Stringing

Flower garden

Embellish an art glass bead with cascading fringe

by **Anna Elizabeth Draeger**

a

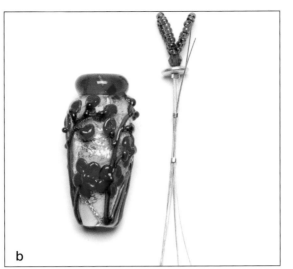

b

c

Let the hues of a lampworked glass bead inspire your color palette for a simple, contemporary necklace.

stepbystep

Pendant

[1] Cut two 20-in. (51 cm) pieces of .010 beading wire. Center 17 11º seed beads on each wire, and string a 4 mm round crystal over all four wire ends. String an 8 mm spacer and a 2 x 2 mm crimp bead **(photo a)**. Flatten the crimp bead (Basics, p. 13).

[2] Cut two 10-in. (25 cm) pieces of .010 beading wire, and string two 2 x 2 mm crimp beads over both ends. Hold the crimp beads about 1 in. (2.5 cm) from the wire ends, and string the four wire ends from step 1 through both crimp beads. Space the crimp beads out, making sure they don't extend past the length of the art glass bead **(photo b)**. Flatten the crimp beads, and trim the 1-in. (2.5 cm) tails close to the middle crimp.

[3] String the art glass bead over all six of the wires.

[4] Trim the wires to various lengths, or leave all the wires the same length, if desired.

[5] Gently curl each wire by dragging it between your forefinger and thumbnail until you achieve the desired curl, leaving about ½–1 in. (1.3–2.5 cm) of straight wire at the end to string the beads on. Do this very carefully; you can always make the wire curl more, but not less. You can also leave the wires straight, if desired.

[6] On one wire, string a pleasing arrangement of 11º seed beads, 4 mms, and 3 mm bicone crystals. Note that the 11ºs may slide into the art glass bead since the hole is larger than the 11ºs, but that will only happen for the first fringe. At the end of the wire, string a microcrimp bead, and crimp it. Trim any excess wire.

[7] Repeat on the remaining wires.

Necklace

[1] On 24 in. (61 cm) of .014 beading wire, string a 2 x 3 mm crimp bead and half of the clasp. Go back through the crimp bead, and crimp it. Trim the short wire close to the crimp, and cover the crimp with a crimp cover.

[2] String a repeating pattern of an 8 mm diagonally drilled glass cube bead and an 8 mm spacer 10 times.

[3] String a repeating pattern of an 8 mm round gemstone and an 8 mm spacer 12 times, and then string an 8 mm round.

[4] String a 3 mm round spacer, one loop of the bail, an 8 mm cube bead, the other loop of the bail, and a 3 mm spacer **(photo c)**.

[5] String the second half of the necklace as a mirror image of the first, and attach the second half of the clasp as in step 1. ●

materials

necklace 19 in. (48 cm)

- art glass bead (Leah Fairbanks, leahfairbanks.com)
- **26** 8 mm round gemstone beads
- **21** 8 mm diagonally drilled glass cube beads
- **25–30** 4 mm round crystals
- **25–30** 3 mm bicone crystals
- **3–4 g** 11º seed beads
- **45** 8 mm flat spacers
- **2** 3 mm round silver spacers
- clasp
- crimp beads
  2 2 x 3 mm
  3 2 x 2 mm
  6 microcrimps
- **2** 3 mm crimp covers
- beading wire, .010 and .014
- chainnose pliers
- crimping pliers
- microcrimping pliers
- wire cutters

Stringing

237

Rock collector

String pyrite chunks, lava lentils, and faceted blue goldstone for a necklace that will capture the eye of an aspiring geologist

by **Tea Benduhn**

Shades of black and silver make a harmonious necklace.

Show your fun and funky side with rough-hewn gemstone beads and nuggets.

step by step

[1] On a 2-in. (5 cm) head pin, string the largest of the 10–15 mm pyrite nuggets. Make a plain loop (Basics, p. 13) at the end of the head pin.
[2] Repeat step 1 twice on two 1½-in. (3.8 cm) head pins, using the remaining pyrite nuggets.

[3] Cut an 18-in. (46 cm) piece of beading wire. String a crimp bead and half of the clasp. Go back through the crimp bead, and crimp it (Basics).
[4] String 25 4 x 6 mm faceted blue goldstone beads.
[5] String three 18–20 mm lentil beads, the loop of a 1½-in. (3.8 cm) head pin, a lentil, the loop of the 2-in.

(5 cm) head pin, a lentil, the loop of a 1½-in. (3.8 cm) head pin, three lentils, and 25 4 x 6 mms.
[6] String a crimp bead and the remaining half of the clasp. Go back through the crimp bead and a few 4 x 6 mms. Crimp the crimp bead, and trim the excess wire.
[7] Using crimping pliers, close crimp covers over the crimp beads. ●

materials
necklace 15 in. (38 cm)
- 8 18–20 mm lava lentil or coin beads (Harlequin Beads, harlequinbeads.com)
- 3 10–15 mm pyrite nuggets (Fire Mountain Gems and Beads, firemountaingems.com)
- 50 4 x 6 mm faceted blue goldstone beads
- clasp
- 2-in. (5 cm) head pin
- 2 1½-in. (3.8 cm) head pins
- 2 crimp beads
- 2 crimp covers
- flexible beading wire, .018
- chainnose pliers
- crimping pliers
- roundnose pliers
- wire cutters

EDITOR'S NOTE:
For a longer necklace, string additional 4 x 6 mm beads at each end to reach the desired length.

Autumn garland

This necklace works up so quickly, you may want to make one for every season.

Vintage-style flowers herald the colors of autumn

designed by **Maria Kirk**

Having worked as a florist for many years, Maria finds that most of her designs reflect her love of flowers and foliage. These Lucite flowers bunch beautifully around your neck, and their featherlight drape won't weigh you down.

step*by*step

[1] On 32 in. (81 cm) of thread, attach a Bead Stopper, leaving a 6-in. (15 cm) tail. String 6º seed beads for the desired necklace length, and attach a Bead Stopper, leaving at least 6 in. (15 cm) for the second tail.

[2] Tie a 1-yd. (.9 m) length of thread to the center of the beaded strand with an overhand knot (Basics, p. 13).
[3] Using one end of the thread, pick up one to three 8º or 11º seed beads, a 26–30 mm flower, a 7–26 mm flower, and one to three seed beads. Sew back through the flowers and the first seed beads

materials

necklace 20 in. (51 cm)
- 7 30–40 mm Lucite leaves
- 7 26–30 mm Lucite flowers
- **35–40** 14–30 mm Lucite leaves
- **25–30** 7–26 mm Lucite flowers
- 11–13 g 6º seed beads, color A
- 1–2 g 8º seed beads, color B
- 2–3 g 11º seed beads, color B
- 2–3 g 11º seed beads, color C
- 2–3 g 11º seed beads, color D
- lobster claw clasp
- 4 5–6 mm jump rings
- nylon beading thread
- beading needles, #12 or #13
- **2** Bead Stoppers
- **2** pairs of pliers

a

b

c

picked up **(photo a)**, then sew through the next 14 6⁰s on the strand.

[4] Working as in step 3, attach three more flowers to one side of the central flower, varying the size, number, and color of seed beads picked up. Using the other end of the thread, attach three more flowers to the other side. With each end of the thread, sew through the remaining 6⁰s on the strand, and secure the tails with the Bead Stoppers.

[5] Repeat step 2.

[6] With one end of the thread, exit a 6⁰ a few beads away from the central flower. Pick up three to five seed beads, a 30–40 mm leaf, and two to four seed beads. Sew back through at least one of the first seed beads picked up **(photo b)**, then sew through the 6⁰s to exit one or two beads from the next flower.

[7] Working as in step 6 and using both ends of the thread, attach a leaf for each flower, varying the size, number, and color of seed beads picked up. With each end of the thread, sew through the remaining 6⁰s on the strand, and secure the tails with the Bead Stoppers.

[8] Repeat step 2, and randomly attach the smaller flowers along the strand. Repeat to attach the smaller leaves. End these threads (Basics).

[9] Test the necklace for fit, and add or remove 6⁰s if necessary. On one end, remove the Bead Stopper. With one tail, pick up 12–15 11⁰ seed beads, sew back into the beaded strand, and end the thread. Repeat with the remaining tails, sewing through the same loop of beads. Repeat on the other end of the necklace.

[10] On one end, open a jump ring (Basics), and attach the beaded loop. Close the jump ring. Attach a second jump ring and a lobster claw clasp **(photo c)**. On the other end of the necklace, attach two jump rings. ●

EDITOR'S NOTE:
If you don't have Bead Stoppers, you can attach a stop bead (Basics) for each thread in the beaded strand.

DESIGNER'S NOTES:
• **Before attaching the smaller flowers and leaves, divide them into two groups of roughly the same number and size. Then divide the groups in half again. Attach one group to half of the necklace at a time so that the overall look of the piece is balanced.**
• **You can mix up the colors of the flowers and leaves, or gradate the colors along the length of the necklace.**
• **If you find a floppy flower or leaf, try sewing through it again for added stability. Or add a smaller flower, leaf, or loop of seed beads behind it.**

Asymmetrical
amethyst

Pair your favorite metal and gemstone in a swingy multistrand

by **Stacy Werkheiser**

When your necklace is done, leftover 6–7 mm round beads, extra chain links, and 3–4 mm spacers can easily be transformed into cute earrings.

step by step

[1] Cut a 2½-in. (6.4 cm) piece of 22-gauge wire, and make the first half of a wrapped loop (Basics, p. 13). String a 6–7 mm round bead, and make the first half of a wrapped loop. Repeat to

materials

necklace 38 in. (97 cm)

- **2** 8-in. (20 cm) strands 10–12 mm round beads
- **8** 6–7 mm round beads
- **36–46** 5–6 mm spacers
- **2** 30–32 mm hammered rings
- 41 in. (1 m) 22-gauge wire, half-hard
- 18 in. (46 cm) chain, 20–22 mm (large) links
- 12 in. (30 cm) chain, 5–6 mm (small) links
- 2-in. (5 cm) head pin
- **3** 7–8 mm jump rings
- **2** crimp beads
- flexible beading wire, .014–.015
- chainnose pliers
- crimping pliers
- roundnose pliers
- wire cutters

make eight bead units.
[2] Attach one loop of a bead unit to a 30–32 mm hammered ring, and complete the wraps. Attach the other loop to the end of a 12-in. (30 cm) piece of small-link chain, and complete the wraps. Open a 7–8 mm jump ring (Basics), and attach the other end of the chain to another hammered ring. Close the jump ring.
[3] Arrange the bead units along the chain as desired. For each bead unit, cut and remove a chain link, attach the loops of the unit to the unattached chain links, and complete the wraps.
[4] Cut an 18-in. (46 cm) piece of beading wire. Center 13 in. (33 cm) of 10–12 mm round beads and 5–6 mm spacers. On each end of the wire, string a crimp bead and a hammered ring. Go back through the crimp bead and the last few beads on each end, crimp the crimp beads (Basics), and trim the excess wire.
[5] Cut a 3-in. (7.6 cm) piece of wire, and make the first half of a wrapped loop. String a spacer, a 10–12 mm round, and a spacer. Make the first half of a wrapped loop. Repeat to make seven 10–12 mm bead units.

[6] Cut an 18-in. (46 cm) piece of large-link chain, and repeat step 3. Use jump rings to attach each end of the chain and a hammered ring.
[7] On a head pin, string a spacer, a 10–12 mm round, and a spacer, and make the first half of a wrapped loop. Attach the jump ring from step 2, and complete the wraps. ●

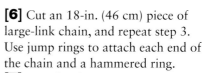

STRINGING

Simple sequences

Transform simple strands into an alluring accessory

by **Anna Elizabeth Draeger**

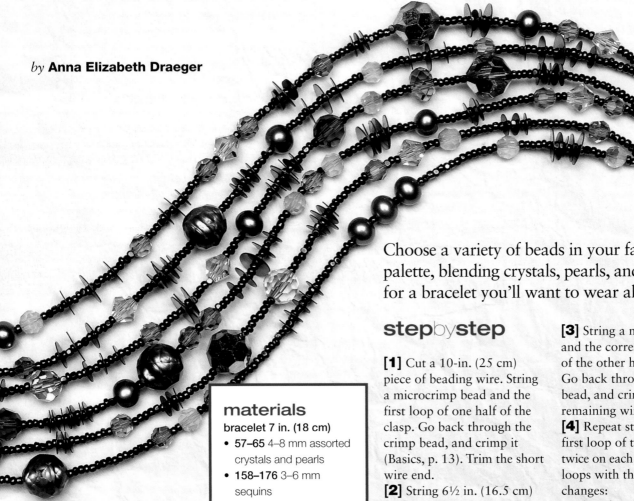

You can easily adapt this design to make a stunning multistrand necklace by stringing about 15–20 in. (38–51 cm) of beads on each strand.

materials
bracelet 7 in. (18 cm)
- **57–65** 4–8 mm assorted crystals and pearls
- **158–176** 3–6 mm sequins
- **4–5 g** 15º Charlottes
- 3-strand clasp
- **12** 1 x 1 mm microcrimp beads
- flexible beading wire, .010
- microcrimping pliers
- wire cutters

Choose a variety of beads in your favorite color palette, blending crystals, pearls, and sequins for a bracelet you'll want to wear all the time.

step by step

[1] Cut a 10-in. (25 cm) piece of beading wire. String a microcrimp bead and the first loop of one half of the clasp. Go back through the crimp bead, and crimp it (Basics, p. 13). Trim the short wire end.

[2] String 6½ in. (16.5 cm) of pearls, crystals, sequins, and 15º Charlottes, stringing the 15ºs between the larger beads and sequins to make a pleasing sequence. String three or more small beads or sequins together, separated by 15ºs, to make clusters along the strand.

[3] String a microcrimp bead and the corresponding loop of the other half of the clasp. Go back through the crimp bead, and crimp it. Trim the remaining wire end.

[4] Repeat steps 1–3 on the first loop of the clasp, then twice on each of the remaining loops with the following changes:
- Alter the number of 15ºs picked up in each sequence.
- Change up the styles and sizes of beads you are using.
- Switch the stringing order of the bead sequences. ●

METALWORK

Just riveting

Create custom bead caps, then use a classic cold-connection technique to make a stunning focal piece

designed by **Jima Abbott**

Jima Abbott's *Sun and Sea* necklace uses riveted hand-made bead caps to highlight Harlan Simon's art glass bead. You can see more of Harlan's beads at harlanbeads.com.

Highlight a bead with handmade bead caps to create a personalized centerpiece. Learning basic metalwork techniques like sawing, texturing, and tube riveting isn't hard, and these skills expand your jewelry-making possibilities to grand proportions.

step by step

Bead caps

[1] Plan how many bead caps you would like to stack on each end of the bead. The largest bead cap should start with a circle that is 10–12 percent larger than the diameter of the bead; for example, a cap for a 20 mm bead should start as a 22 mm diameter circle. Additional bead caps will be progressively smaller.

[2] Using the dividers or an appropriately sized template, draw a circle on the metal sheet using the felt-tip pen. Using the ruler, draw a line through the center of the circle. Draw a perpendicular line through the circle, then divide each of the four segments in half **(photo a)**. If you want a more detailed edging,

continue dividing each segment in half until you have the desired number of segments for your edging.

[3] Using your ruler or a template, mark each line an equal distance from the edge. Draw in your edging using the felt-tip pen **(photo b)**. This sample shows a large cap with a scalloped edge that comes in 1 mm from the outer circle. The outer cap on Jima's bead features an organic, irregular flame design, which comes in further from the outer circle. Once your design is finalized, trace it with the permanent marker. If desired, you can scribe the design with a scribe or sharp object before tracing it with the permanent marker to make the line sharper and easier to follow with your saw.

[4] Using the jeweler's saw, cut along the outer edge, following your lines. Use a hole punch, or a center punch and drill, to create a hole in the center of the disk **(photo c)**. Because dapping the disk into the dome shape will enlarge the hole, create a hole slightly smaller in diameter than your metal tubing.

[5] To decorate the disk with stampings, set the disk on an anvil or bench block, position the stamp where you would like the design to appear, and hit the end of the stamp with your hammer **(photo d)**. You can also use the hammer itself, a vibrating engraver, a flexible shaft, or other tools to create the textures and patterns you desire.

[6] Set the disk face down in the largest depression on your dapping block, and place the appropriate dapping punch above it. Hit the top of the dapping punch with your hammer to shape the disk **(photo e)**. Turn the disk several

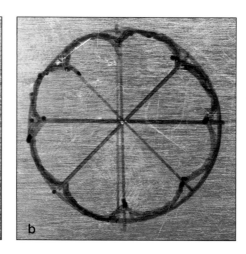

a

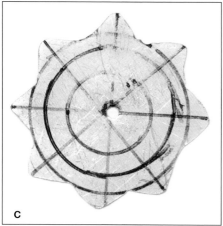

c

d

materials

one bead

- 18–25 mm focal bead with 5 mm or larger hole
- **1–3** 4 x 2-in. (10 x 5 cm) pieces of 22-gauge sterling silver or 24-gauge copper or brass sheet
- ⅞–1¼ in. (2.2–3.2 cm) sterling silver tubing, ³⁄₁₆-in. (5 mm) outside diameter
- anvil or bench block
- ball-peen hammer
- bench pin
- dapping block and dapping punches
- dividers or circle templates
- files: round, flat, and half round
- fine-tip permanent marker
- hole punch, or center punch and drill
- jeweler's fine-grit sandpaper
- jeweler's saw and 4/0 blades
- liver of sulfur or Black Max oxidizer (optional)
- metal stamps or other materials for texturing metal
- nonpermanent felt-tip pen
- plumb bob or tapered tool
- polishing cloth
- ruler
- scribe (optional)
- vibrating engraver or flexible shaft (optional)

e

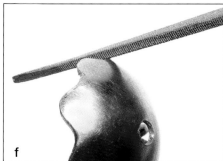

f

g

h

i

EDITOR'S NOTE:
Jima has been making riveted beads for 10 years, but if you're just getting started with metalwork, here are a few tips:
• **Start with a simple design.** It takes time to learn to saw well, so large scallop or star designs are easier for beginners than finely detailed designs.
• **Practice, practice, practice.** Use inexpensive brass or copper sheet metal to practice sawing, texturing, and shaping your bead caps before you start using more expensive metals.
• **Experiment with focal beads.** If you're nervous about using a hammer near a beautiful art glass bead, start out using sturdy resin beads as your focals.
• **If your beads keep rolling as you start your rivets,** set them back in the dapping block for the first few taps.

times, and continue dapping until the disk conforms to the dome of the depression. Remove the disk from the depression, and set it in the next smallest depression. Continue dapping, changing dapping punches as needed and checking the size of the bead cap against the bead frequently. Smaller bead caps may not need to be dapped as tightly as larger bead caps; check the size of the cap against the cap it will sit next to.

[7] Refine the edges of the bead cap with the files **(photo f)**. If necessary, enlarge the hole in the bead cap using a round file.

[8] Repeat steps 2–7 to make the desired number of bead caps for both ends. If desired, oxidize the caps using liver of sulfur or Black Max according to the manufacturer's instructions. Polish the pieces with a polishing cloth.

Assembly

[1] String the bead caps and focal bead on the tubing in the desired order, leaving 1/16 in. (2 mm) of the tubing protruding from the end. Mark the tubing 1/16 in. (2 mm) from the other side of the bead with the permanent marker **(photo g)**.

[2] Remove the pieces from the tubing, and use the jeweler's saw to cut the tubing at the marked line. Replace the pieces on the tubing, and set them securely on a hard surface, such as a work bench or bench block. The bead needs to be held firmly in place so it will not wobble or roll as you work, and you need to be able to turn the piece over repeatedly.

[3] Position the plumb bob or tapered tool in the tubing **(photo h)**, and strike twice with the hammer to begin flaring the tubing. Flip the bead over, and repeat on the other side. Repeat again on each side as necessary to get a flare started that will hold the beads in place.

[4] Progress to using the small dapping punch in your set, and increase the size of the flared tube on each side. Use the hammer to flatten the rivet so it is almost flush with the surface of your bead **(photo i)**.

[5] Sand the bead caps as necessary to remove any hammer marks, and polish with the polishing cloth. ●

Dressed up in black and silver, this three-loop necklace and bracelet (left) are perfect for a holiday gathering or evening out. Dressed down in shades of purple and indigo, the two-loop bracelet (right) is great as a casual-wear accessory.

An easy way to bead crochet

Crochet loops of beads into quick-and-easy jewelry

bracelets designed by **Adele Rogers Recklies**
necklace designed by **Keiko Seki**

While the origin of this variation of bead crochet is unclear, Adele Rogers Recklies calls it Turkish Loops because she learned it from a Turkish beader in 2007 while in Turkey for the International Bead and Beadwork Conference. The technique, also known as perlen crochet or jewelry crochet, has appeared in Japan, Germany, and Austria, among other places. Regardless of the origin, it is an easy-to-learn variation on a technique that sometimes makes beginners want to cry in frustration. Try the two-loop bracelet first to get the hang of the technique. Next, move on to the three-loop bracelet and the necklace. After that, work out your own variations, and let us know how they come out!

step by step

Two-loop bracelet

[1] With a twisted-wire or Big Eye needle attached to the end of the cord, string a repeating pattern of four 11º seed beads, a color A 4 mm fire-polished bead, four 11ºs, and a color B 4 mm fire-polished bead 41 times. Make a slip knot (Basics, p. 13) about 8 in. (20 cm) from the end of the cord, and insert your hook into the slip knot.

[2] Slide the first group of one 4 mm and four 11ºs down to the knot, and,

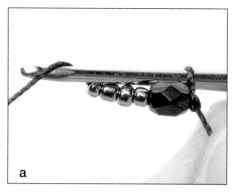

a

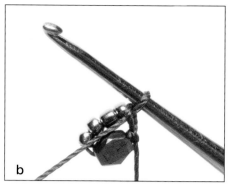

b

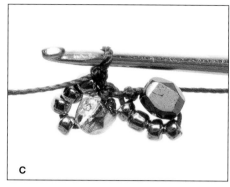

c

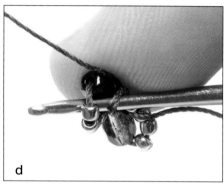

d

e

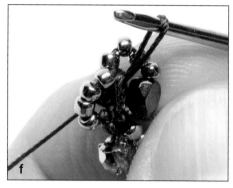

f

with the hook, grasp the cord right after the fourth 11º **(photo a)**. Pull the cord through the loop on the hook to work a chain stitch **(photo b)**. Grasp the cord with the hook, and pull it through the loop on the hook to work another chain stitch without beads.

[3] Repeat step 2 **(photo c)**. You have now completed the stitches for round 1, which consists of two beaded loops. It will be pulled into a tubular form in the next round.

[4] Insert the hook in the middle of the first loop in the previous round, sliding it between the 4 mm and the first 11º. Make sure the 4 mm is behind the hook and the 11ºs are in front of the hook **(photo d)**. Slide the next group of beads up to the previous stitch. The 4 mm in the new stitch should be the same color

as the 4 mm in the stitch into which you inserted your hook. With the hook, grasp the cord after the fourth 11º **(photo e)**, and pull it through the loop on the hook to work a slip stitch **(photo f)**. Grasp the cord again, and pull it through the loop on the hook to work a slip stitch without beads, making sure it is worked between the two groups of 11ºs. Repeat in the second loop of the previous round.

[5] Work as in step 4 until the rope is about 1½ in. (3.8 cm) short of the desired length. Place a paper clip or safety pin in the last stitch to temporarily hold your place.

[6] Attach a beading needle to the tail, and string a bead cap, three or four 11ºs, the button, and three or four 11ºs.

[7] Sew back through the bead cap, and continue into the crochet stitches at the end of the bracelet **(photo g)**. Sew around the cord in the core of the bracelet, and retrace the thread path through the bead cap, the 11ºs, and the button, exiting through the core of the bracelet. Tie a half-hitch knot (Basics), weave the tail through the bracelet core a few times, and trim.

[8] Remove the paper clip or safety pin, and continue working in two-loop crochet until the rope is the desired length or you've used all the beads. Work one more round without beads to close up the end. Leaving a 12-in. (30 cm) tail, trim the cord, and pull it through the last stitch.

[9] Attach a beading needle, and string a bead cap and enough 11ºs to make a loop around the button. Sew back through the bead cap, and continue into the crochet stitches at the end of the bracelet. Secure and end the cord as in step 7.

Three-loop bracelet
Work as in the two-loop bracelet, with the following changes:
• Begin by stringing a repeating pattern of four 11ºs and a 4 mm 111 times.

A monochromatic color palette suits this design well, enhancing the elegant lines and spiraling pattern.

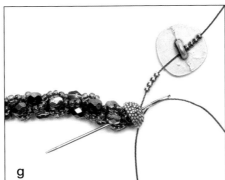

g

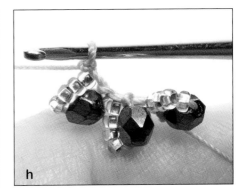

h

i

Wear it two ways: Dangle the drop in front for a Y-necklace, or wear it in back for a classic round neckline.

- Make round 1 with three loops instead of two (photo h).
- Work three sets of stitches per round.

Necklace

[1] String the following sequence a total of 55 times: a color A 6 mm bugle bead, two color A 11º seed beads, a 4 mm pearl, a color B 6 mm bugle bead, four color B 11º seed beads, a color C 6 mm bugle bead, and four color C 11º seed beads. Make a slip knot 12 in. (30 cm) from the end of the cord, and insert the hook into the slip knot.

[2] To work the first round, slide the first group of color C beads up to the slip knot, and work a chain stitch. Work another chain stitch without any beads. Slide the group of color B beads up, and work two chain stitches. Slide the group of color A beads up, and work two chain stitches.

[3] Work in three-loop crochet as in the bracelet, inserting the hook after the bugle in each stitch. Continue until

you've stitched all the beads. Work three more stitches without beads to tighten up the end, trim the cord to 8 in. (20 cm), and pull the tail through the last stitch.

[4] Attach a beading needle to the 12-in. (30 cm) tail, and pick up an alternating sequence of fire-polished beads and spacers to equal about 2½–3 in. (6.4–7.6 cm). Pick up five 11ºs in your choice of color, the loop half of the toggle clasp, and five 11ºs, and sew back through the beads just added and into the core of the crochet rope (photo i). Retrace the thread path through all the beads and the clasp, and end the cord within the rope, as in step 7 of "Two-loop bracelet."

[5] Attach a beading needle to the other end, and pick up a spacer, five 11ºs, the bar half of the clasp, and five 11ºs. Sew back through the spacer, and continue into the end of the crochet rope. Retrace the thread path, and end the cord.

[6] To add the dangle, on 18 in. (46 cm) of beading thread, pick up a 4 mm pearl, a spacer bead, a 6 mm fire-polished bead, a spacer, a 10 mm fire-polished bead, a spacer, the 20 x 12 mm bead, and three seed beads. Skip the seed beads, and sew back through the rest of the beads added in this step.

[7] Pick up 10 11ºs and the toggle loop, and retrace the thread path through the dangle beads. Sew back through them again so both the working thread and the tail are coming out between the same beads, and tie a square knot (Basics). End the threads (Basics). ●

materials

all projects

- beading cord, size E or F or equivalent
- twisted-wire or Big Eye needle
- beading needle, #10
- 1.5 mm crochet hook
- paper clip or safety pin

two-loop bracelet 7 in. (18 cm)

- **41** 4 mm fire-polished beads in each of **2** colors: A, B
- **5** g 11º seed beads
- shank button
- **2** 6–8 mm bead caps

three-loop bracelet 7 in. (18 cm)

- **111** 4 mm fire-polished beads
- **5** g 11º seed beads
- shank button
- **2** 9–10 mm bead caps

necklace 17 in. (43 cm) plus 2½-in. (6.4 cm) dangle

- 20 x 12 mm glass or gemstone focal bead
- **7** 6–12 mm fire-polished beads
- **56** 4 mm faux pearls, color A
- **55** 6 mm bugle beads in each of **3** colors: A, B, C
- 11º seed beads
  3 g color A
  5 g in each of **2** colors: B, C
- **10** 5–8 mm spacers
- toggle clasp
- nylon or GSP beading thread, size D or 6 lb. test

Contributors

Jima Abbott is a self-taught jeweler who started pounding on a piece of brass wire on the cement floor of his store on Hollywood Boulevard in 1967 and got carried away. He creates jewelry and works on new metal bead ideas in Caspar, Calif., on the Pacific Ocean's edge. Contact him via e-mail at jima@mcn.org.

Full-time designer and instructor **CJ Bauschka** lives in Adrian, Mich. Contact CJ at (517) 442-4093, via e-mail at angeldesigner@frontier.com, or visit her online at 4hisglorycreationsbycj.com.

Tea Benduhn is an associate editor at *Bead&Button* magazine. Contact her at tbenduhn@beadandbutton.com.

Merle Berelowitz is a beader from Cape Town, South Africa, who now resides in New York City. She loves beading with Lucite flowers and beads. Contact her via e-mail at msmaddiesbeads@nyc.rr.com, or visit her website, msmaddiesbeads.com.

Kimberly Berlin's jewelry designs are influenced by history, nature, and ancient cultural art. She has been creating wire art for many years, teaches wire art classes in San Antonio, Texas, and is the author of a 2012 wire art book from Kalmbach Books. Contact Kimberly via e-mail at berlik@flash.net.

Jimmie Boatright is a retired school teacher and lifelong crafter who teaches jewelry making at the Atlanta Bead Market in Buford, Ga. Contact Jimmie at (678) 714-8293, via e-mail at atlantabeadmarket@hotmail.com, or see a list of her classes at atlantabeadmarket.com.

Babette Borsani of Savannah, Ga., has been beading since 2004. Contact Babette at borsani@att.net.

Kathryn Bowman is all about making jewelry, marketing jewelry, and teaching jewelry making. She picked up stitching as a child, which was a natural fit when she later started working with beads. She also works with metal to create components for her jewelry. Visit her website, 1beadweaver.com, or e-mail her at 1kathrynbowman@gmail.com.

April Bradley, originally from Alaska, now lives in Valley Forge, Pa., with her husband and children. Beading and the art of applying old-world styles to everyday modern life continues to be a driving force in her life. Contact April at april_bradley@comcast.net, or visit her website, aprilbradley.com.

Dina Broyde was a New York City art teacher for more than 30 years. She took her first beading class in 2002 and loved it. Since then, Dina has taken workshops with many inspiring teachers and learned a variety of new techniques. Her years of teaching color and design have come into play in her beadwork. E-mail Dina at broyde-beads@hotmail.com.

Contact **Antonio Calles** in care of Kalmbach Books, books@kalmbach.com.

Cindy Caraway is an award-winning beadwork designer and beading teacher from Dubuque, Iowa. She finds inspiration in everything from nature to architecture to trips to the hardware store, and her style ranges from very organic to repetitive symmetry. Visit her online at cindycaraway.com or caraway.etsy.com, or e-mail her at cindycarawaybeadwork@yahoo.com.

Luan Carnevale is co-owner of Life's a Bead in Belmont, Mass., where she teaches a range of techniques and shares her love of beading with others. Contact Luan at (617) 489-7222, via e-mail at lifesabead@comcast.net, or visit her online at lifesabead.com.

Carolyn Cave is a self-taught bead artist from Alberta, Canada, who loves to fulfill her creative passions by making jewelry and other articles with beads. Contact her via e-mail at carton@nucleus.com.

Lilian Chen is an internationally known bead and wire artist from California whose designs have been featured in several beading magazines. Lilian was named a CREATE YOUR STYLE with SWAROVSKI ELEMENTS Ambassador in 2009. Visit community.create-your-style.com/user/51489/goldgatsby to view Lilian's designs, or contact her via e-mail at lilian888crystals@yahoo.com.

Melanie Colburn is an Oregon bead designer who designs quilt kits, hats, and jewelry with her sisters. Visit her online at sibling-arts.com, or contact her via e-mail at mainydawn@msn.com.

Jennifer Curran's art-therapy work with children led her to beading in 2004. She enjoys getting absorbed in the creative process, and she's always on the lookout for new products, tools, and findings. Through her program, "Beads for the Brave," she sends donated beads and materials to women serving overseas. E-mail Jennifer at simplybeadnaround@yahoo.com.

Cynthia Newcomer Daniel has been making jewelry for more than 40 years. Her latest design interest is adapting filigree and lace-making techniques to bead weaving. Visit Cynthia's website, jewelrytales.blogspot.com, where she writes short vignettes about her creations, or contact her via e-mail at jewelrytales@charter.net.

Keeping with a long family tradition, **Donna Pagano Denny** is always working with her hands. She's crocheted and tatted with beads and has been bead weaving since 1990. Seed beads are her passion, and her motto is "the smaller the beads the better." When not beading, you'll find Donna playing tennis or out riding her recumbent bicycle. She sells her work at Lush Beads in Lowell, Mass. Contact her via e-mail at lacetatter@aol.com.

Anna Elizabeth Draeger is an associate editor at *Bead&Button* magazine and author of *Crystal Brilliance*. Contact her via e-mail at adraeger@beadandbutton.com, or visit her website, http://web.mac.com/beadbiz.

Stephanie Eddy is a jewelry designer and teacher with more than 40 years of experience. Contact Stephanie at (208) 853-7988, via e-mail at kitsforsale@stephanieeddy.com, or visit her website, stephanieeddy.com.

Julia Gerlach is Editor of *Bead&Button* magazine. Contact her at jgerlach@beadandbutton.com.

Judith Golan of Rehovot, Israel, began beading after receiving her master's degree in plant sciences in 2006. She enjoys 3D beadwork and often finds inspiration in the natural world. Contact Judith at judith27k@ gmail.com, or visit her blog, http://judith27k.blogspot.com.

Beading is a natural fit for **Melissa Grakowsky**, who has a bachelor's degree in physics and a Bachelor of Fine Arts degree in painting. The craft combines science and artistry in a creative outlet that fits into her busy life. Melissa started beading in 2007 and now teaches beading classes worldwide. Contact Melissa by e-mail at grakowsky@ gmail.com, or visit her website, grakowsky.net.

Amanda Shero Granstrom lives in Portland, Ore. She loves color, whether working with beads, fibers, polymer clay, glass, or chain mail. Amanda has been designing and crafting jewelry since 2001. Contact her via e-mail at amanda@redeftshibori.com, or visit her website, craftycatjumprings.com.

Smadar Grossman is a full-time jewelry designer who lives in Israel. She fell in love with bead weaving a few years ago and has been exploring its possibilities ever since. Contact Smadar at smadarstreasure@gmail.com, or visit her blog, smadarstreasure.blogspot.com.

Lora Groszkiewicz is the editorial assistant at *Bead&Button* magazine. Contact Lora at lgroszkiewicz@beadandbutton.com.

Aasia Hamid is a bead weaver and jewelry designer who loves to create unique jewelry in her studio in Gilbert, Ariz. She enjoys sharing her knowledge of color and beading techniques through teaching. Contact her at (480) 586-1843, via e-mail at aasia@aasiajewelry.com, or visit her website at aasiajewelry.com.

Wendy Hunt is a jewelry designer who lives in Ontario, Canada. She began designing chain mail and beaded jewelry in 2004. Contact Wendy via e-mail at hunt7897@rogers.com.

Diane Hyde is an award-winning beader from Waukesha, Wis. Visit her website, beadpunk.net, to see a gallery of her beadpunk designs, purchase beadpunk supplies, and get inspired.

Virginia Jensen is the author of *Cube Bead Stitching* and *Cube Bead Stitching II*. With many years of graphic design experience, it's no surprise that her greatest joy in beadwork is the design process. She lives in Grand Junction, Colo. Visit her website, virjenmettle.com.

Lisa Keith has been beading for several years, and her favorite techniques include right-angle weave, herringbone, and unique tribal stitches. Contact Lisa via e-mail at lkeith@lj-studio.com, or visit her website, lj-studio.com.

Maria Kirk of Nottingham, England, has been designing, teaching, and creating kits for over 15 years. In 1999, one of her pieces was selected to adorn the Royal Christmas Tree at Buckingham Palace, and in 2009 she designed a crystal poppy to raise funds for the Royal British Legion Poppy Appeal. Contact Maria at 0044-1773-712240, maria@nostalgiaribbon.com, or visit her website, www.nostalgiabeads.com.

Barbara Klann has been beading for more than 20 years and is constantly amazed at what can be accomplished with a small pile of beads, a needle, and thread. Her main materials of choice are seed beads with a few crystals or pearls sprinkled in here and there. Contact Barbara in care of Kalmbach Books, books@kalmbach.com.

Sonia Kumar began making jewelry with paper clips about six years ago. She now works mainly with wire and gemstones. To see more of Sonia's work, visit catchalljewelry.etsy.com.

Heidi Kummli is a bead embroidery artist, and co-author of *The Art of Bead Embroidery*. Her second bead embroidery book will be published in 2012. Contact her via e-mail at freespiritheidi@dishmail.net, or visit her website, freespiritcollection.com.

Cathy Lampole of Newmarket, Ontario, Canada, enjoys the fine detail that can be achieved with bead weaving, especially with crystals. Besides designing jewelry, Cathy owns a bead shop, That Bead Lady. Visit her website, thatbeadlady.com, or e-mail her at cathy@ thatbeadlady.com.

Shirley Lim resides in Singapore and has been beading since 2000. She loves combining peyote with herringbone, her favorite stitch. Contact Shirley at beadingfantasy@me.com, visit her online at web.me.com/beadingfantasy or beading-fantasy.blogspot.com.

Connie Lorig has been beading and designing her own work in Manitou Springs, Col., for more than 25 years. Contact Connie at cmlorig@comcast.net.

Susan Matych-Hager, professor emeritus of music at Siena Heights University, works as a full-time bead maker and jewelry designer. She and Kathy Petersen recently collaborated on a necklace that was juried into the Convergence II exhibit co-sponsored by the International Society of Glass Beadmakers (ISGB). Contact Susan at susan@hagerstudiosglass.com, or visit her website, hagerstudiosglass.com.

Laura McCabe maintains a working studio in Old Mystic, Conn. Visit her website, justletmebead.com.

When not traveling with her family, **Callie Mitchell** beads at her home studio in Houston, Texas. Her jewelry pieces are primarily designed as "souvenirs" of beloved and beautiful places. Contact Callie via e-mail at peregrinebeader@gmail.com, or visit peregrinebeader.etsy.com.

Samantha Mitchell designs jewelry as a way to express her creativity when she's not busy caring for her young son. Contact her at samantha@crystyles.com, or visit her website, crystyles.com.

Marilyn Mullins began beading seven years ago after she saw a cute bracelet in a department store and thought to herself, "This can't be that hard to make." Contact Marilyn at marilyn.mullins@ymail.com, or visit her online at marilynbeads.etsy.com and double-m-enterprises.com.

Teacher and jewelry designer **Marina Nadke** lives in Dortmund, Germany. During a trip to Canada, she saw her first beading magazine and fell in love with the craft. She says that creating new projects is "like dreaming with open eyes." Visit her website at marina-original.de, or contact her via e-mail at marina.nadke@t-online.de.

Elizabeth Nance started beading in 2004 after going to a bead shop to replace the findings on a pair of earrings. When she's not beading, Elizabeth is a landscape designer, estate gardener, wife to Steven, and mother to three children. Visit her website, beaddiddy.com, or e-mail her at enance@gmail.com.

Nancy Owens, from Attica, Mich., crochets, knits, makes cards, and work in stained glass, cake decorating, and lampworking, among other crafts, but says bead weaving is her favorite. Contact Nancy at (810) 724-7825, or via e-mail at catmom@intouchmi.com.

Cindy Thomas Pankopf teaches beading in Brea, Calif., and at the Bead&Button Show, and is a senior instructor for Art Clay Silver. She is the author of books *BeadMaille* and *Absolute Beginners Guide: Making Metal Clay Jewelry*. Contact her via e-mail at info@cindypankopf.com, or visit her website, cindypankopf.com.

Nealay Patel is a graphic designer and the author of the book, *Jewelry for the New Romantic*. He has been beading since 2003 and enjoys the challenge of rendering architectural design ideas in beads. Visit Nealay online at facebook.com/nealay.

Contact **Rebecca Peapples** via e-mail at rspeapples@aol.com.

Kathy Petersen is a school psychologist who enjoys metalwork, lapidary, wire weaving, and chain mail. She and Susan Matych-Hager recently collaborated on a necklace that was juried into the Convergence II exhibit co-sponsored by the International Society of Glass Beadmakers (ISGB). Contact her at kpetersendesigns@aol.com.

Lisa Phillips is an avid beader who hasn't tried an off-loom stitch she hasn't enjoyed creating with. She especially enjoys mixing fibers and beads in a variety of ways. Contact Lisa via e-mail at beadwoman@hotmail.com.

Elizabeth Pullan of Calgary, Alberta, enjoys beading with all her friends and thanks them all for their inspiration, friendship, and most of all, e-mails. Contact her via e-mail at elizabeth1762@hotmail.com or visit her website, brilliansea.com.

Ludmila Raitzin is a renowned sweater designer featured at Saks Fifth Avenue, Neiman Marcus, Bloomingdale's, and more. Her background in fashion led her to become a successful jewelry designer known for her color sense and strong design abilities. Her work has been exhibited in the Museum of Art and Design and has been published in several books and magazines. Contact Ludmila via e-mail at raitzinl@yahoo.com.

Adele Rogers Recklies is the author of *Bead Crochet Snakes: History and Technique*. When she is not beading, Adele knits, crochets, and embroiders costumes for Broadway shows, feature films, opera, and dance. Visit her website, beadcrochetsnakes.com, or her blog, recklessbeading.blogspot.com.

Jean Ann Reeves began beading as a four-year-old, stringing buttons from her mother's button box. She still has the box and a few strands of the carefully strung buttons. She is now a full-time jewelry artist who resides in San Antonio and teaches jewelry making throughout south Texas. Contact her via e-mail at buyalot6@aol.com, or visit her website, etsy.com/shop/jewelrygeniebyjean.

Susan Jo Rochlin is a Southeast Florida artist and private instructor who specializes in beading and bead embroidery. Her style focuses on colorful and whimsical designs for her jewelry, which incorporates pearls, stones, and crystals. Contact Susan via e-mail at susan@mermaidsjewelz.com, or visit her website, mermaidsjewelz.com.

Maggie Roschyk is the author of an upcoming bead stitching book from Kalmbach Books. Visit her blog, Maggie's Musings, at BeadAndButton.com/MaggiesMusings.

Keiko Seki became interested in beading in 1998 when a friend gave her a handmade piece of beaded jewelry. Now, she enjoys the pleasure other people experience when they receive her gifts of hand-crafted bead jewelry. Contact Keiko in care of Kalmbach Books, books@kalmbach.com.

Candice Sexton has been beading since 2001, and enjoys the relaxing, meditative, and creative qualities of wireworking, bead crochet, and bead weaving. The author of a 2013 book from Kalmbach Books on bead crochet, she also likes coming up with new ways to work with materials and techniques, such as using wire as a "thread" to "sew" beads. Visit her website, candicesexton.com.

Michelle Skobel has been beading for most of her life and started designing jewelry three years ago. You can see more of her work, kits, and patterns on her website, michelleskobel.com, or e-mail her at michelle@michelleskobel.com.

Kerrie Slade lives in Mansfield, England, carrying on a family tradition of making beaded flowers — her grandmother made French beaded-flower pins during the 1930s. Contact Kerrie via e-mail at mail@kerrieslade.co.uk, or visit her website, kerrieslade.co.uk.

The late **Gillian "Gill" Slone** was a beader for more than 12 years, had more than 20 projects published in magazines and books, and created finished jewelry on commission and for sale to the public. Gill lived in Wharfedale, North Yorkshire, England.

Kim Spooner is a jewelry designer and instructor based in central Massachusetts. Contact her via e-mail at cisraydesigns@yahoo.com, or view her website, cisraydesigns.etsy.com.

Jenny Van is a frequent contributor to *Bead&Button* magazine. Contact her at (714) 848-5626, or via e-mail at jamie@jjbead.com. View products and class information on her website, jjbead.com.

Stacy Werkheiser is an associate editor for *Bead&Button* magazine. Contact her at swerkheiser@beadandbutton.com.

Laura Zeiner lives in Austin, Texas, with her husband, John, a calico cat named Millibob, and Ginger, her spoiled-rotten shelti. Laura teaches beadwork and, in her spare time, trains for triathlons. Contact Laura at laurazeiner@yahoo.com, or visit her online at sticklizarddesigns.etsy.com. or sticklizarddesigns.blogspot.com.

Index

Make hundreds of
CREATIVE JEWELRY PIECES
with the techniques and projects in these volumes

Each volume contains more than

80

projects and is just $29.95!

Creative Beading
62288

Creative Beading, Vol. 3
62625

This stunning collection of hardcover volumes contains hundreds of fabulous step-by-step projects and fresh ideas selected from the pages of *Bead&Button* magazine. Be a creative beader with the thorough Basics sections, project sections grouped by technique, and a range of editor-tested stringing, wirework, embroidery and crochet designs.

From easy strung bracelets to sleek crocheted bead ropes, there's a project to excite and inspire everyone.

Creative Beading, Vol. 4
62892

Creative Beading, Vol. 5
62922

KALMBACH BOOKS

P13127

Available at your favorite bead or craft shop!
Order online at www.KalmbachStore.com or call 1-800-533-6644
Monday–Friday, 8:30 a.m. – 4:30 p.m. Central Time. Outside the U.S. and Canada, call 262-706-8776 x661.

XBB